MW01622288

Table of Contents

People......5
Emotions, faces, people, professions

Childhood heroes......21
Superheroes, video game characters, movie heroes, games

Leisure and Entertainment......42
Entertainment, music

Festivals and celebrations......45
Christmas, Halloween, Birthday, Wedding

House and Home......52
Mobili, arredamento, cibo, tecnologia, scuola

Hobby......82
Handicrafts, renovation, sports

Countries and Travel......94
Travel, traditions, sights

Landscapes......105
Buildings, nature, weather, space

Vehicles......112
Road traffic, vehicles, airplanes, ships

Animals......122
Marine life, pets, insects

Clothes......134
Clothes, shoes, accessories, finance

Index......141

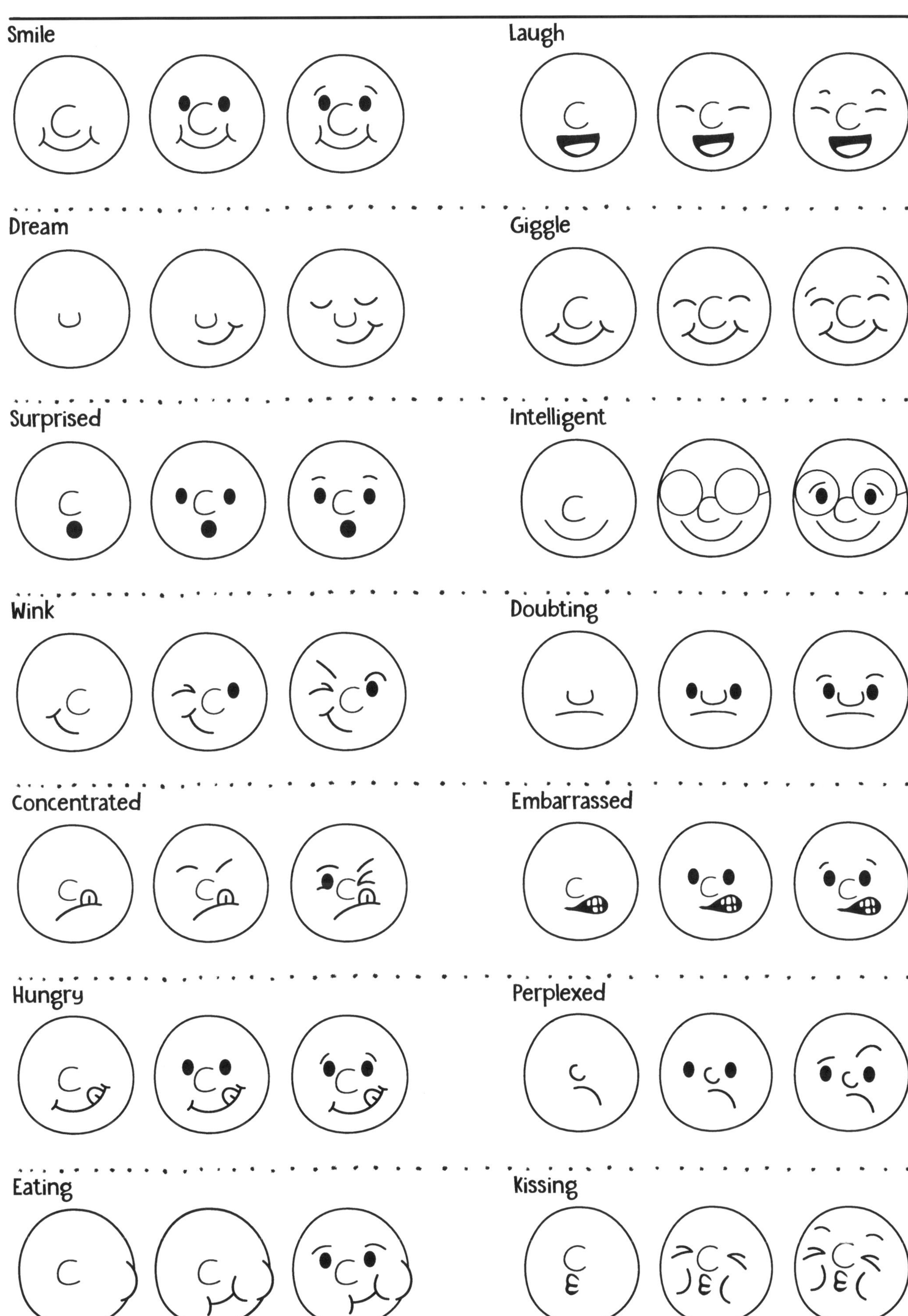
Smile
Laugh
Dream
Giggle
Surprised
Intelligent
Wink
Doubting
Concentrated
Embarrassed
Hungry
Perplexed
Eating
Kissing

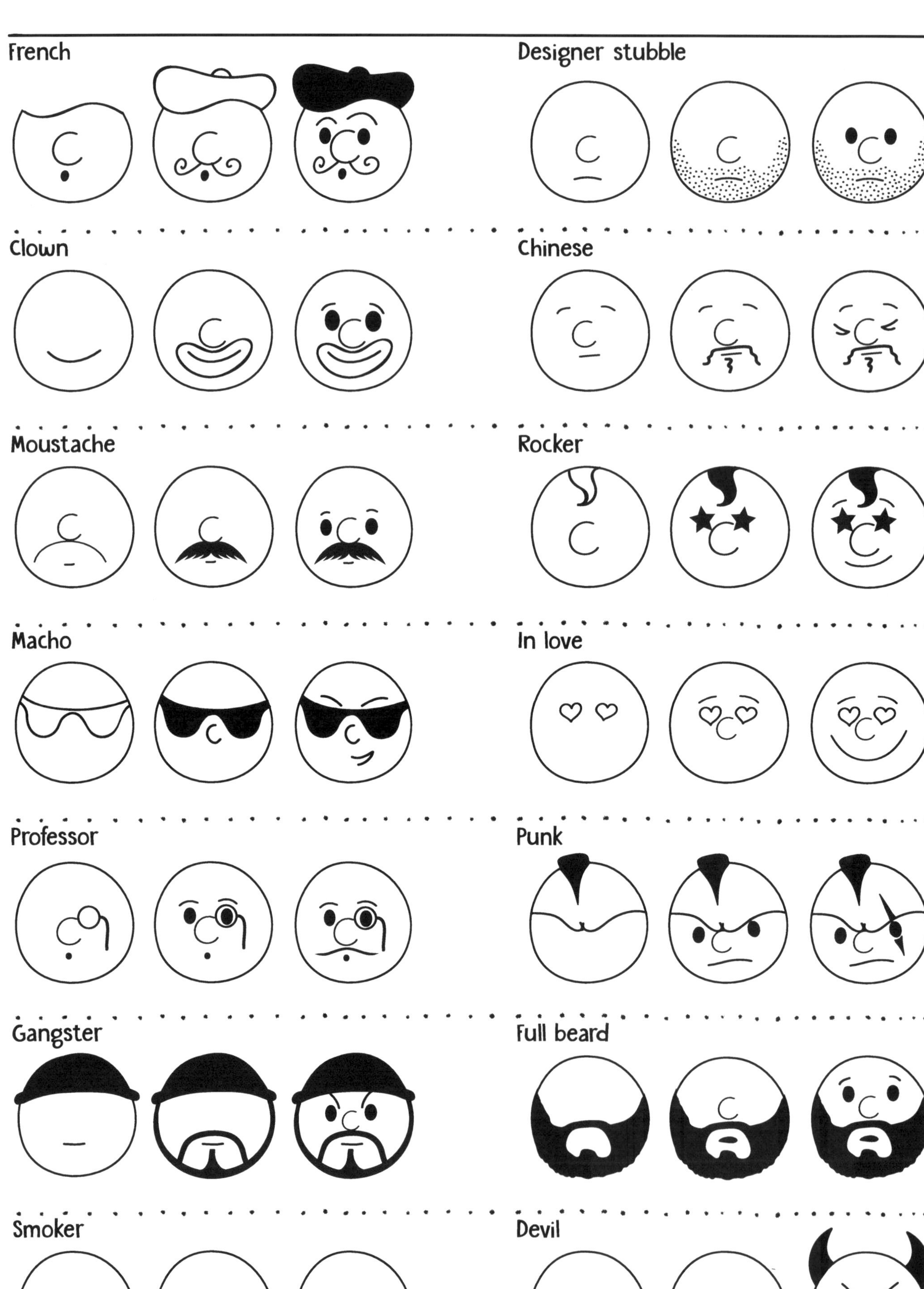
French
Designer stubble
Clown
Chinese
Moustache
Rocker
Macho
In love
Professor
Punk
Gangster
Full beard
Smoker
Devil

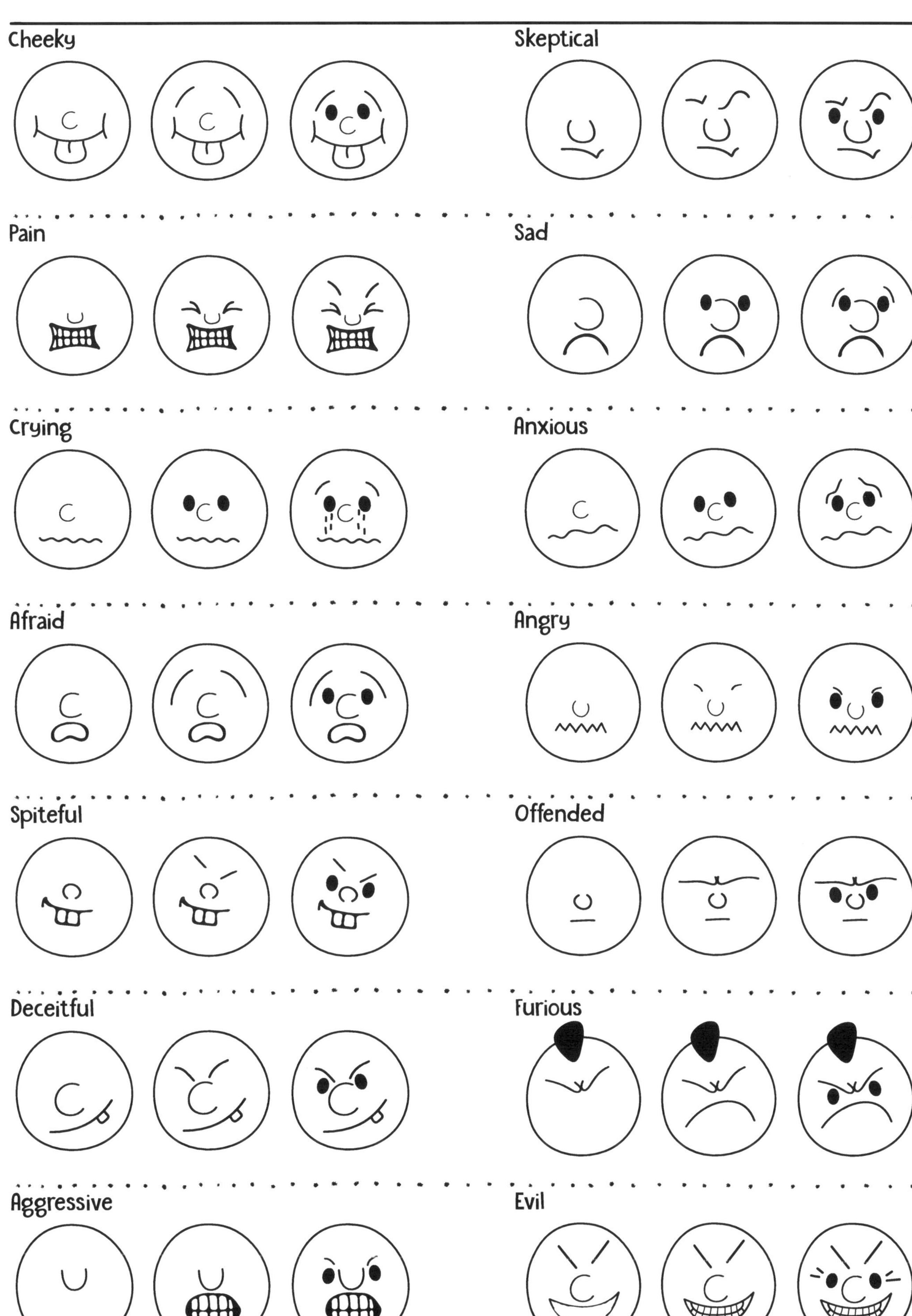
Cheeky
Skeptical
Pain
Sad
Crying
Anxious
Afraid
Angry
Spiteful
Offended
Deceitful
Furious
Aggressive
Evil

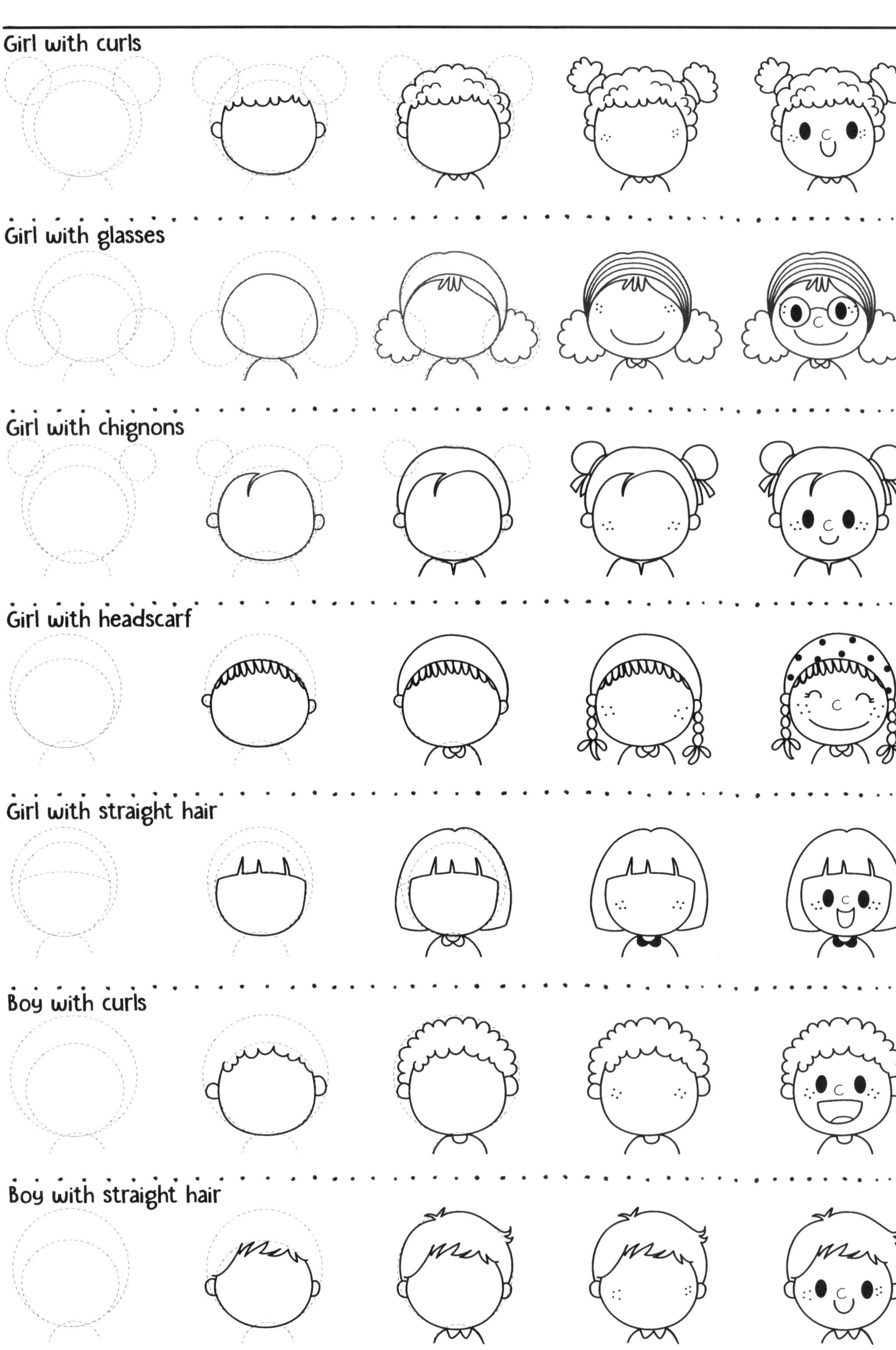
Girl with curls
Girl with glasses
Girl with chignons
Girl with headscarf
Girl with straight hair
Boy with curls
Boy with straight hair

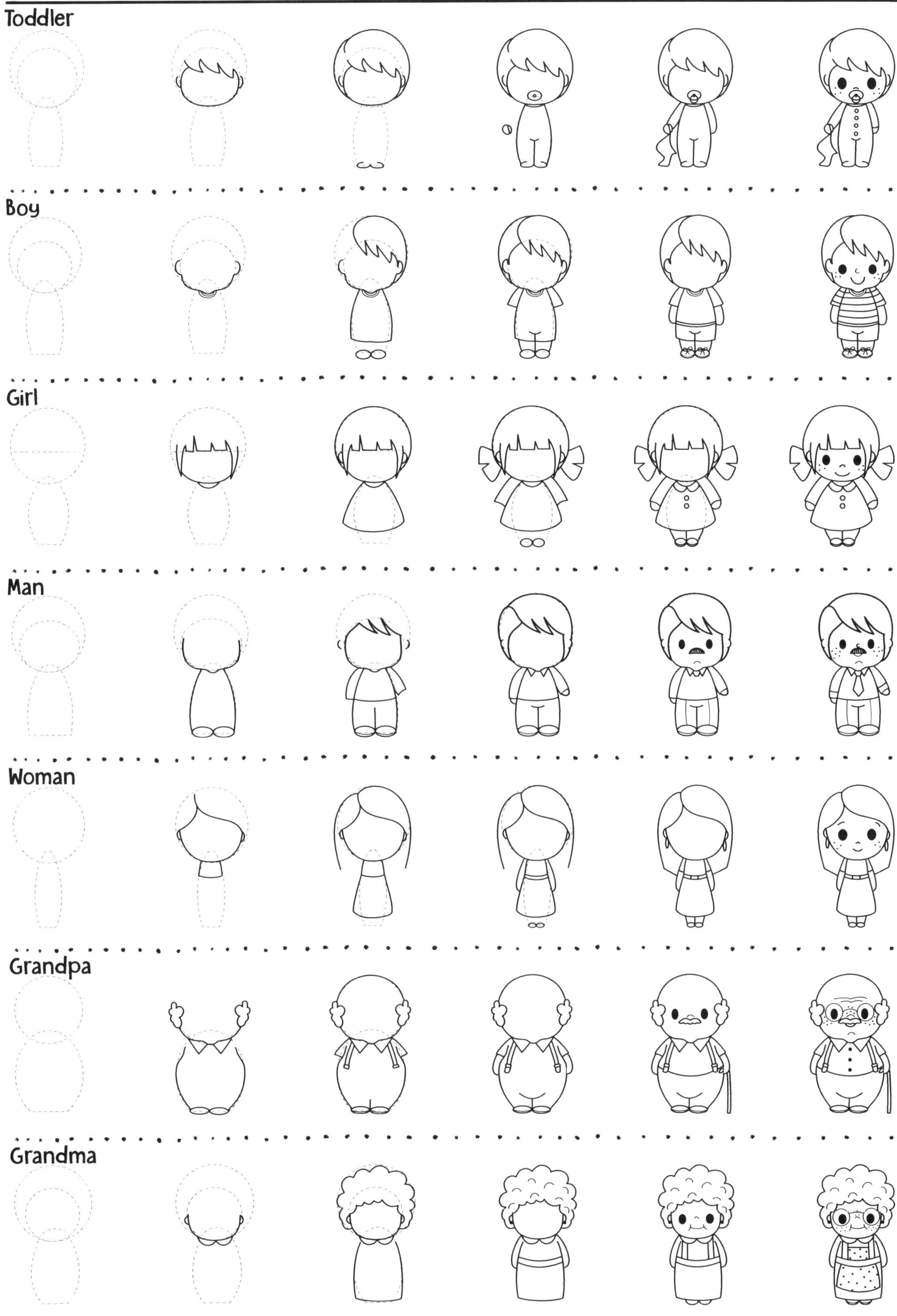
Toddler
Boy
Girl
Man
Woman
Grandpa
Grandma

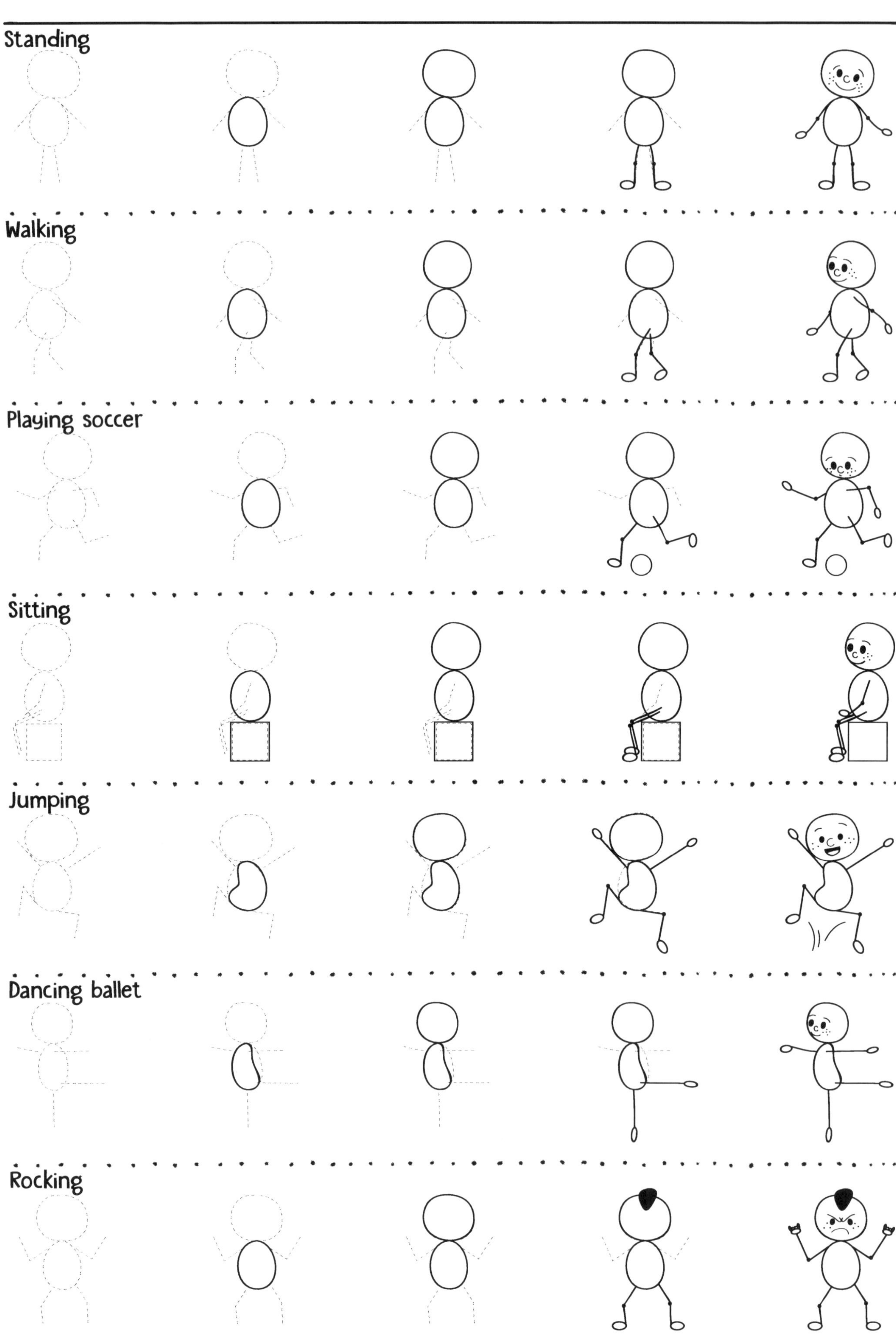
Standing
Walking
Playing soccer
Sitting
Jumping
Dancing ballet
Rocking

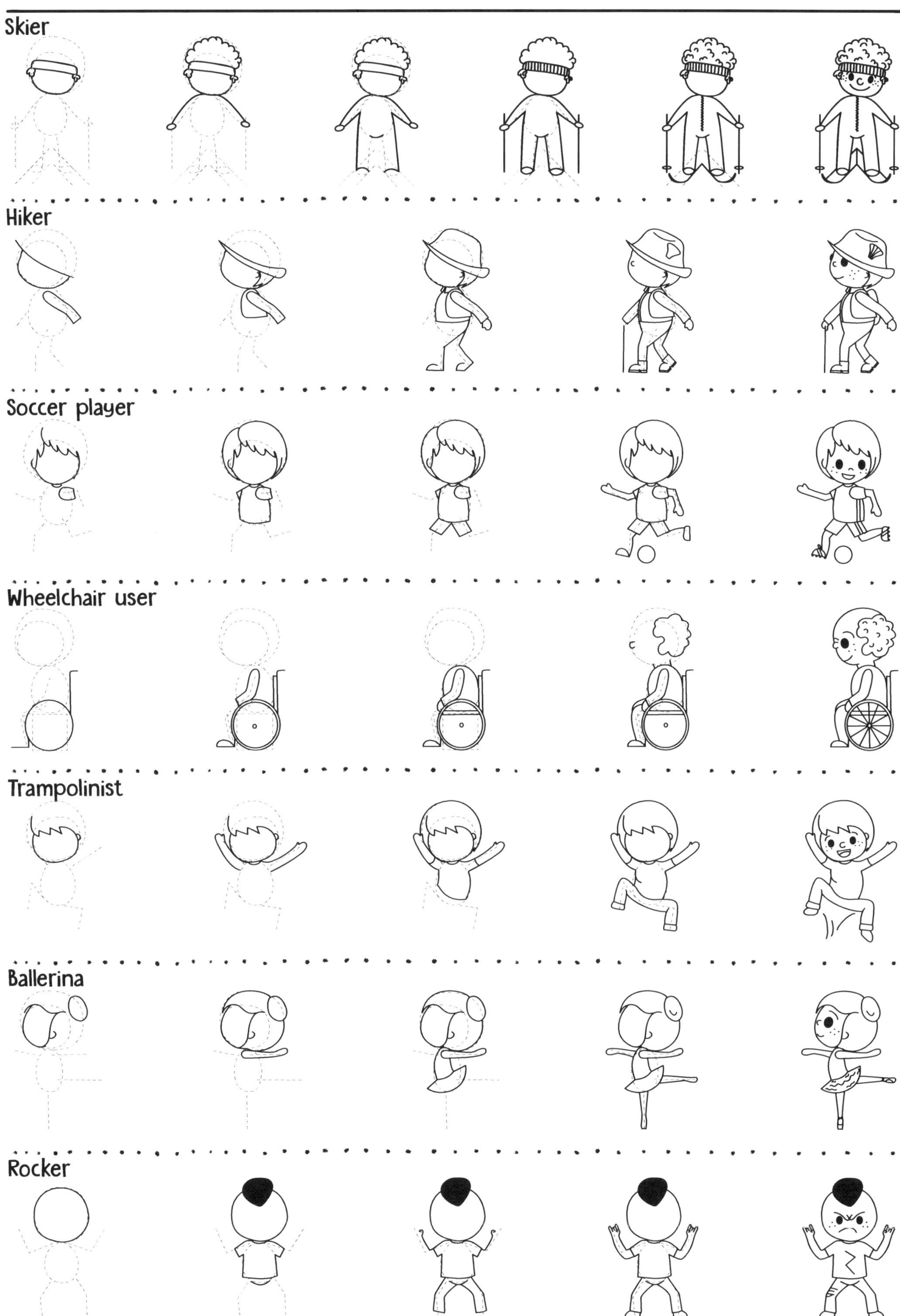
Skier
Hiker
Soccer player
Wheelchair user
Trampolinist
Ballerina
Rocker

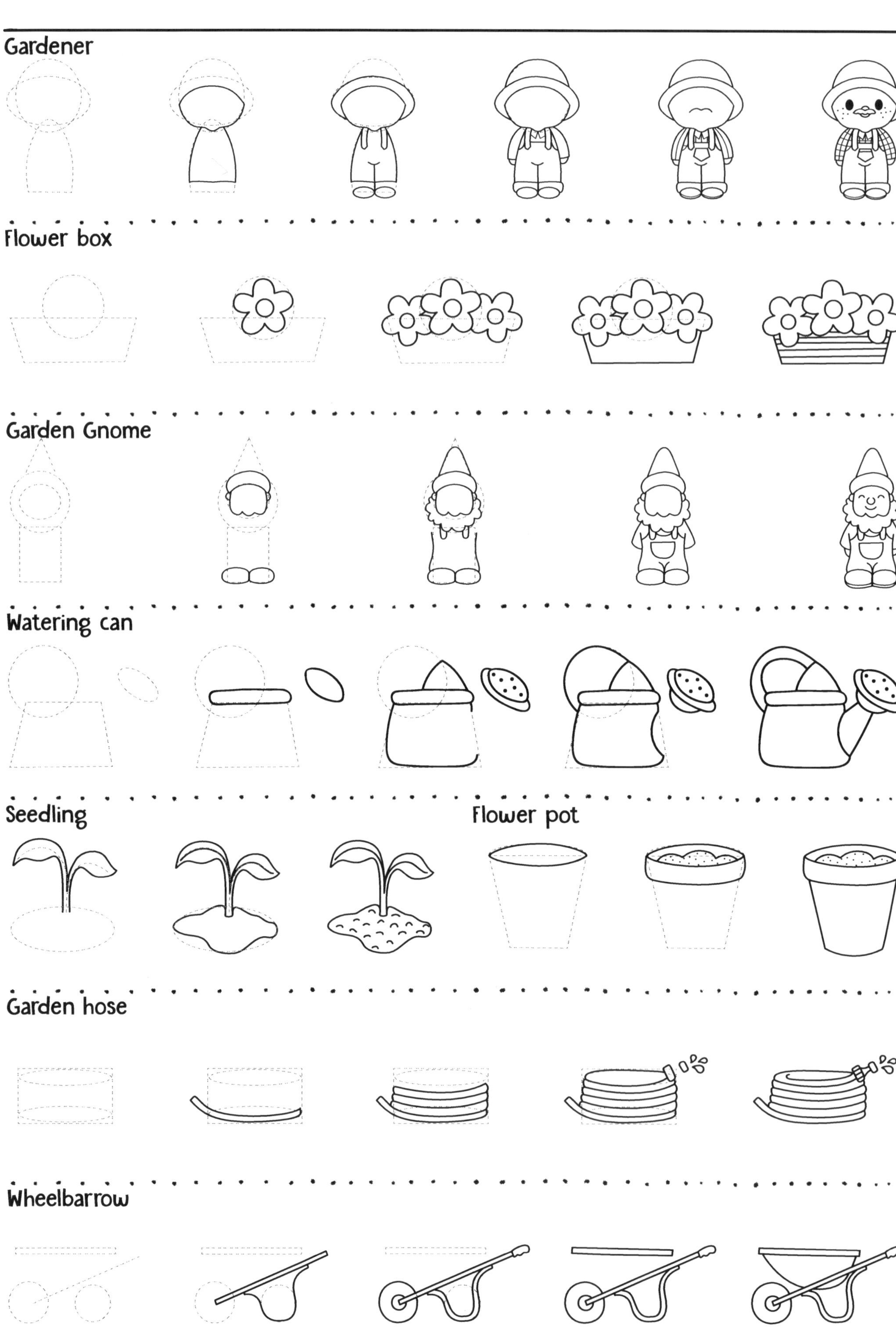
Gardener
Flower box
Garden Gnome
Watering can
Seedling
Flower pot
Garden hose
Wheelbarrow

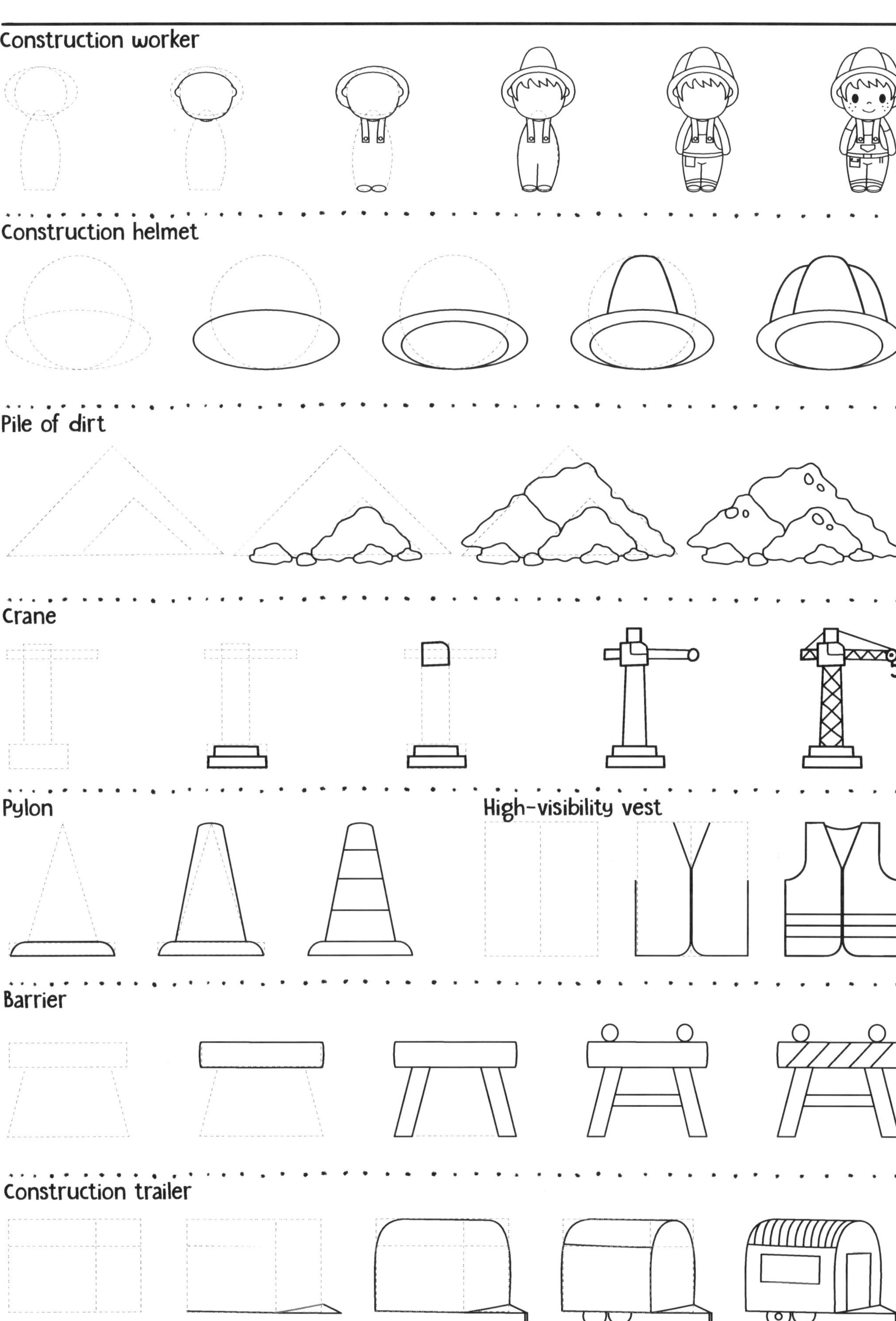
Construction worker
Construction helmet
Pile of dirt
Crane
Pylon
High-visibility vest
Barrier
Construction trailer

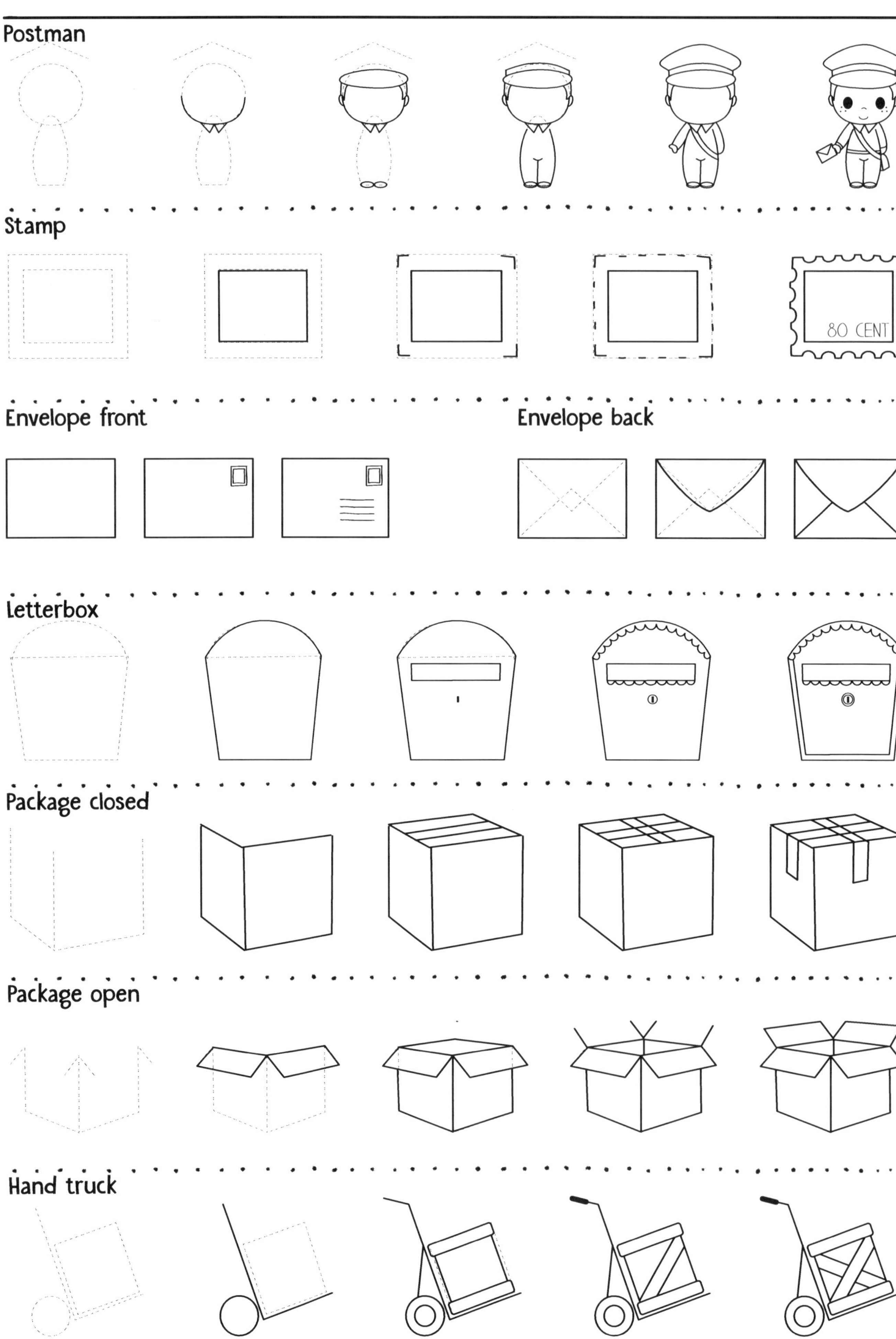
Postman
Stamp
80 CENT
Envelope front
Envelope back
Letterbox
Package closed
Package open
Hand truck

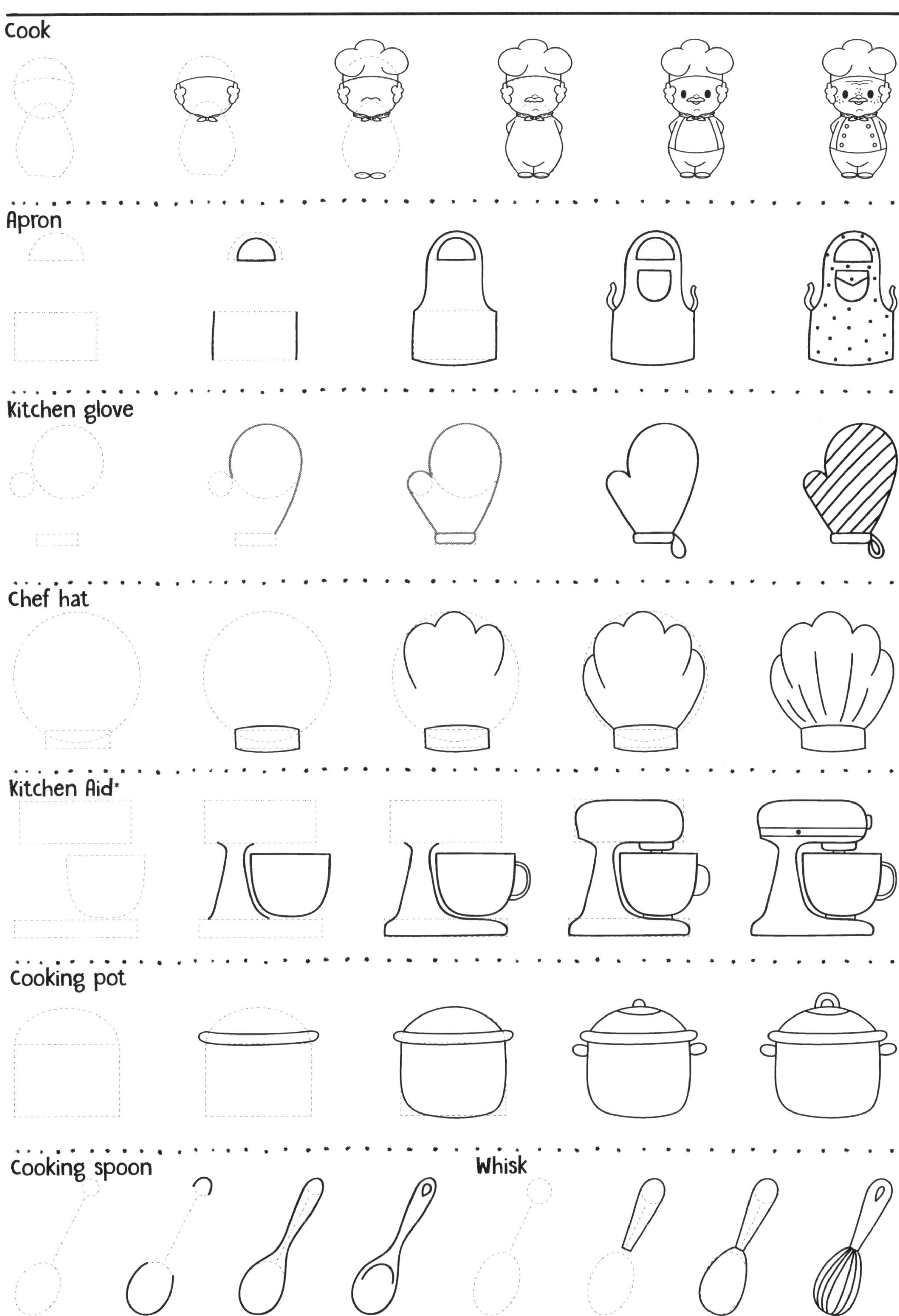
Cook
Apron
Kitchen glove
Chef hat
Kitchen Aid*
Cooking pot
Cooking spoon
Whisk

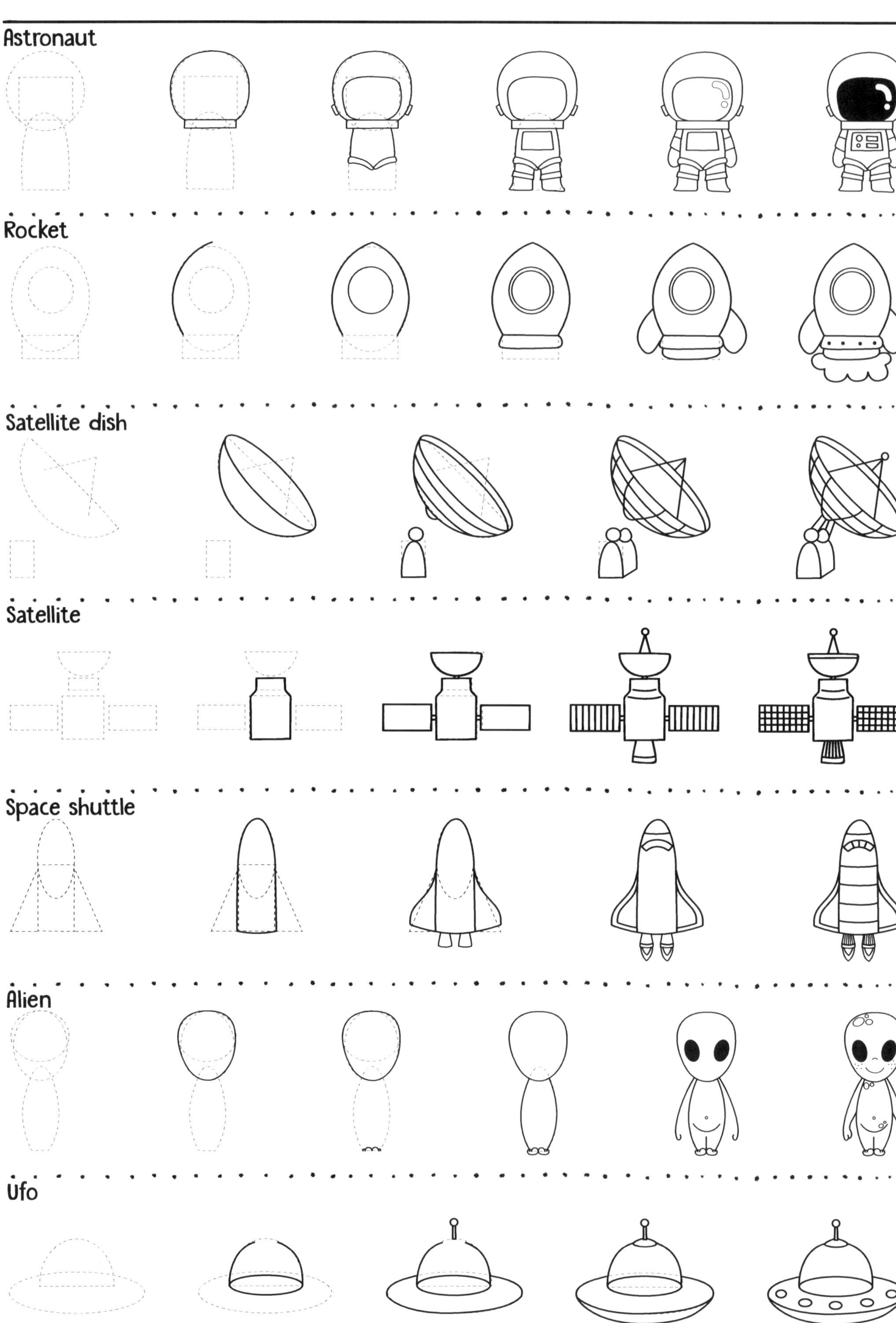
Astronaut
Rocket
Satellite dish
Satellite
Space shuttle
Alien
Ufo

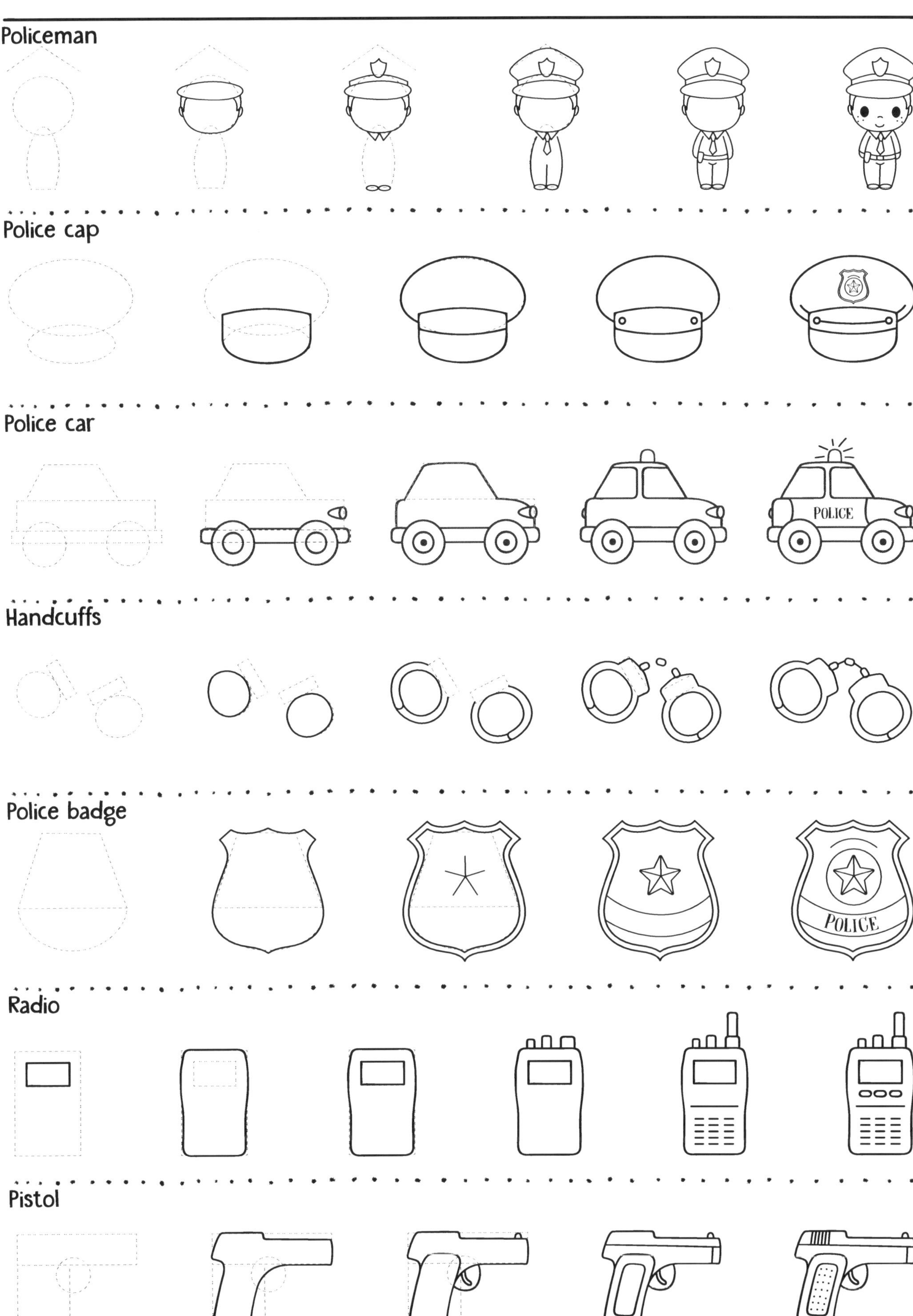
Policeman
Police cap
Police car
POLICE
Handcuffs
Police badge
POLICE
Radio
Pistol

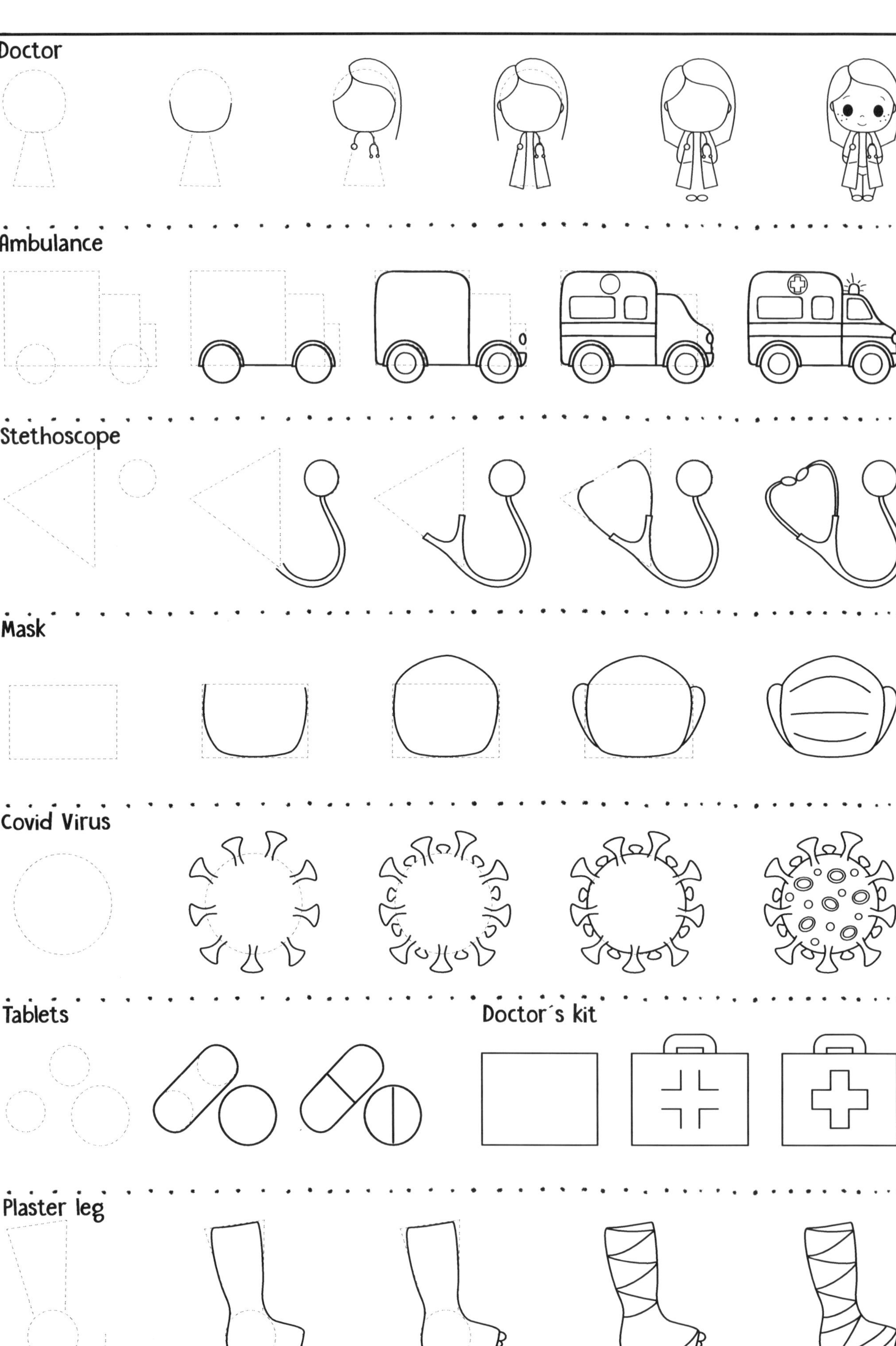
Doctor
Ambulance
Stethoscope
Mask
Covid Virus
Tablets
Doctor´s kit
Plaster leg

Nurse

Syringe

Plaster

Clinical thermometer

Tooth

Atom

Denture

Braces

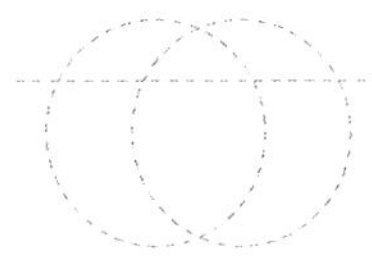
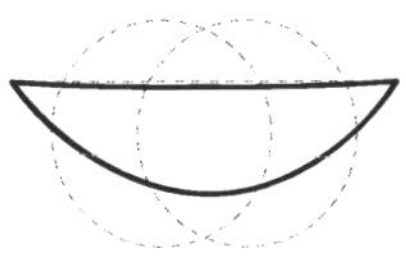
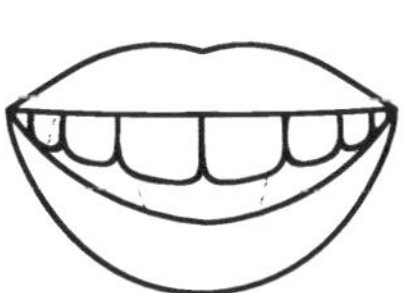
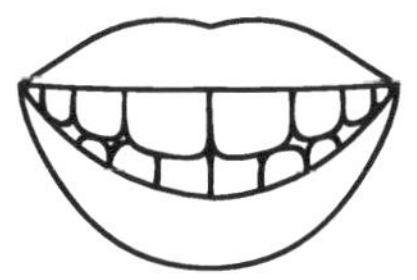
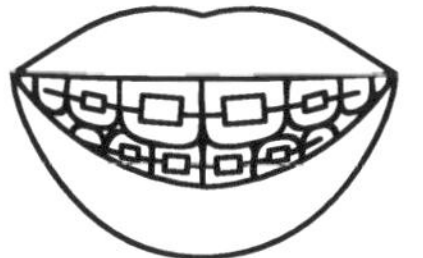

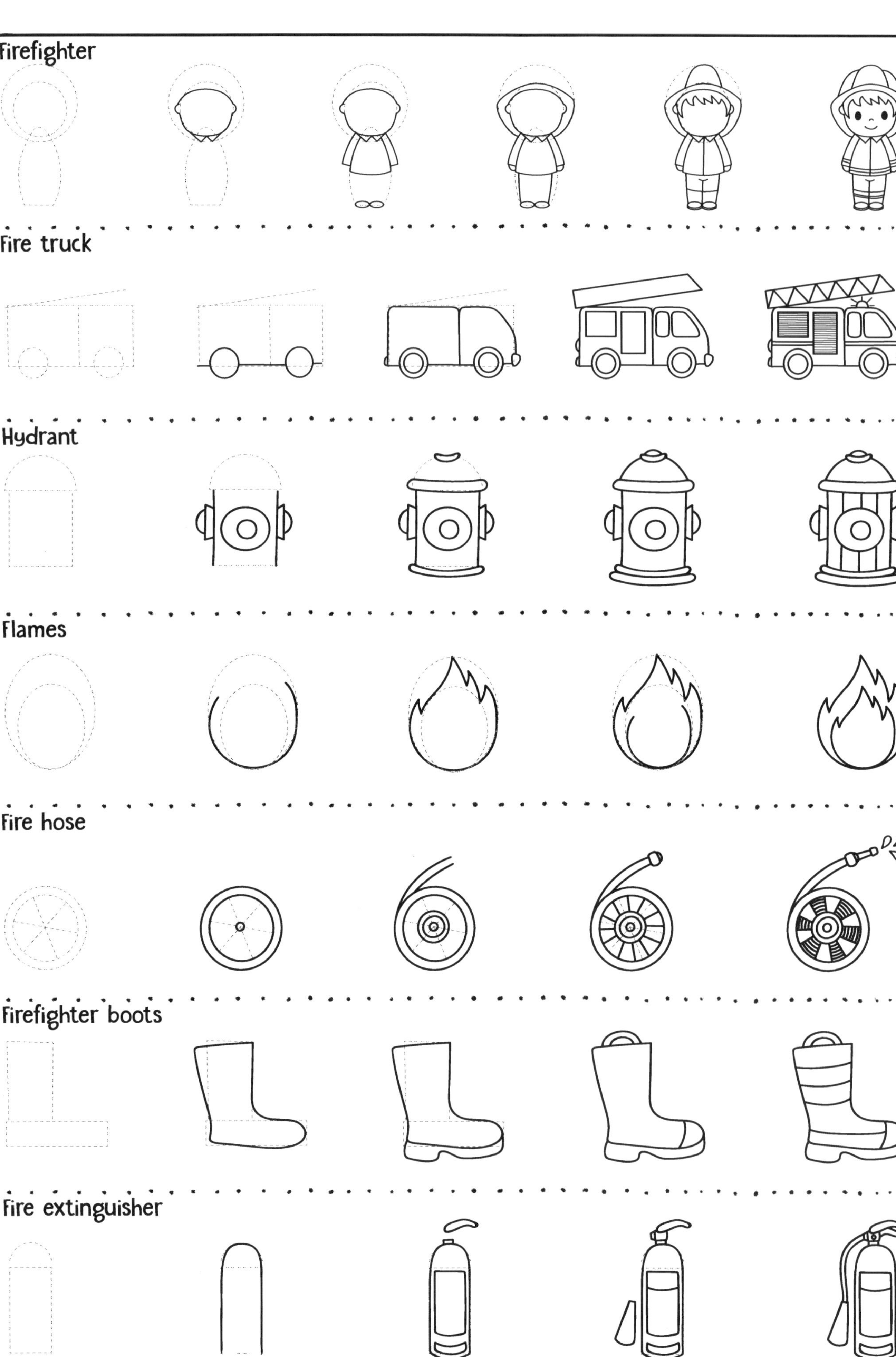
Firefighter
Fire truck
Hydrant
Flames
Fire hose
Firefighter boots
Fire extinguisher

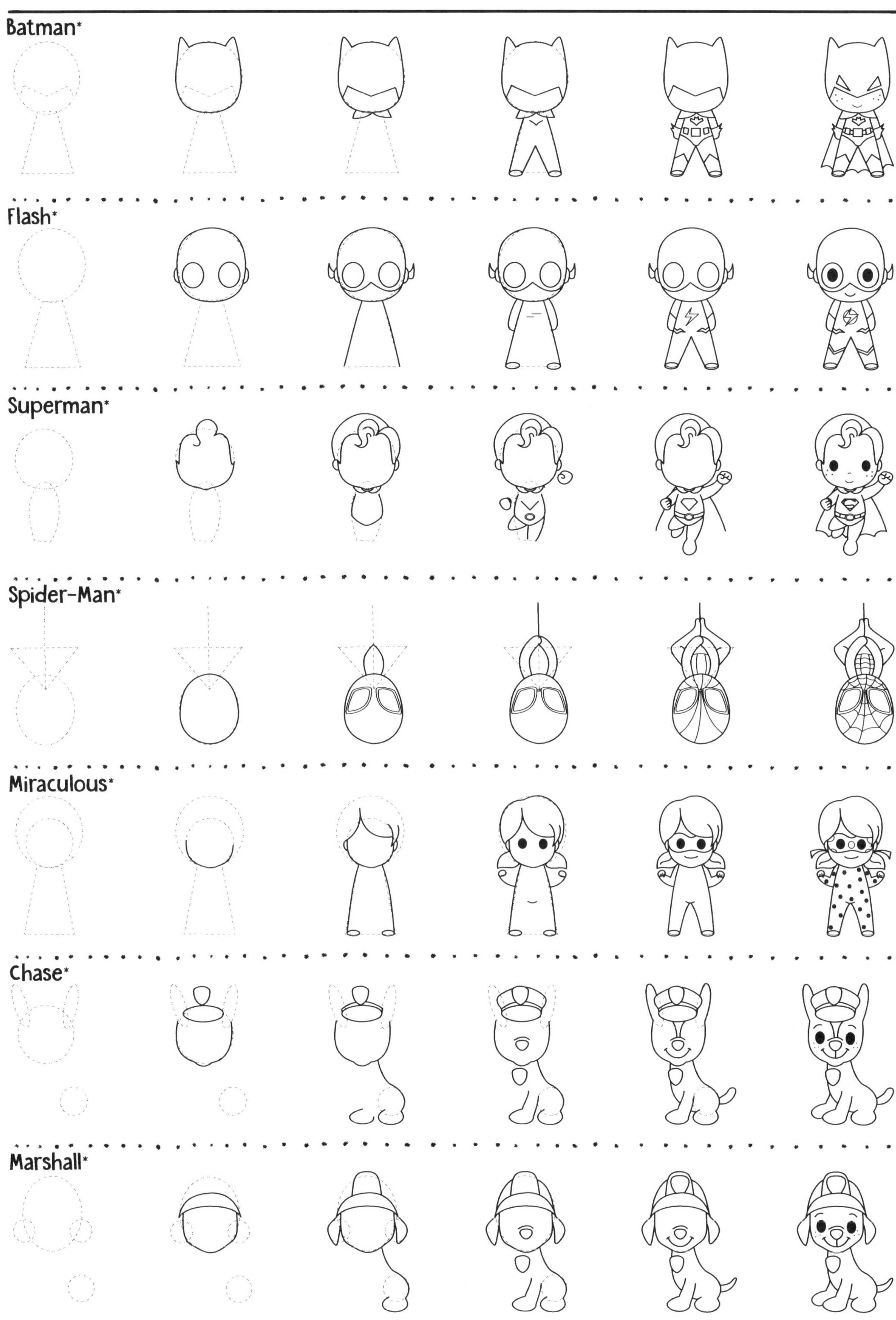
Batman*
Flash*
Superman*
Spider-Man*
Miraculous*
Chase*
Marshall*

Mario*

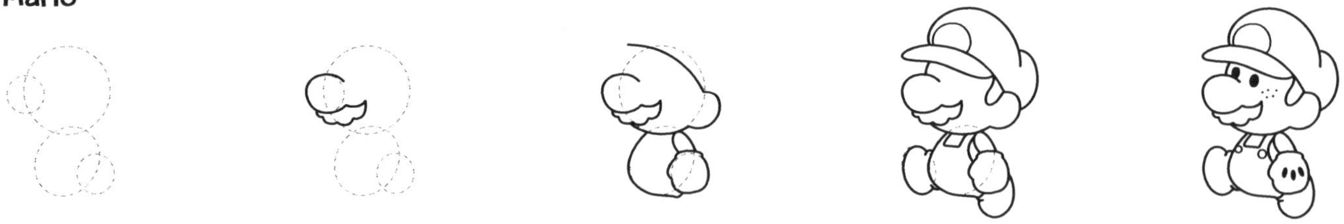

Luigi*

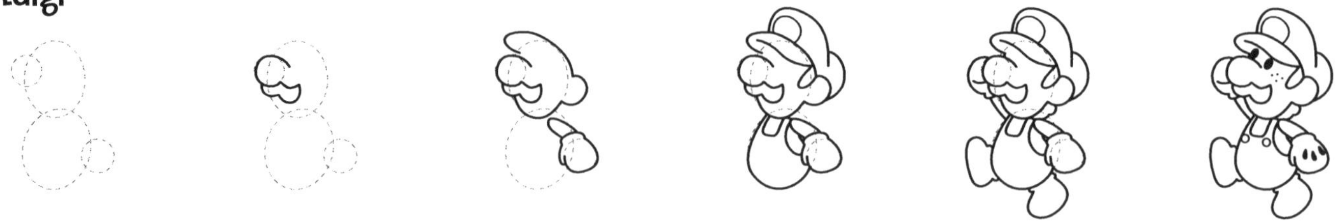

Joshi*

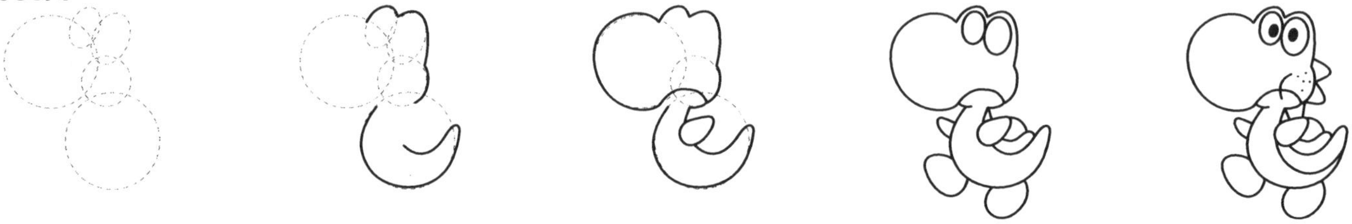

Toad*

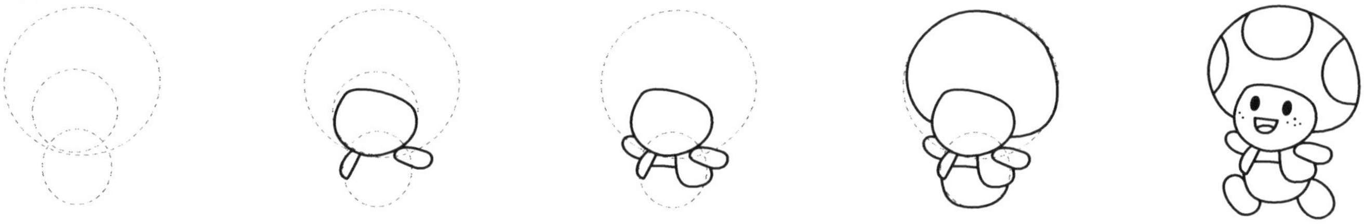

Princess Peach*

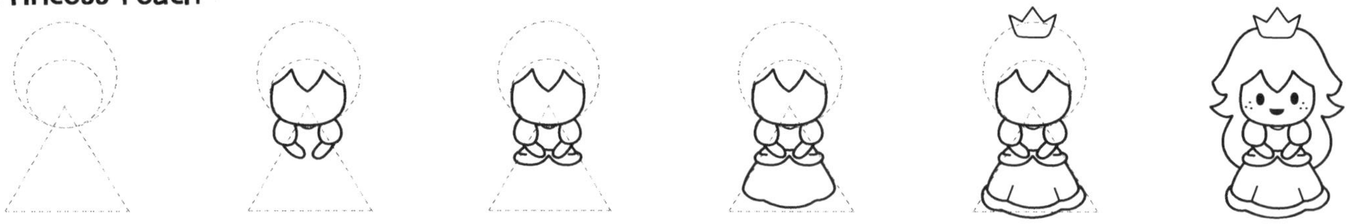

Super Star

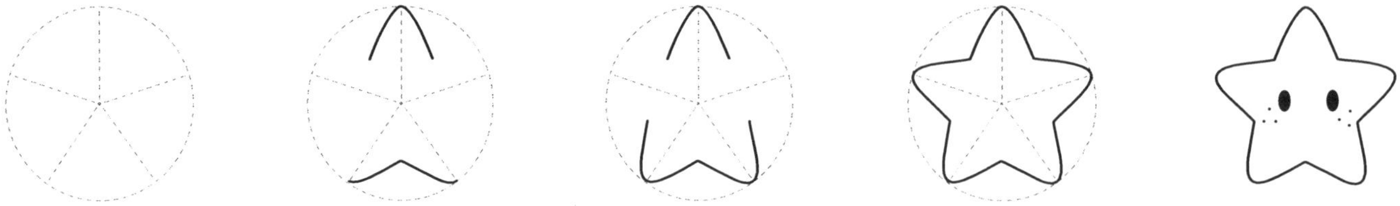

Bombette*

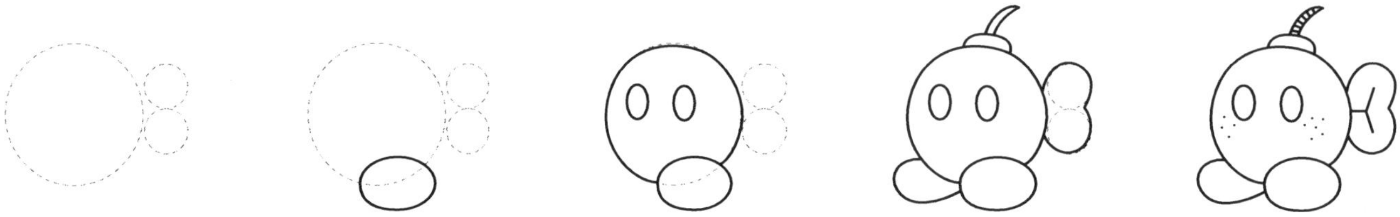

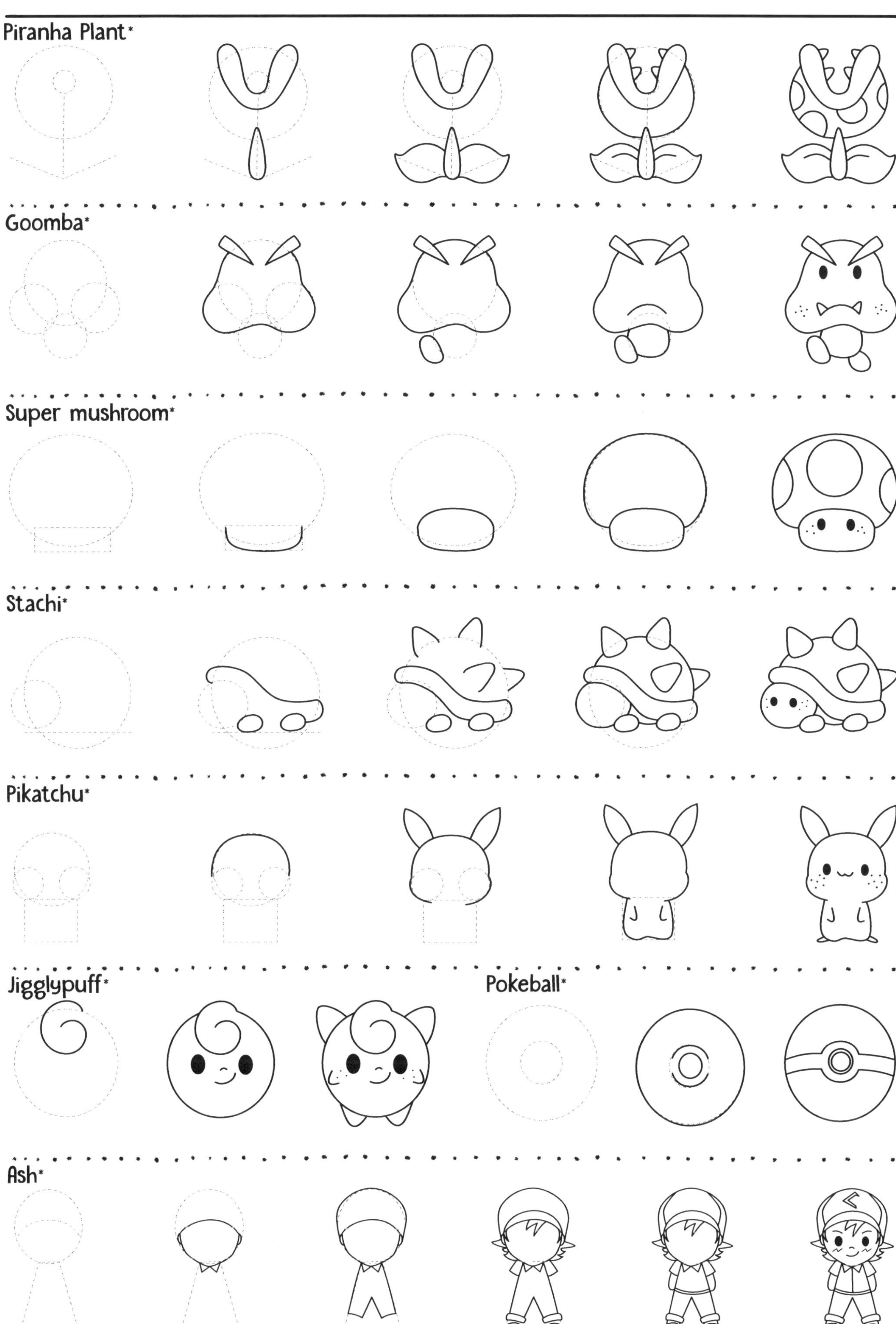
Piranha Plant*
Goomba*
Super mushroom*
Stachi*
Pikatchu*
Jigglypuff*
Pokeball*
Ash*

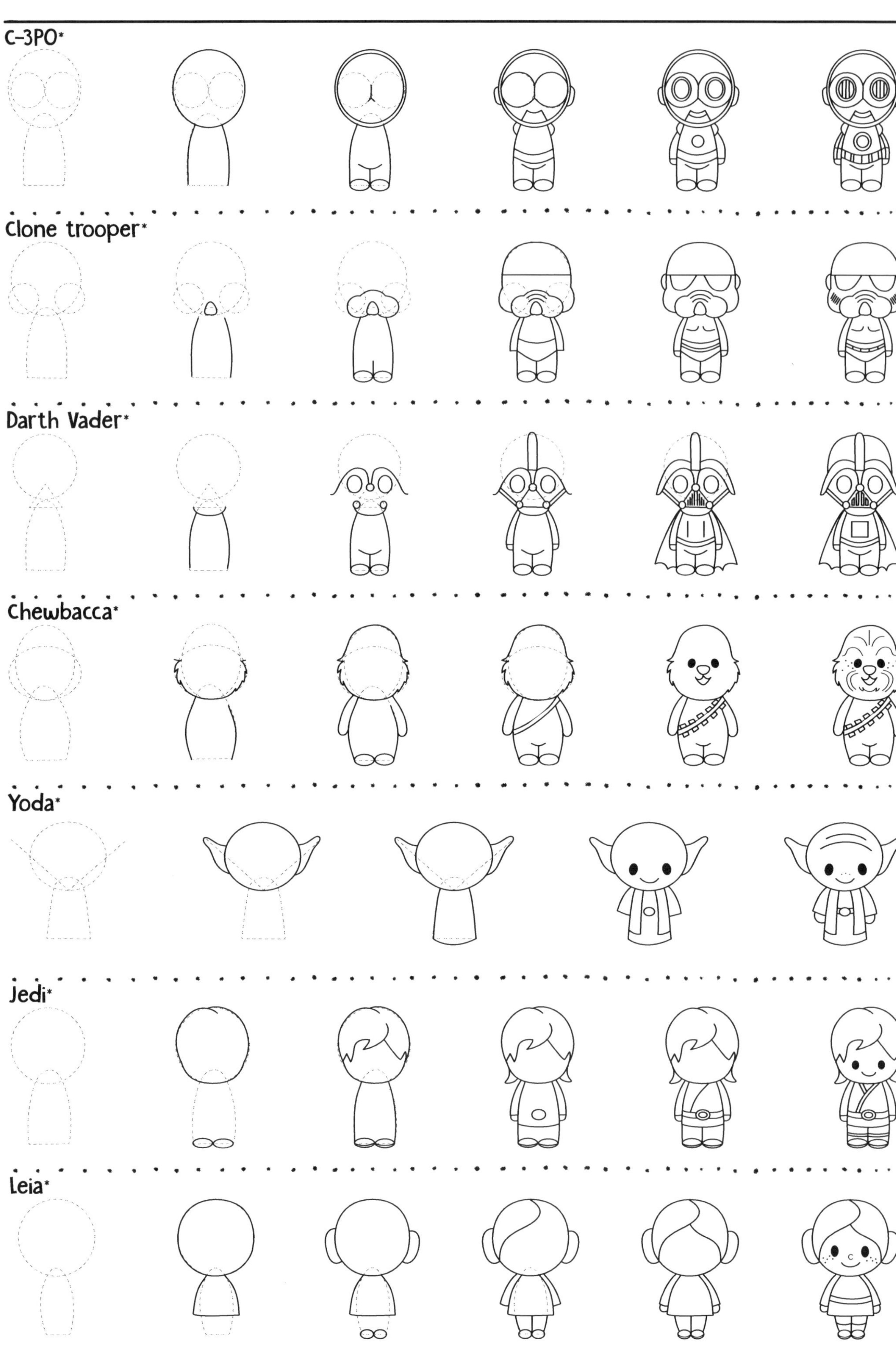
C-3PO*
Clone trooper*
Darth Vader*
Chewbacca*
Yoda*
Jedi*
Leia*

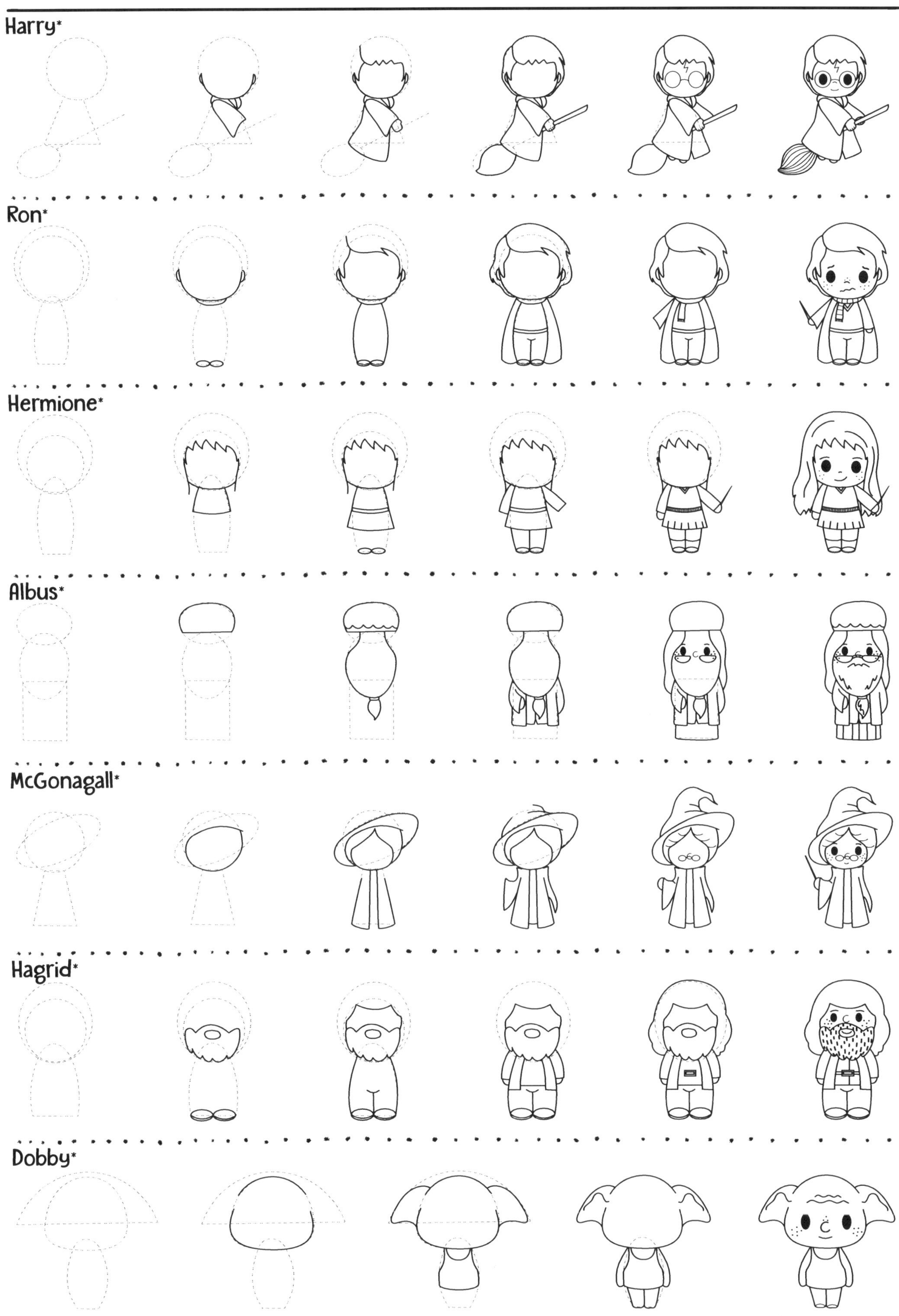
Harry*
Ron*
Hermione*
Albus*
McGonagall*
Hagrid*
Dobby*

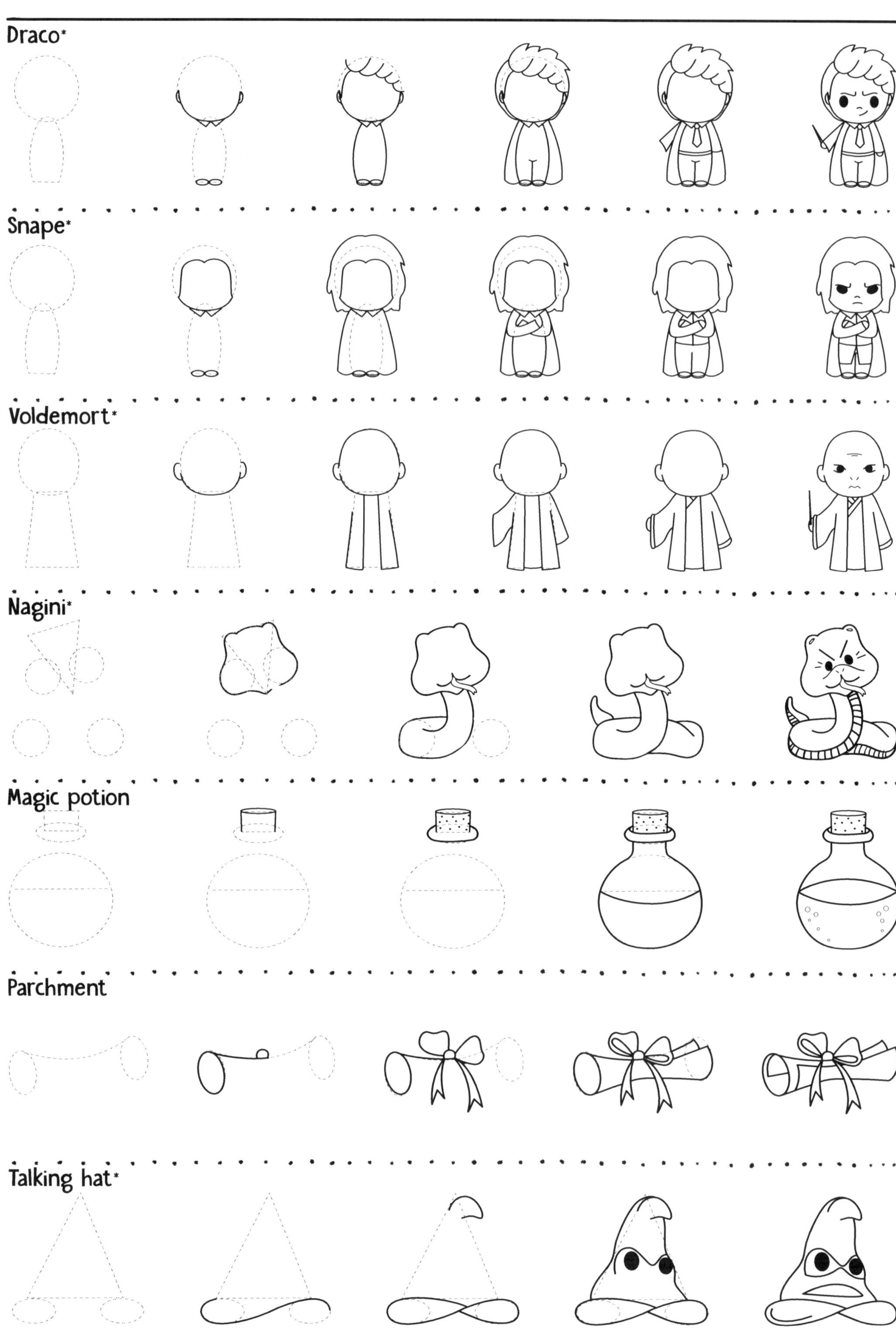
Draco*
Snape*
Voldemort*
Nagini*
Magic potion
Parchment
Talking hat*

Firebolt*

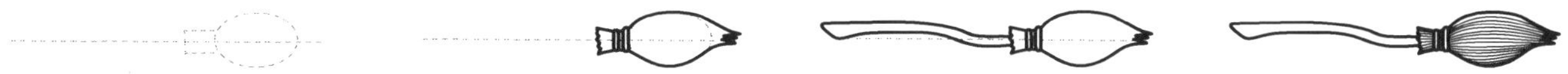

Snitch*

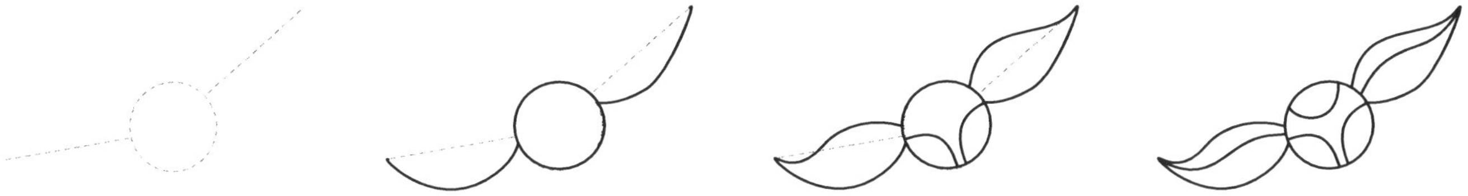

Giant

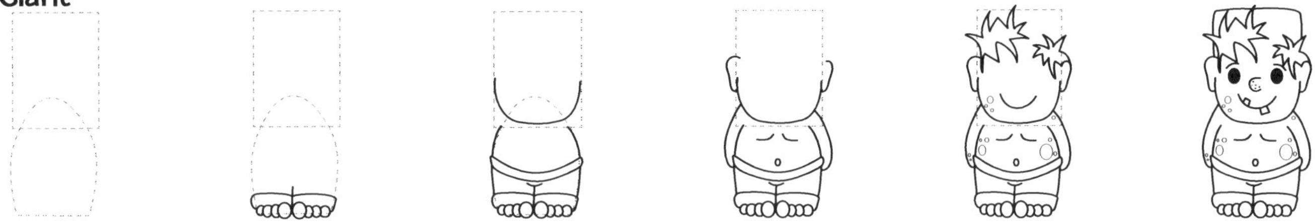

Yeti

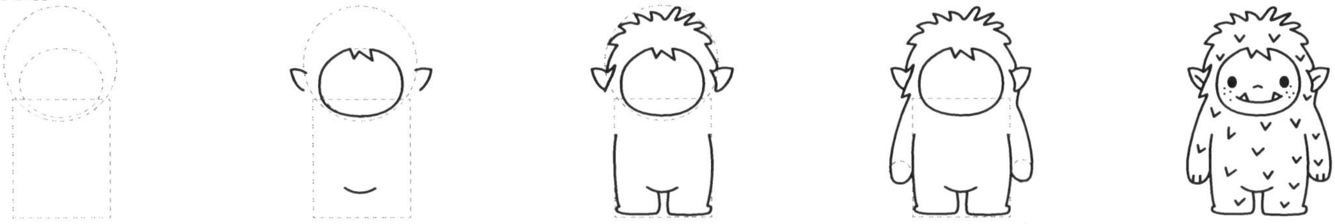

Mammoth

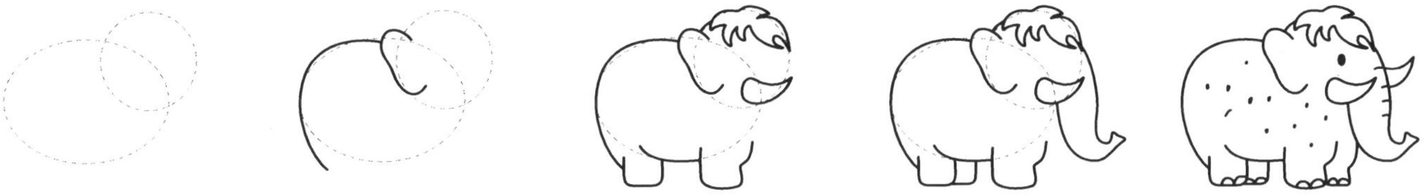

Dragon

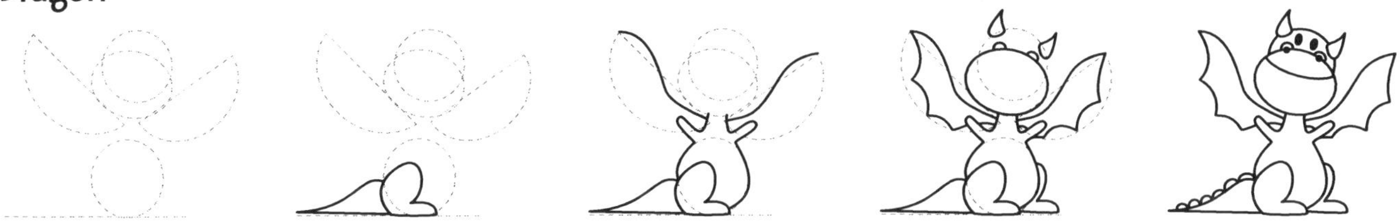

Knight castle

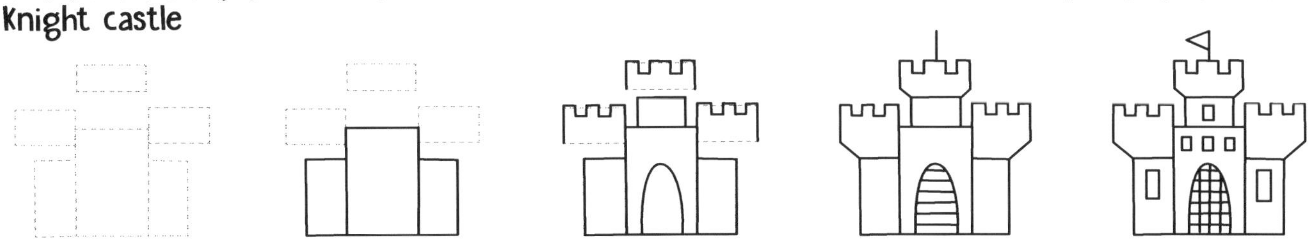

Knight

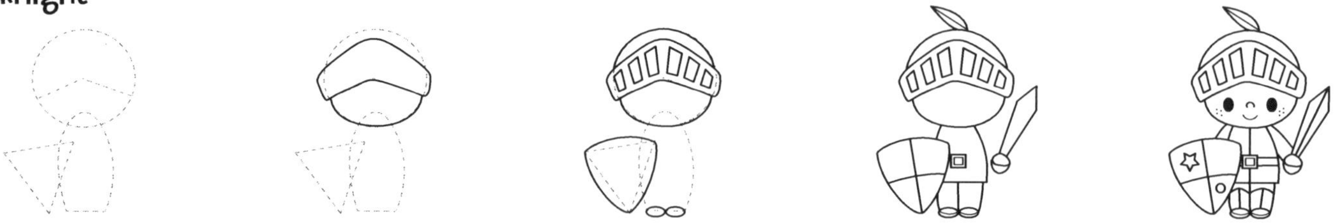

Knight helmet

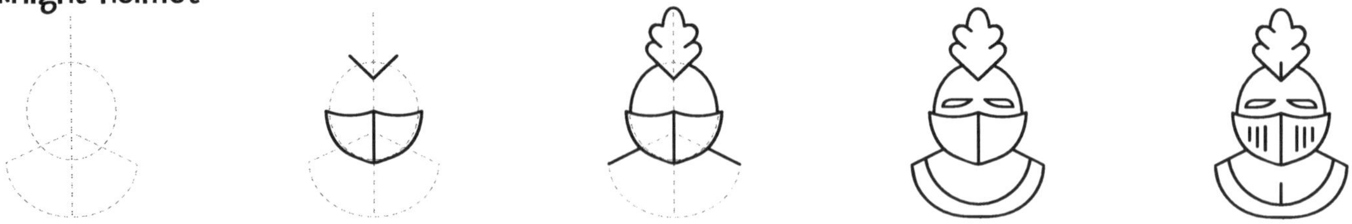

Sword

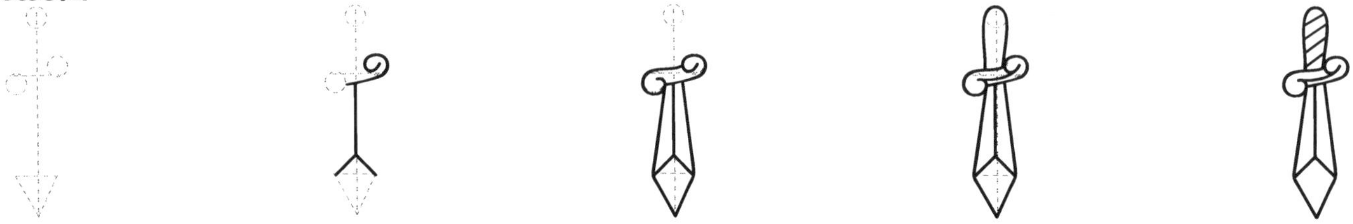

Viking

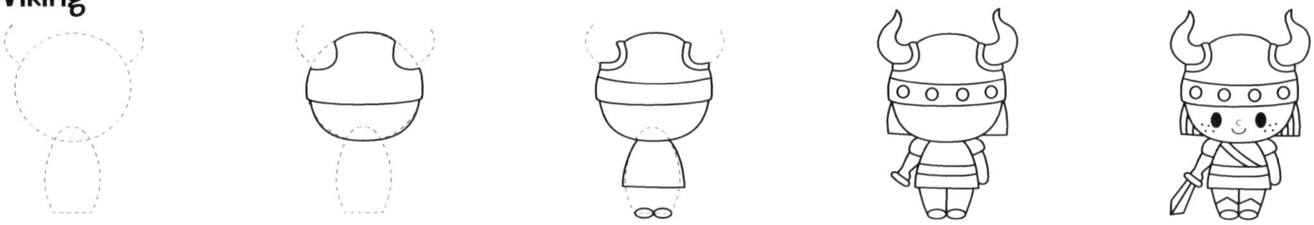

Viking ship

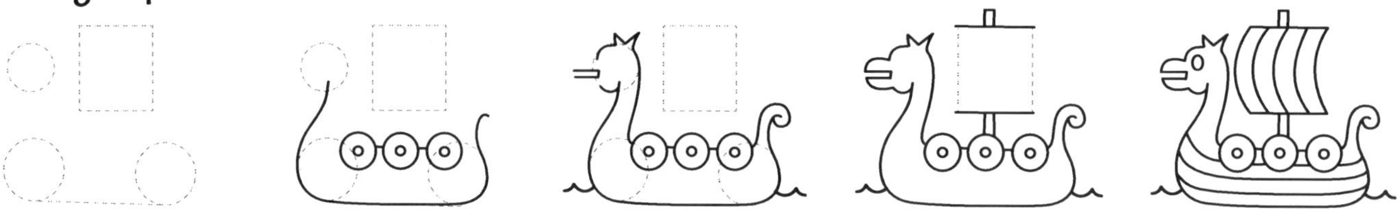

Viking helmet

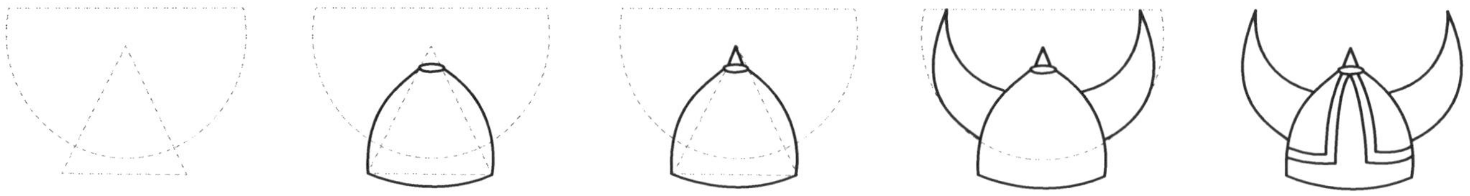

Pirate

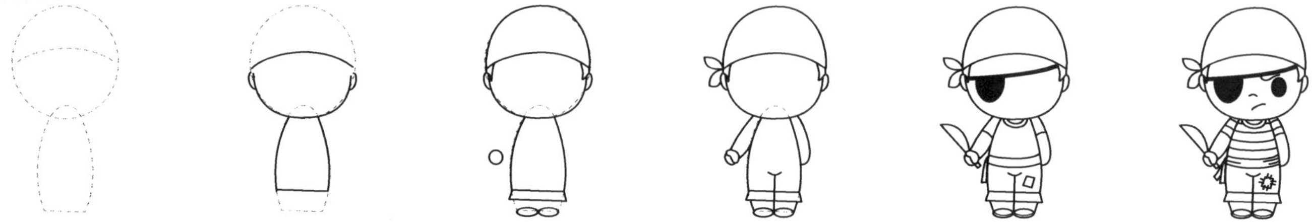

Telescope

Treasure map

Message in a bottle

Treasure chest

Skull

Pirate ship

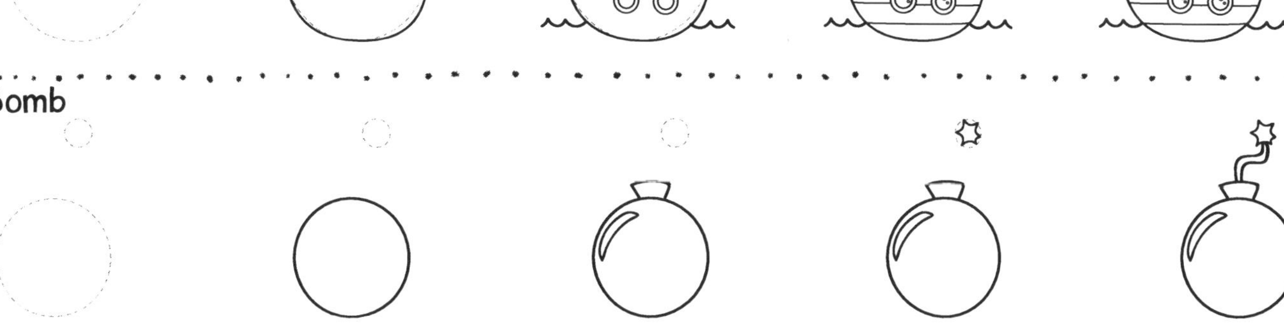

Bomb

Pirate hat

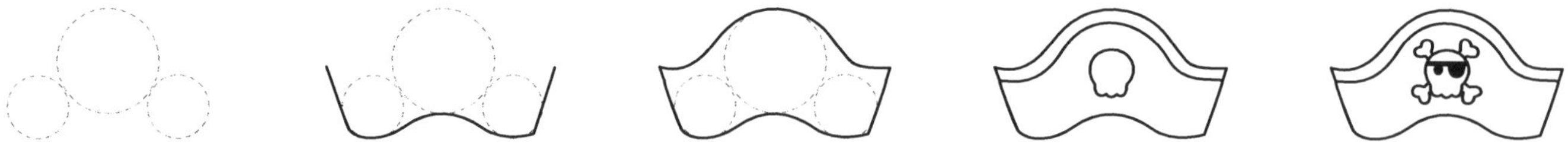

Hook

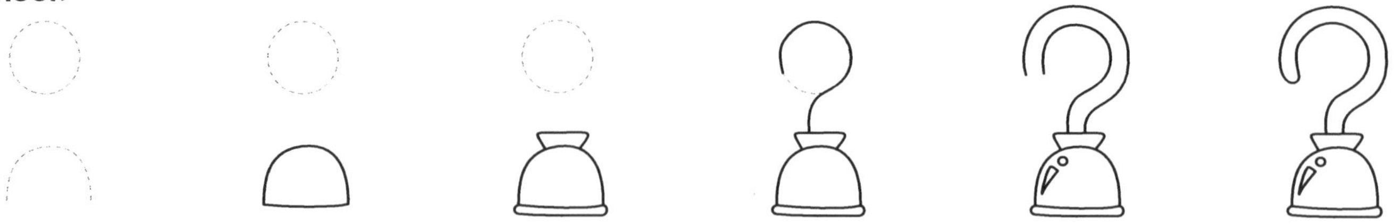

Saber

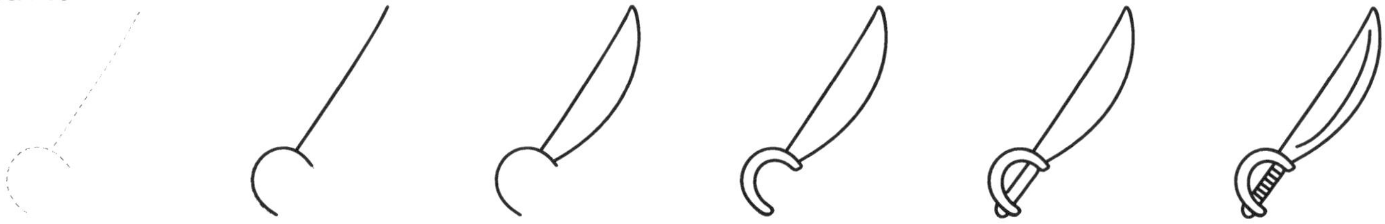

Cannon

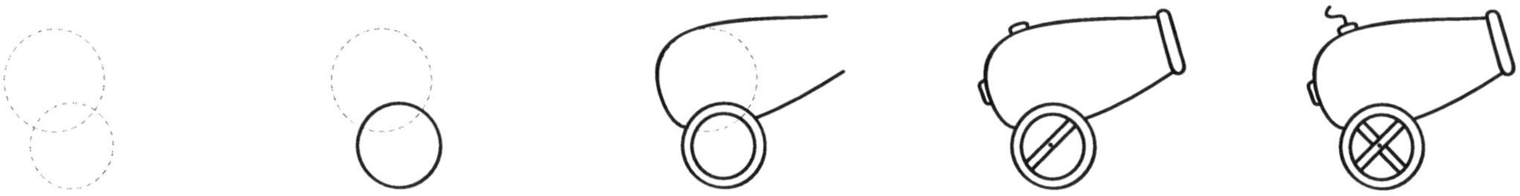

Revolver

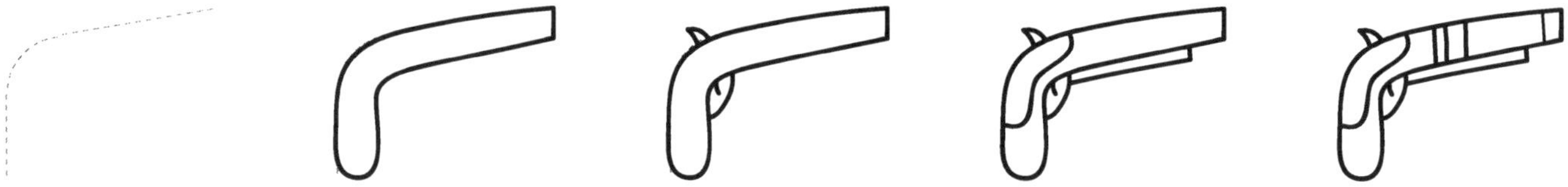

Dinamite

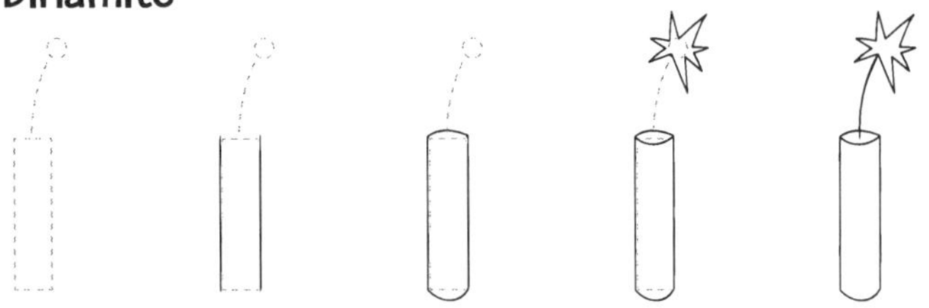

Dinosaur Egg

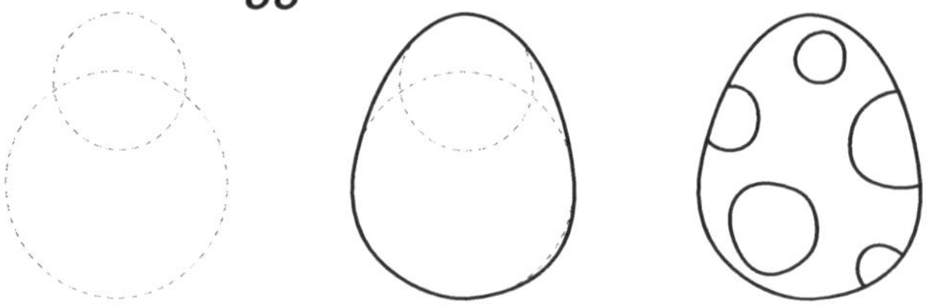

Stone age man

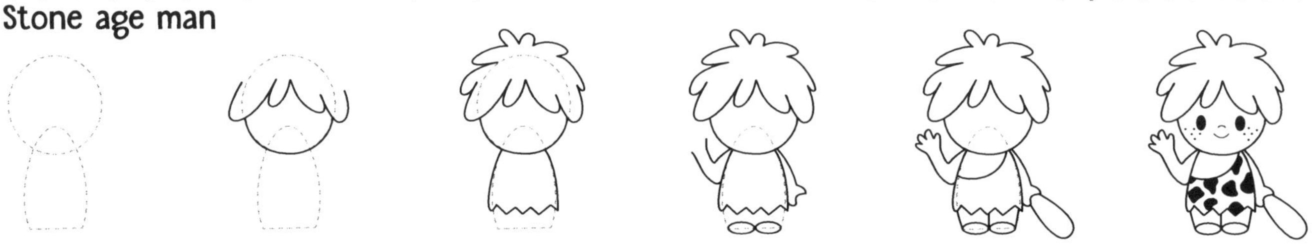

Tyrannosaurus

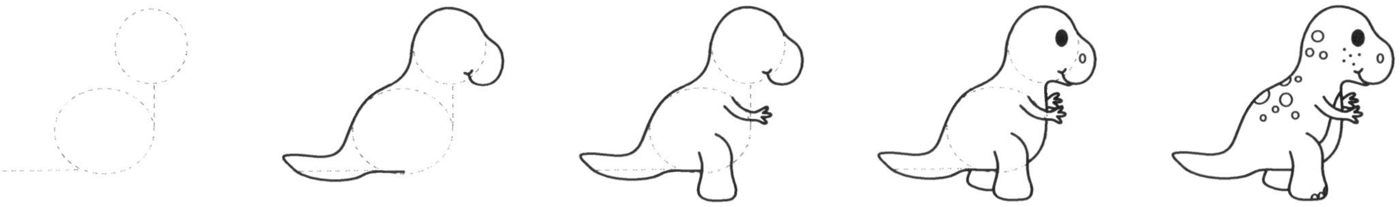

Stegosaurus

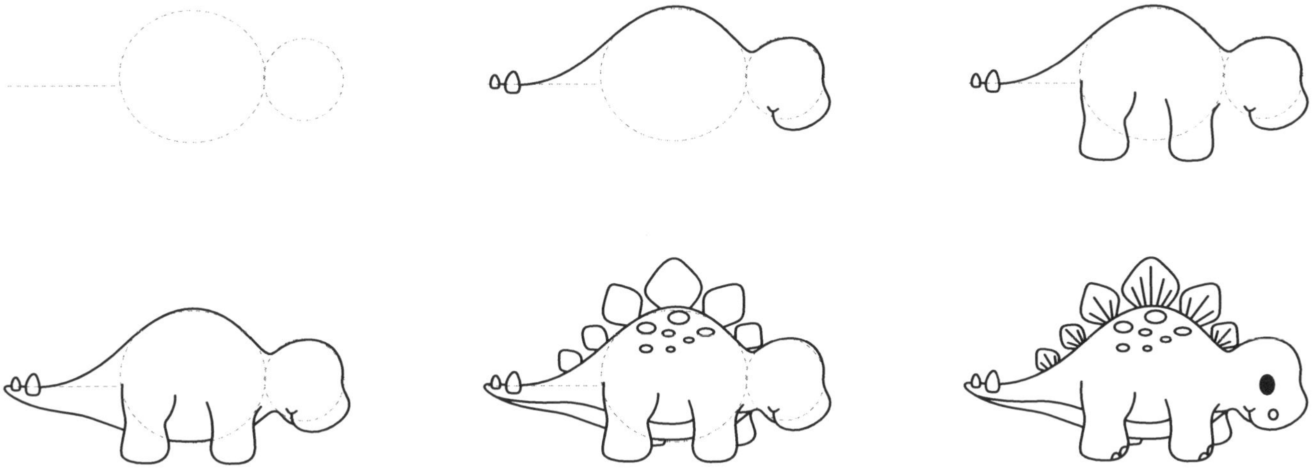

Brachiosaurus

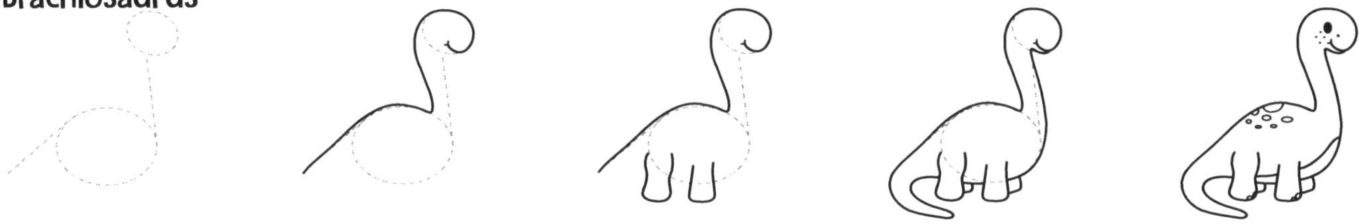

Native American

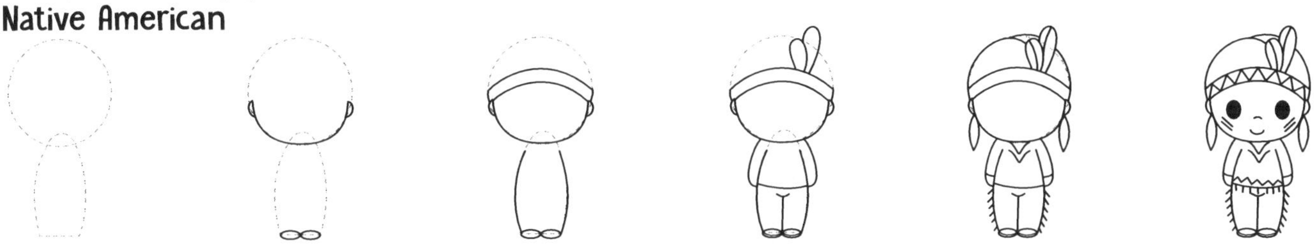

Tepee

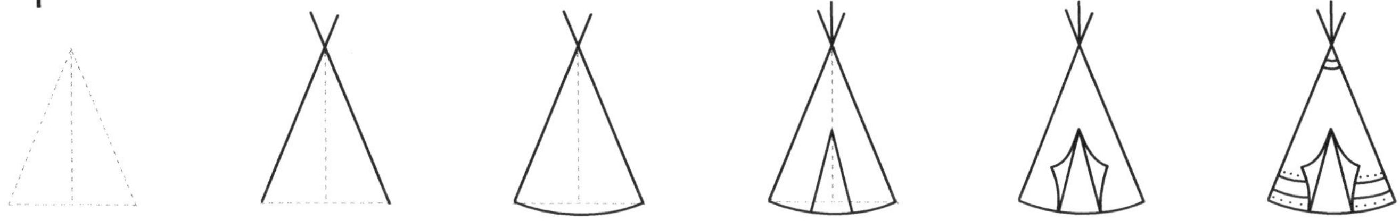

Bow and arrow

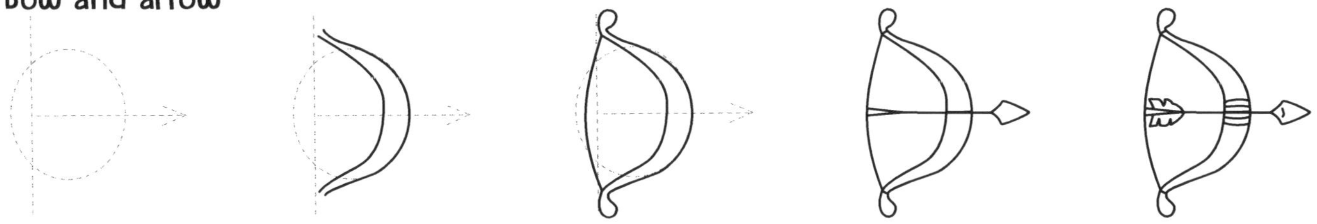

Cowboy

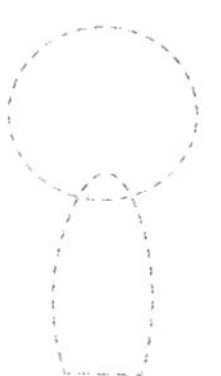 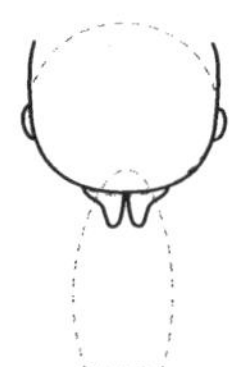 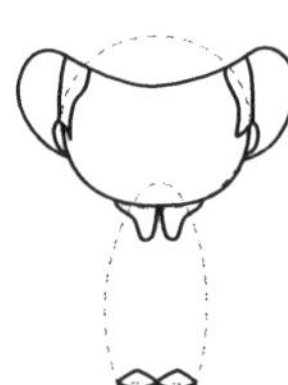 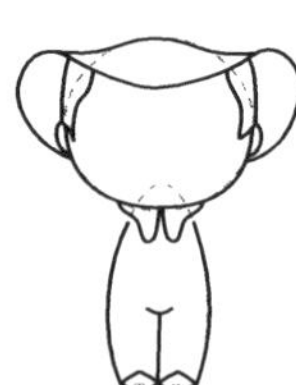 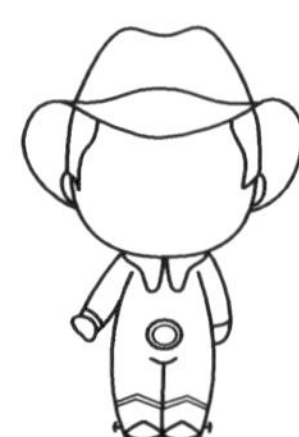 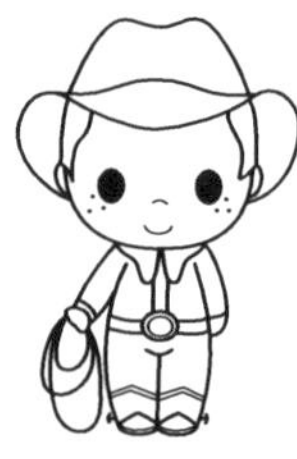

Cowboy hat

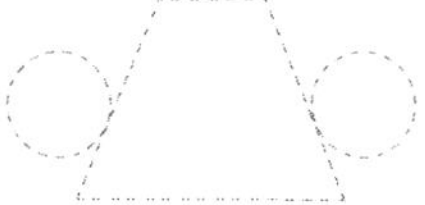 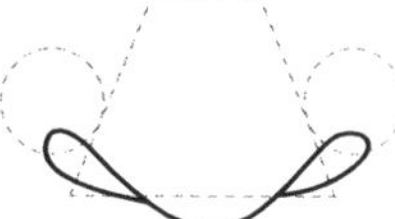 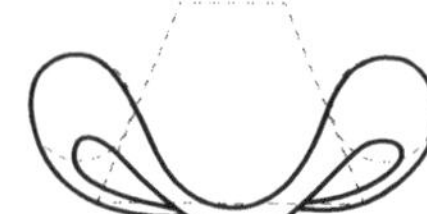 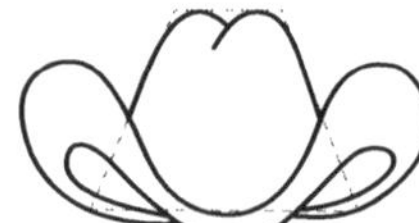 

Sultan

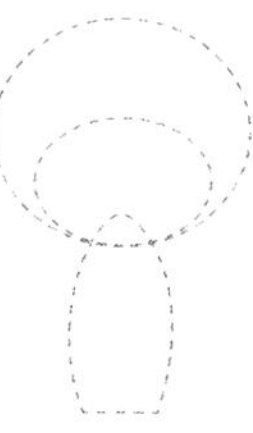 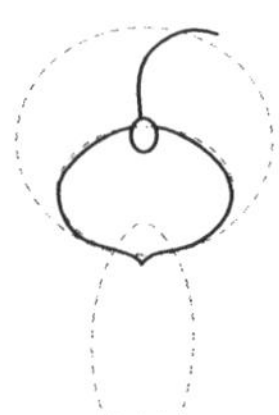 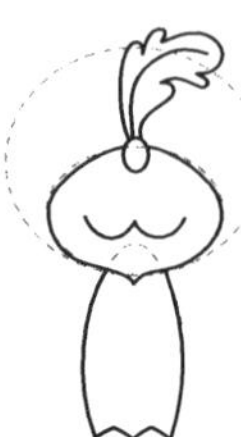 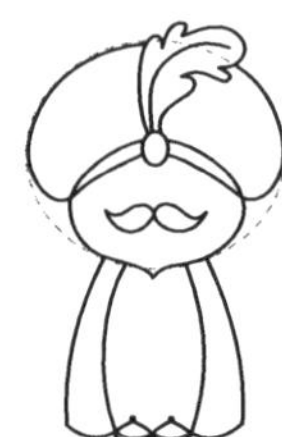 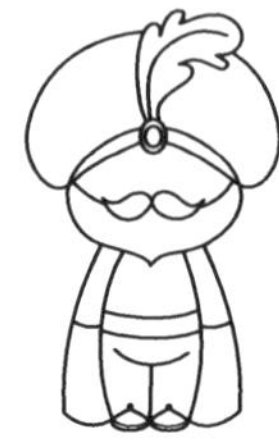 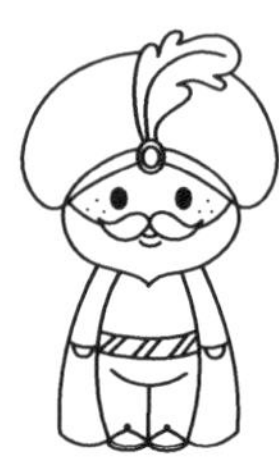

Palace

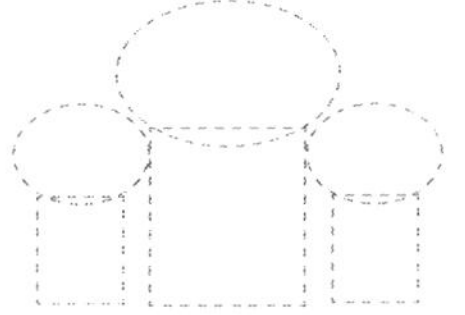 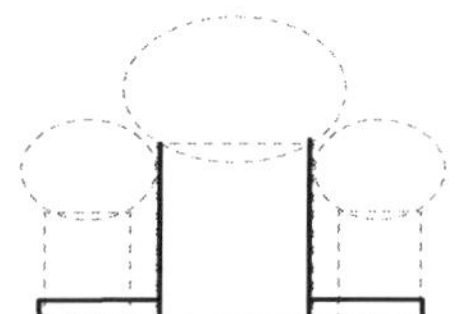 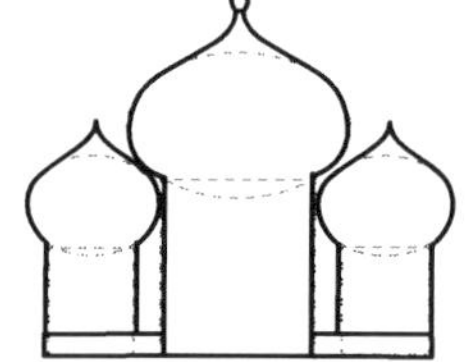 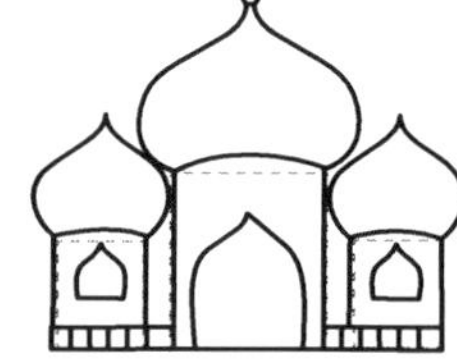 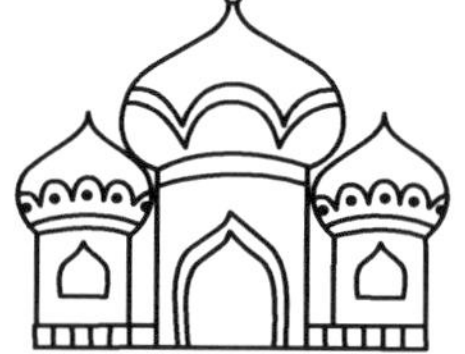

Magic lamp

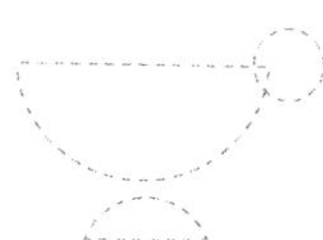 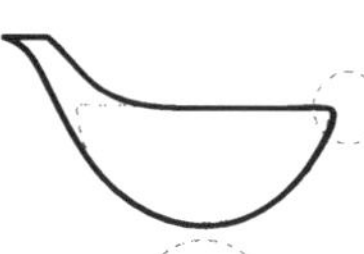 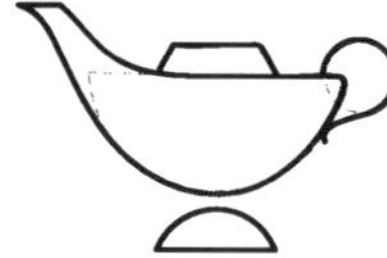 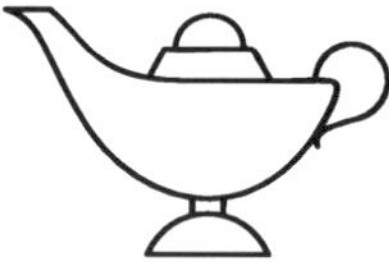 

Genie

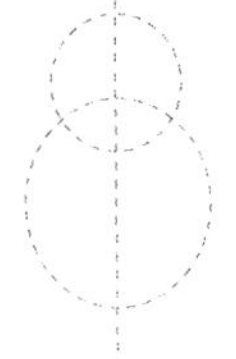 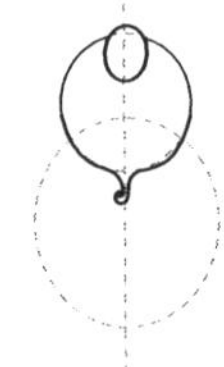 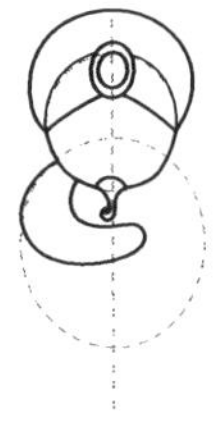 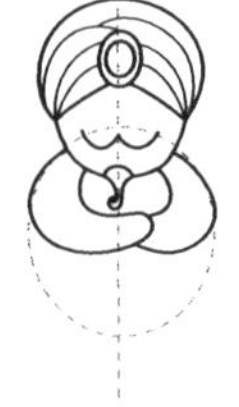 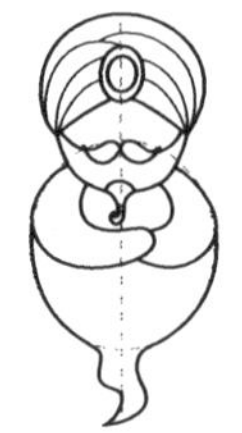 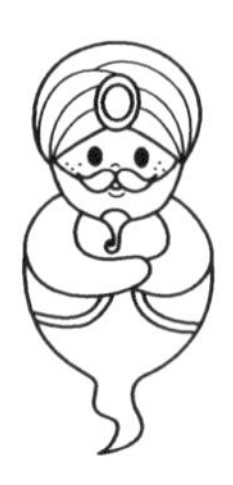

Peter Pan

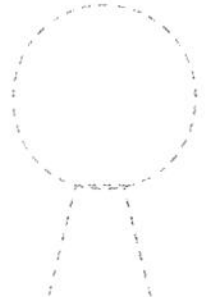 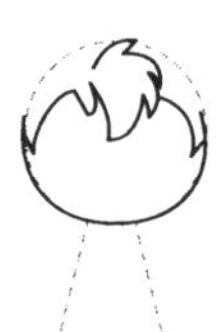 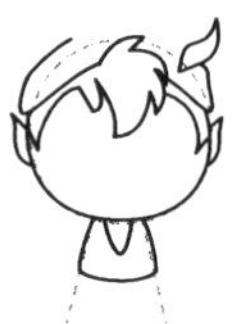 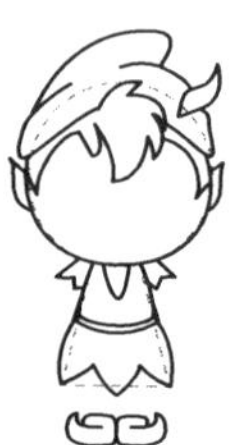 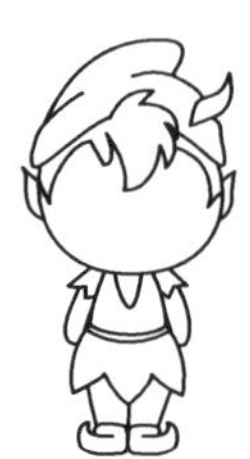 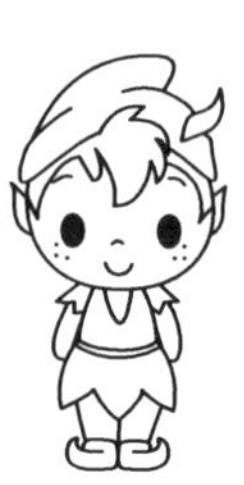

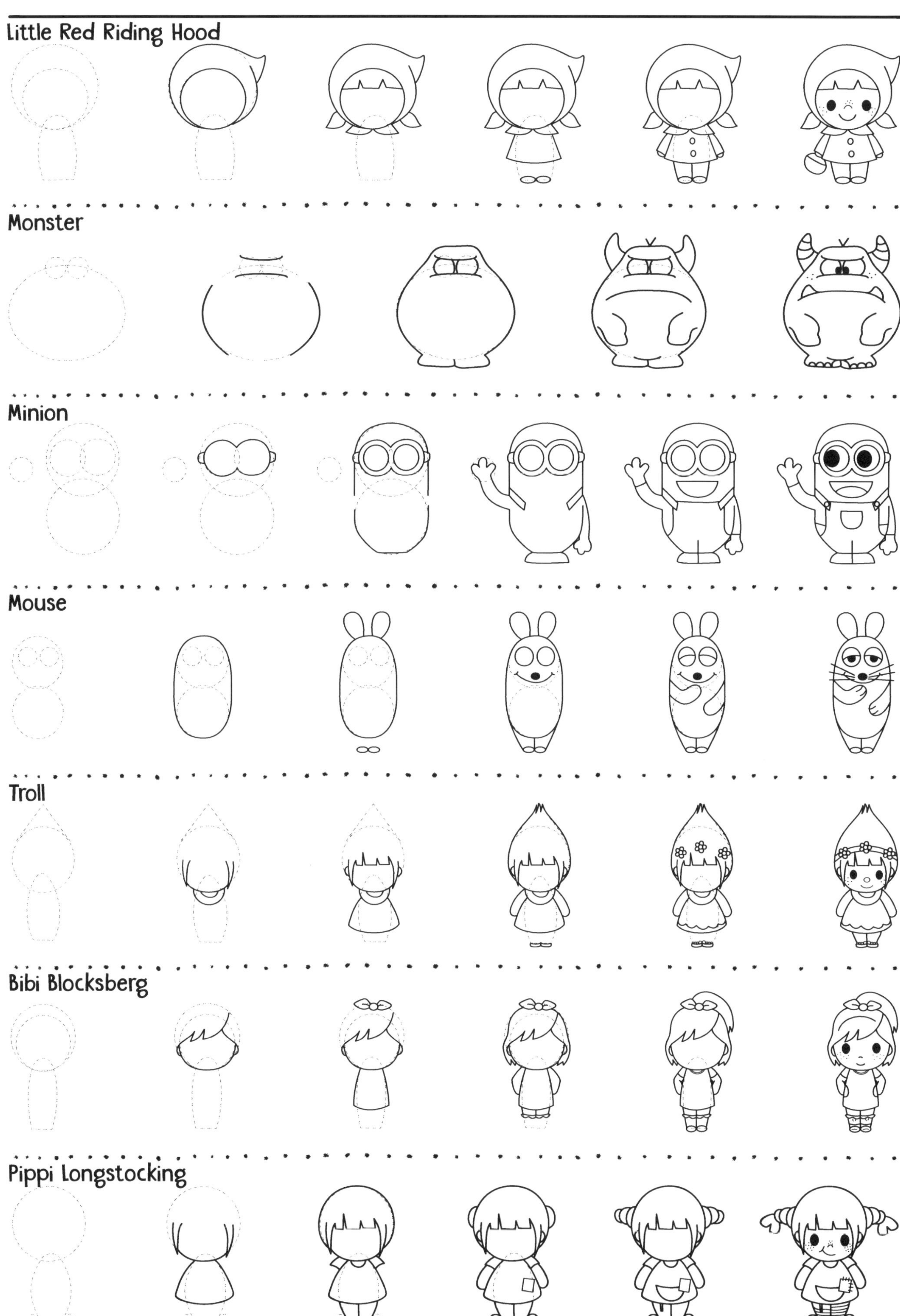
Little Red Riding Hood
Monster
Minion
Mouse
Troll
Bibi Blocksberg
Pippi Longstocking

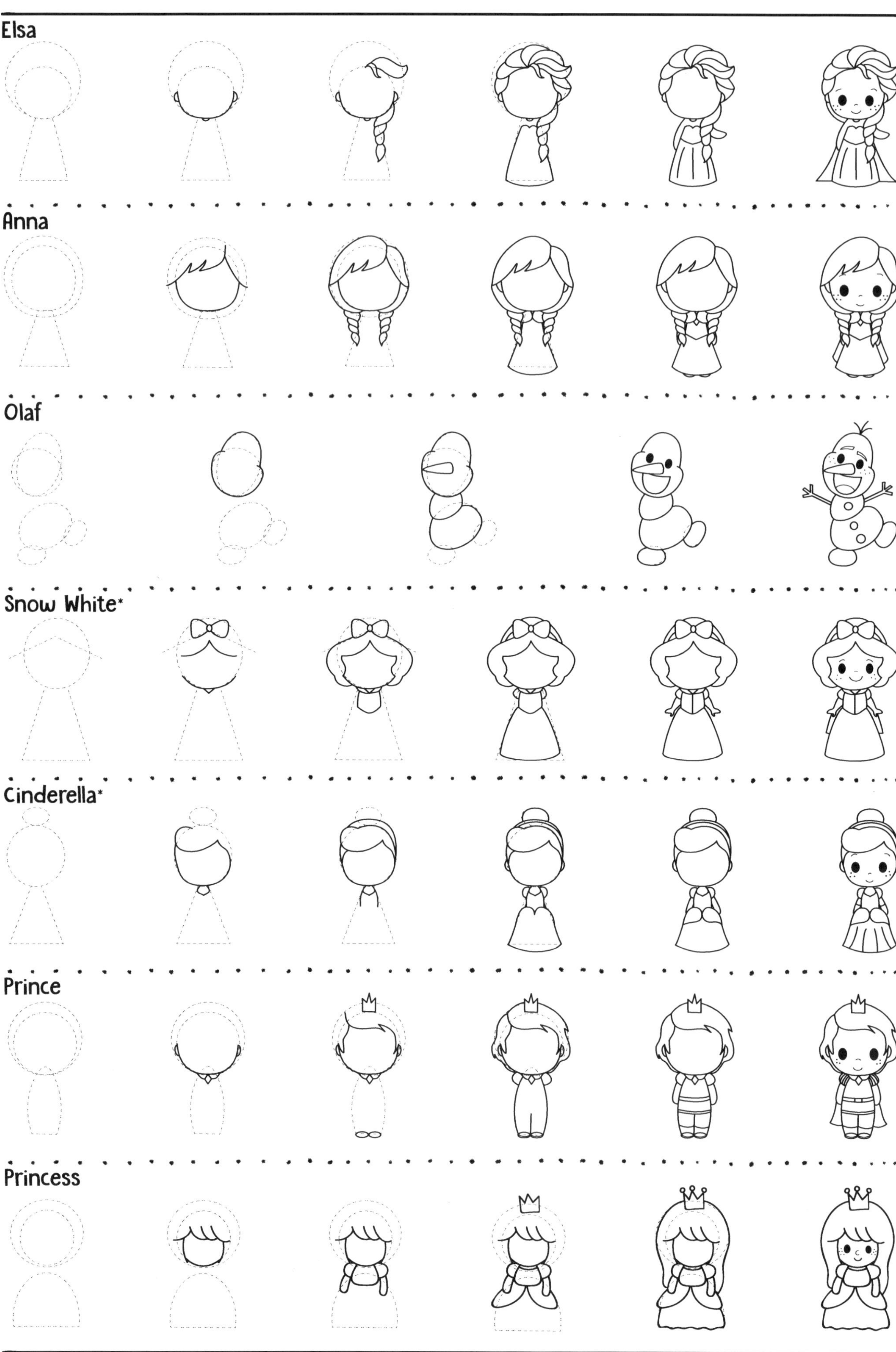

Elsa
Anna
Olaf
Snow White*
Cinderella*
Prince
Princess

Castle

Carriage

Crown

Ball gown

Tiara

Fairy

Fairy wand

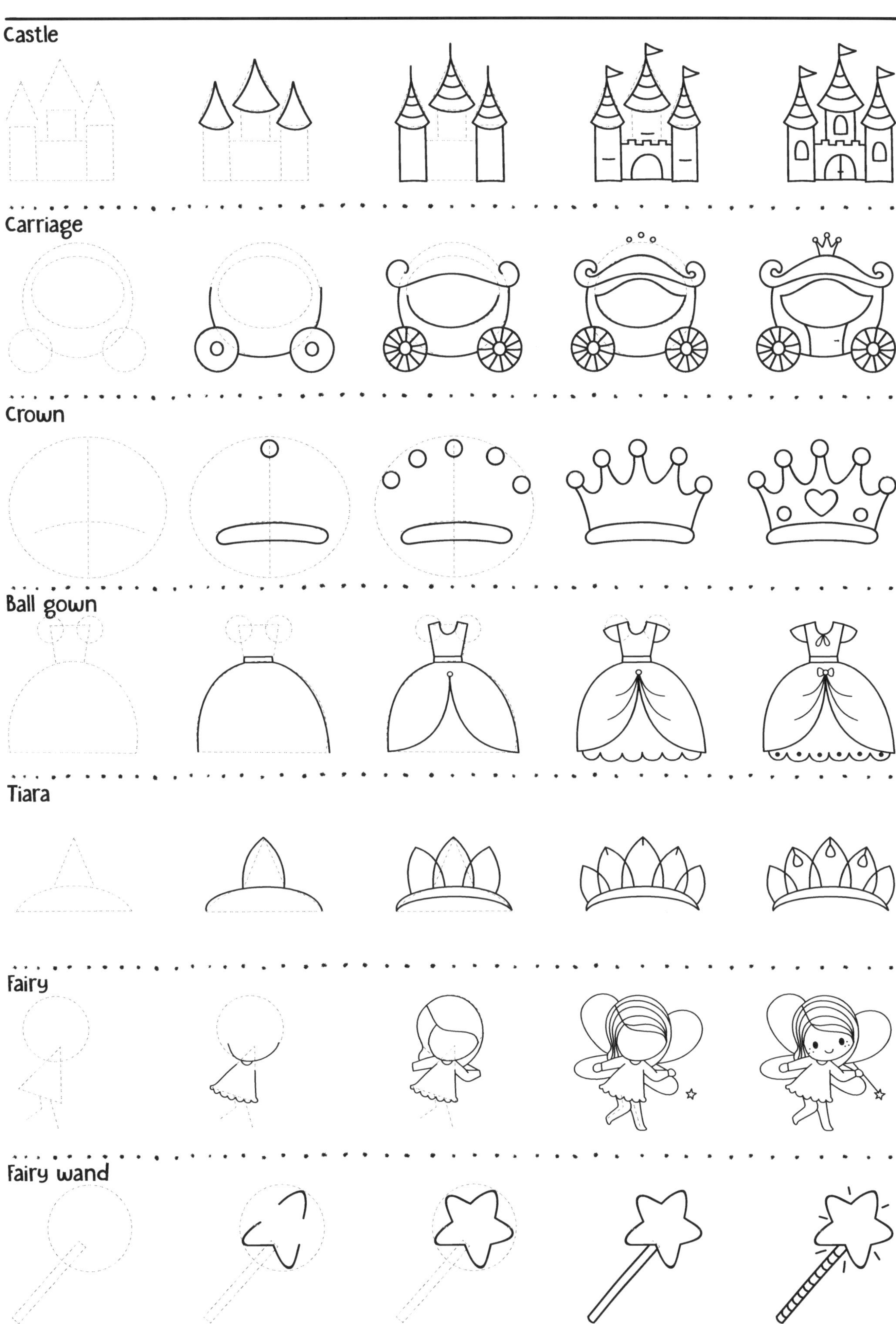

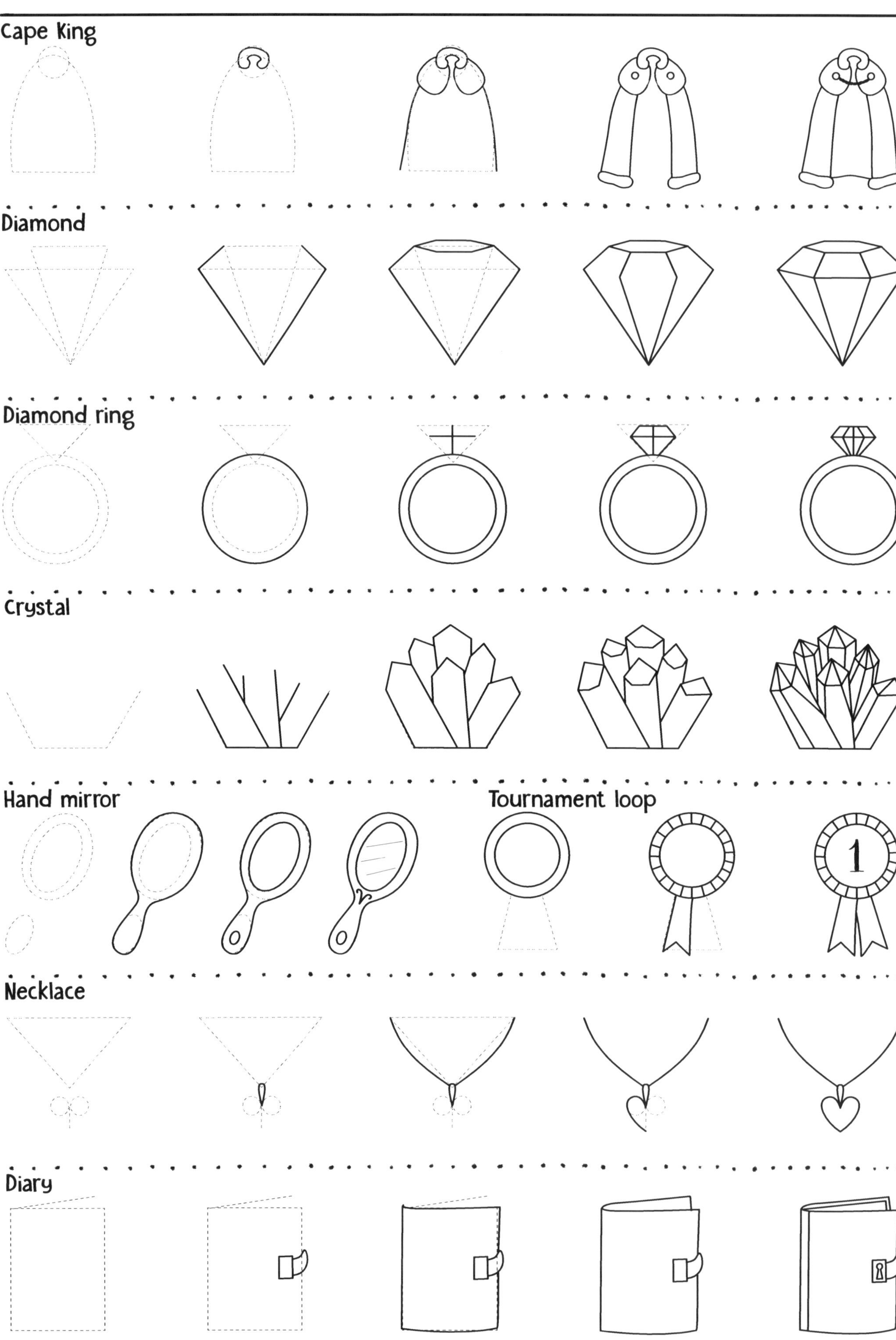
Cape King
Diamond
Diamond ring
Crystal
Hand mirror
Tournament loop
1
Necklace
Diary

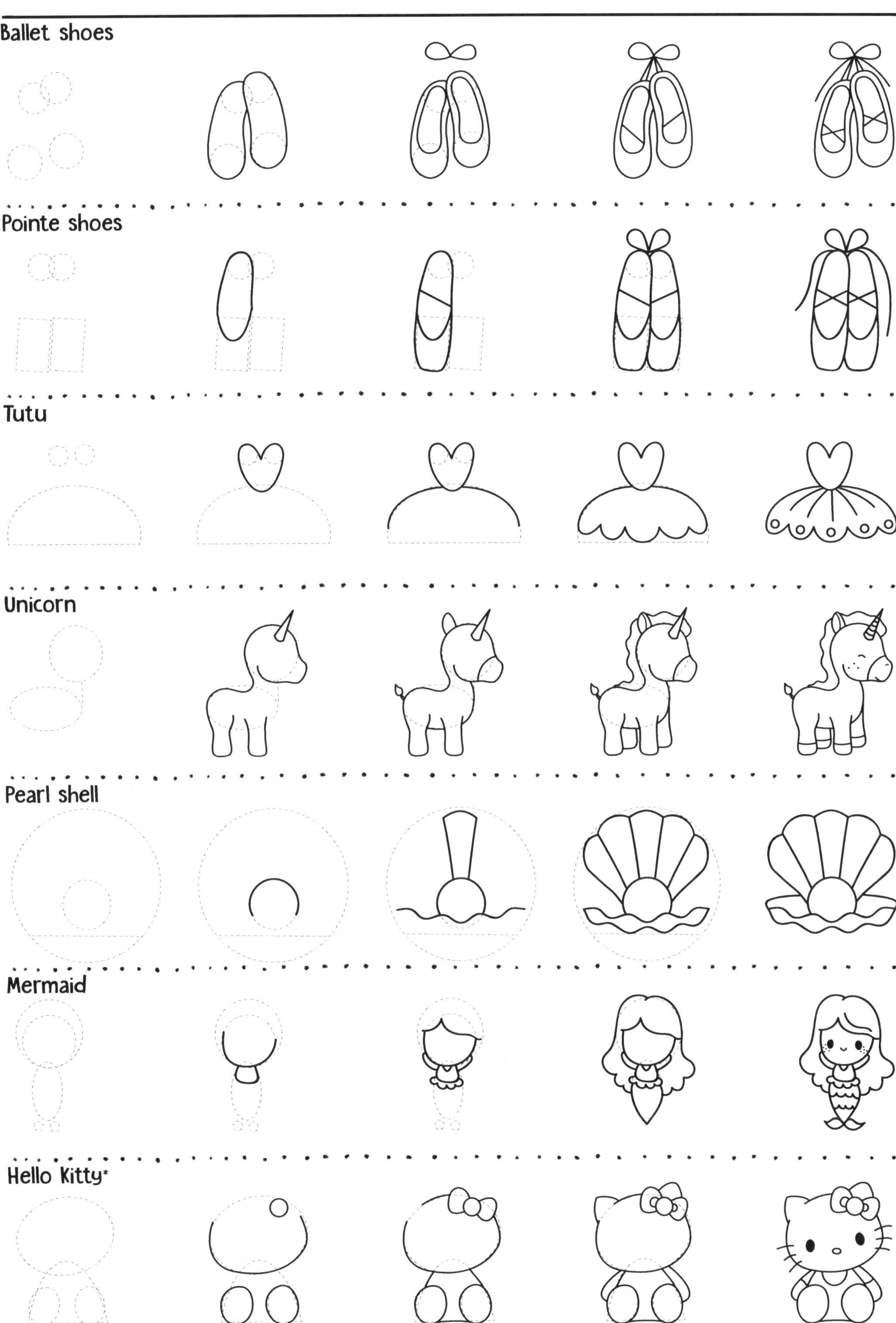
Ballet shoes
Pointe shoes
Tutu
Unicorn
Pearl shell
Mermaid
Hello Kitty*

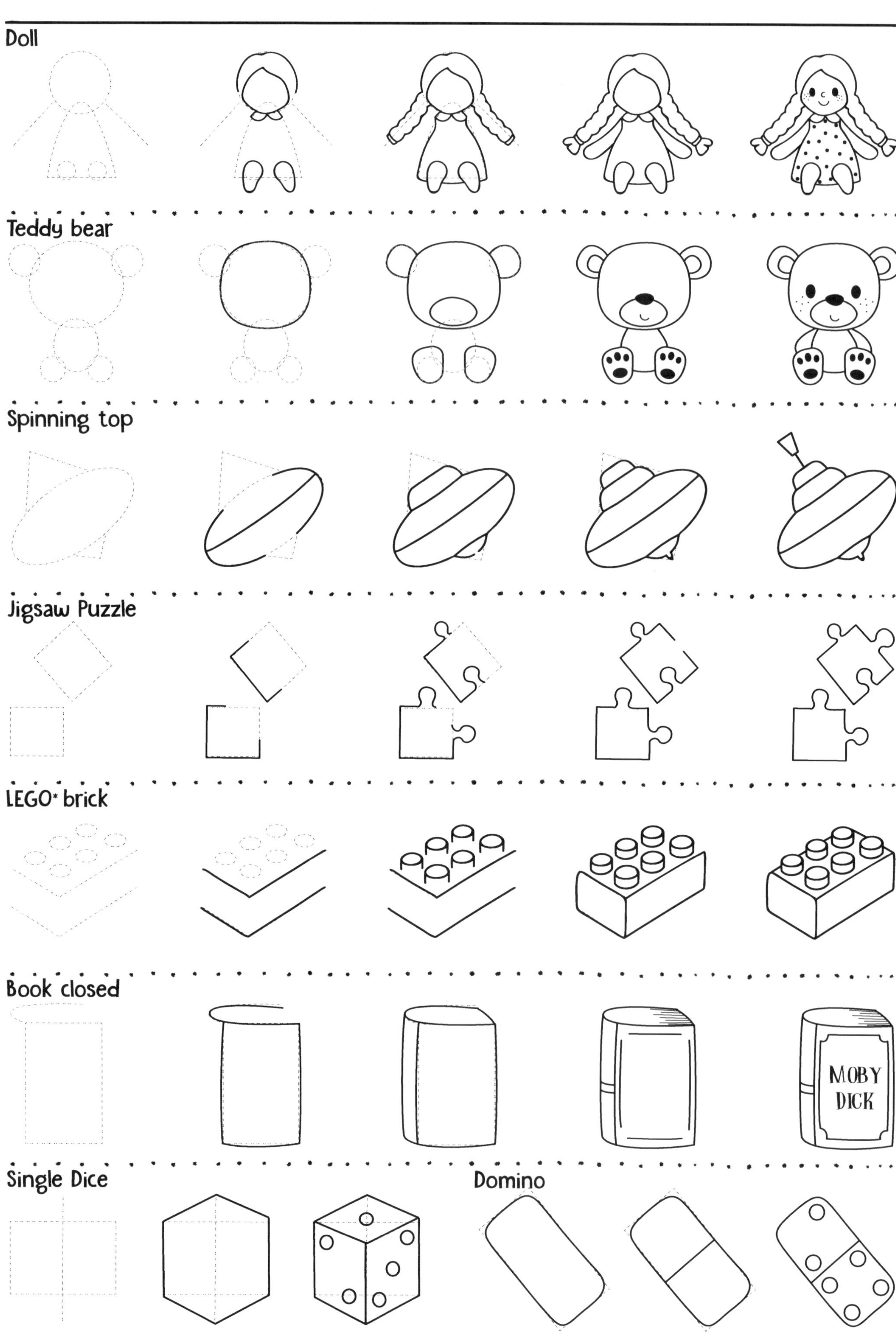
Doll
Teddy bear
Spinning top
Jigsaw Puzzle
LEGO* brick
Book closed
MOBY DICK
Single Dice
Domino

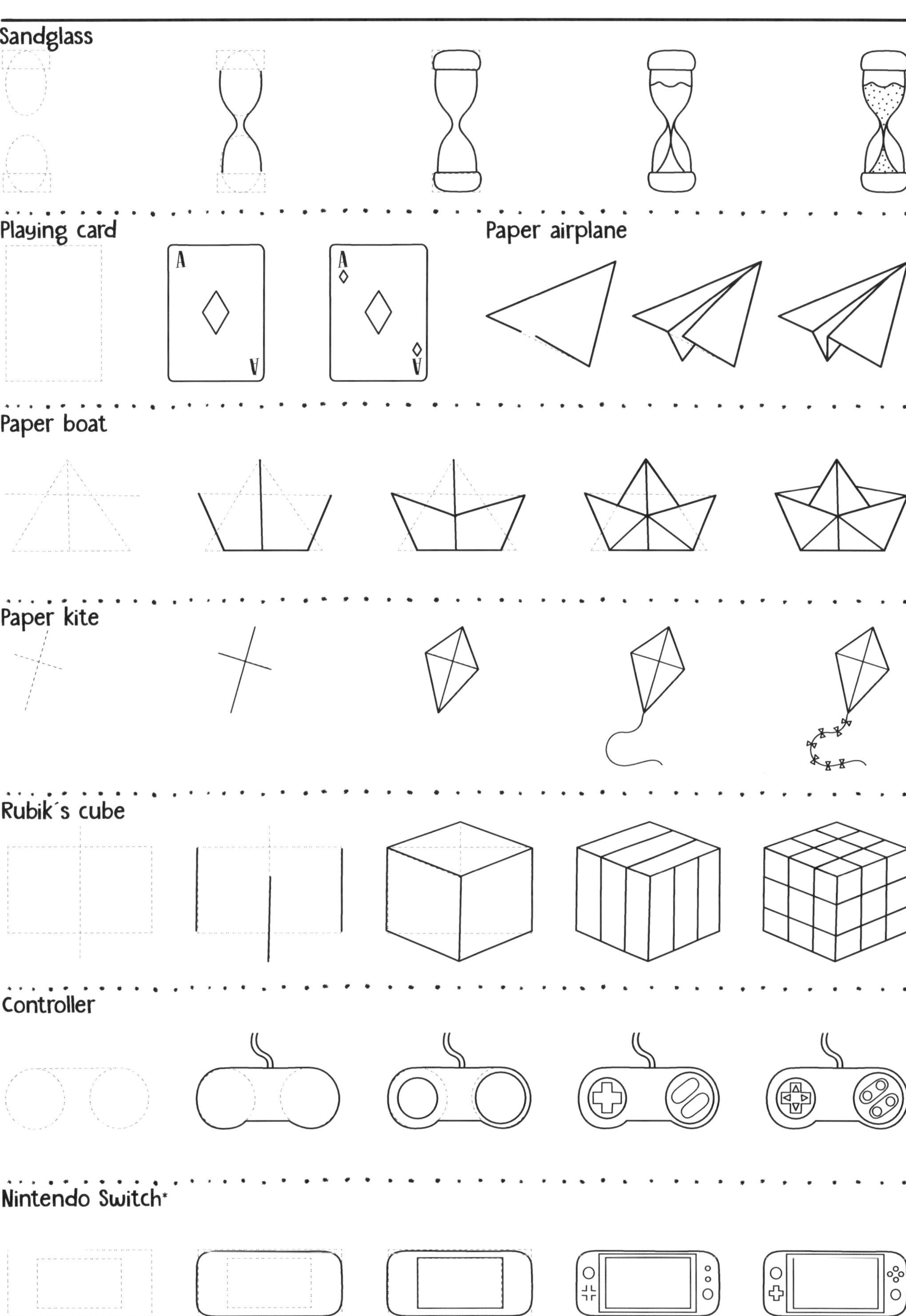
Sandglass
Playing card
Paper airplane
Paper boat
Paper kite
Rubik´s cube
Controller
Nintendo Switch*

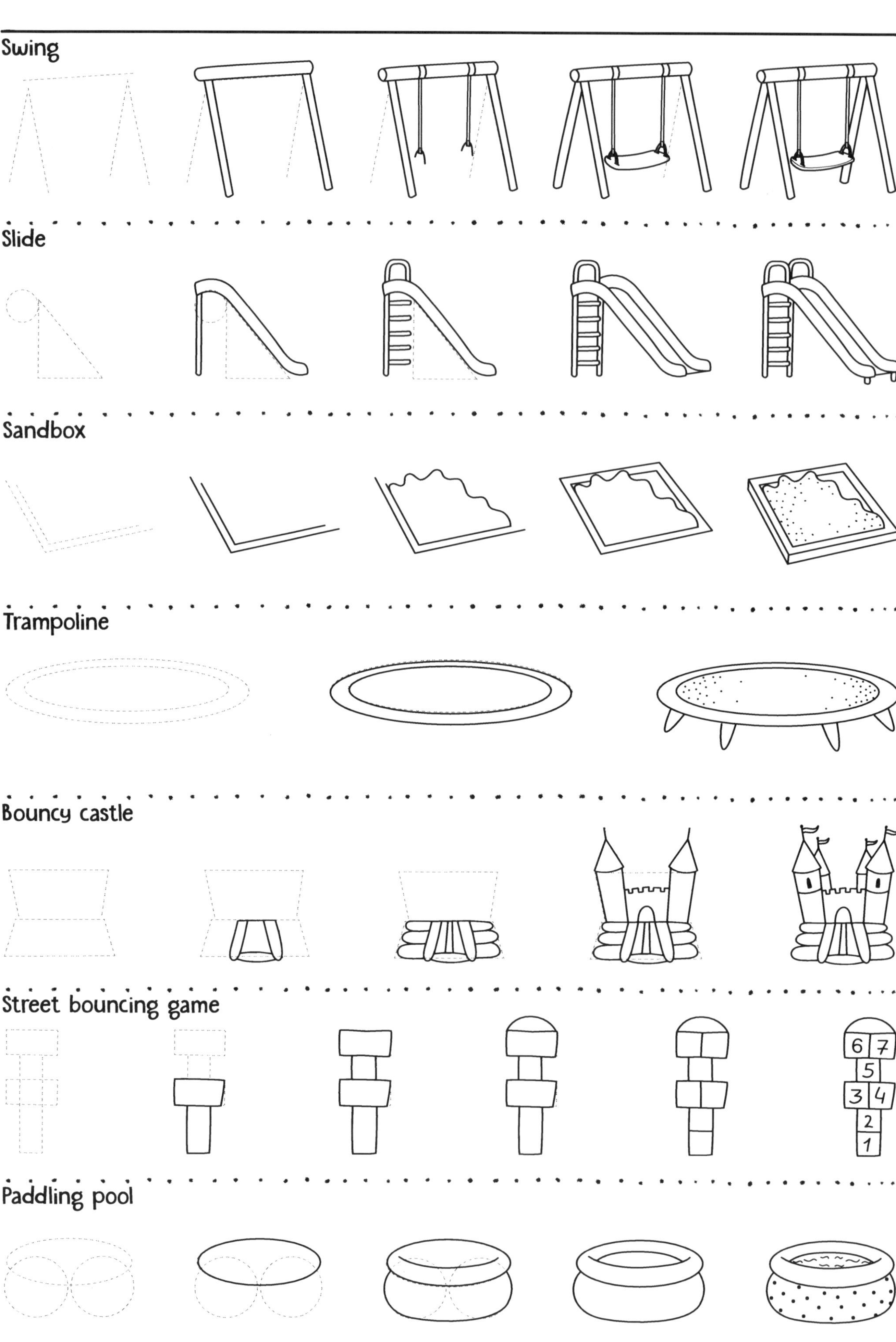
Swing
Slide
Sandbox
Trampoline
Bouncy castle
Street bouncing game
6 7
5
3 4
2
1
Paddling pool

Squirt gun

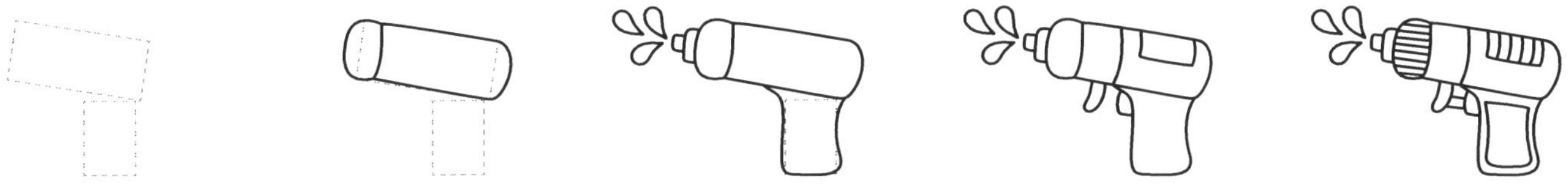

Martins lantern

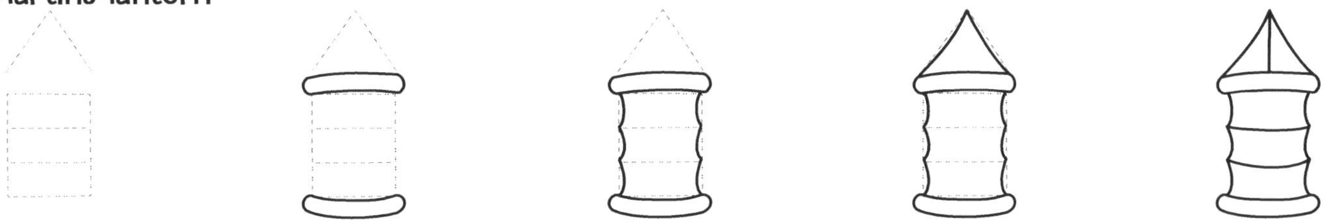

Target

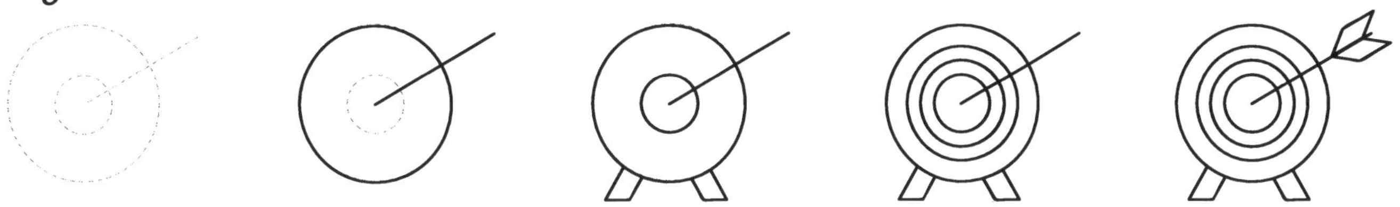

Handcart

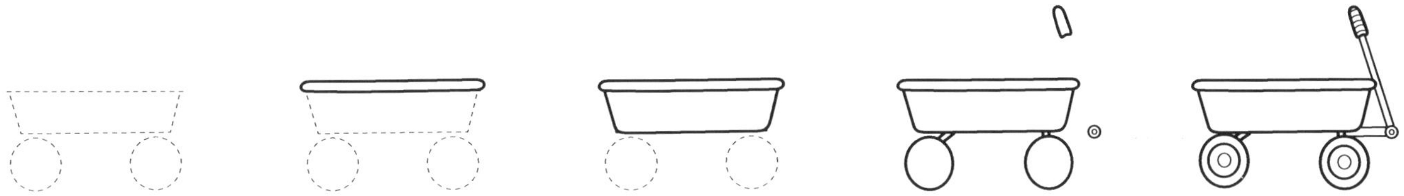

Giant swingboat

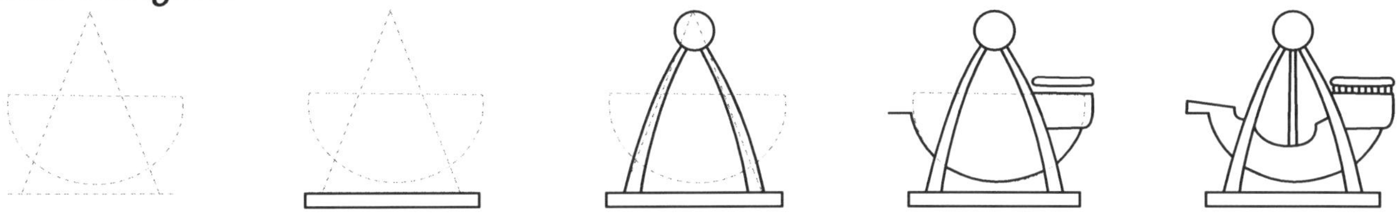

Bumper car

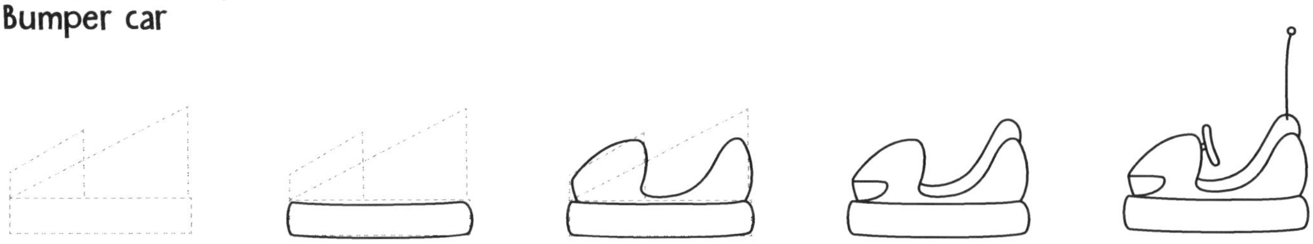

Ferris wheel

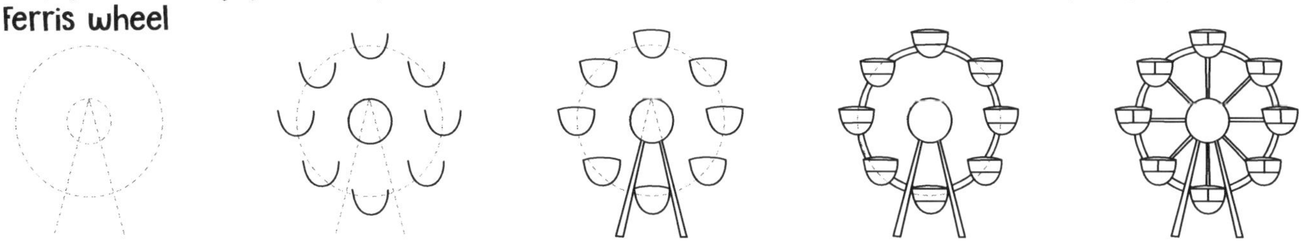

River ride

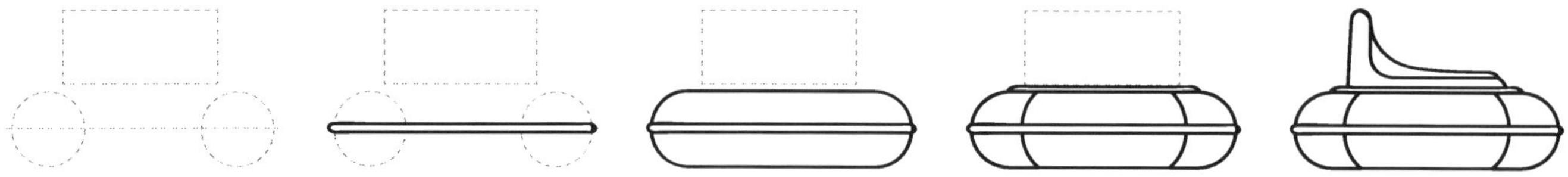

Chairoplane

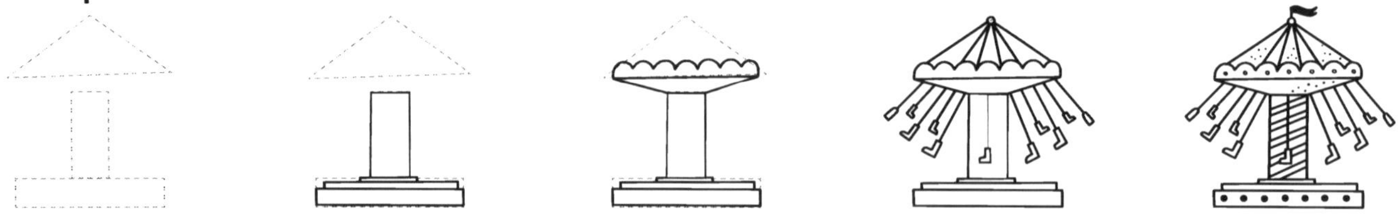

Big top

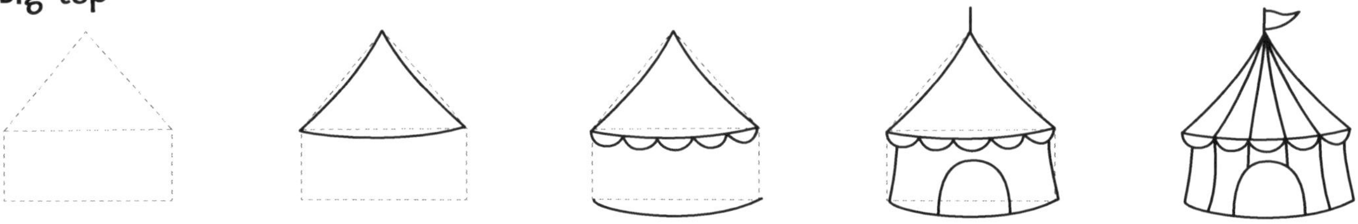

Clown

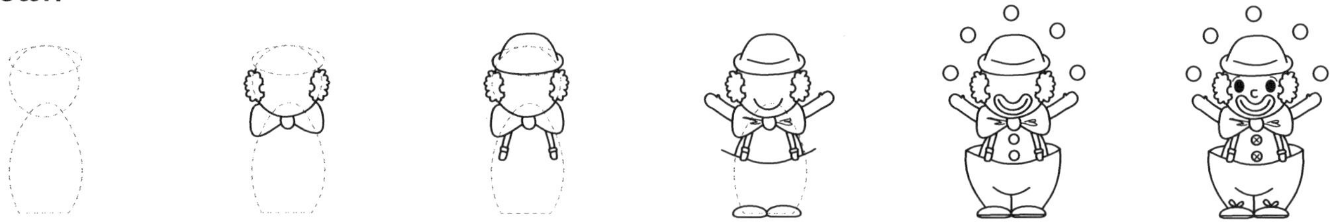

Stage

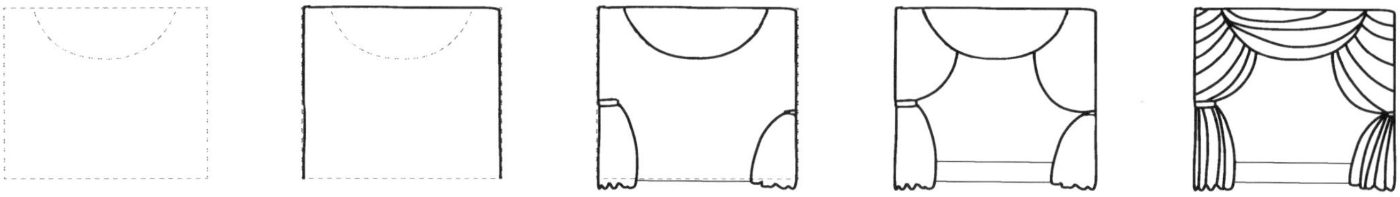

Movie ticket

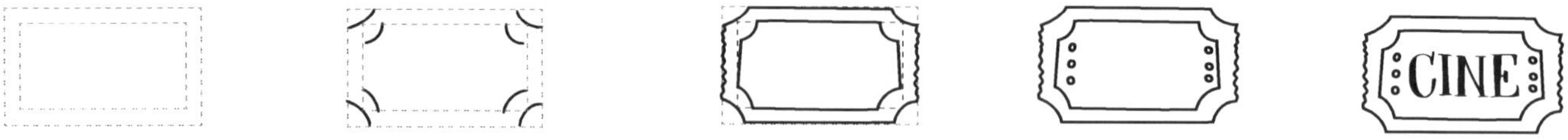

CINE

Popcorn

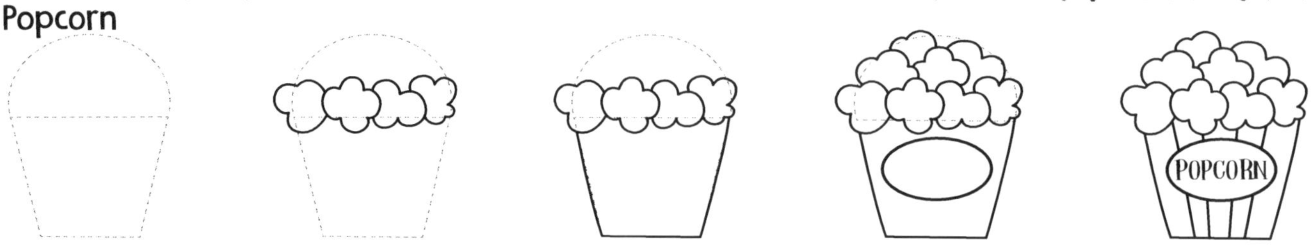

POPCORN

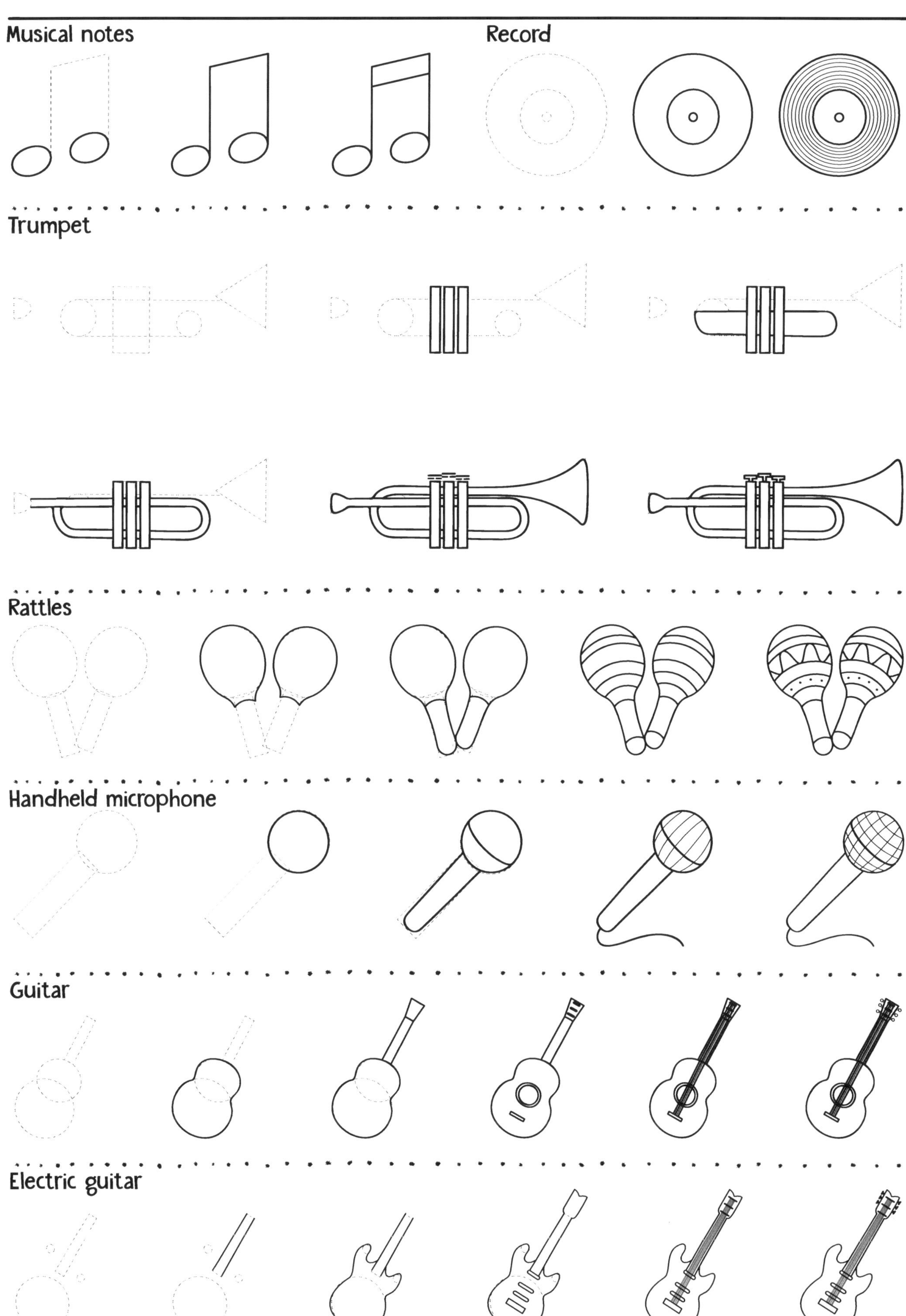
Musical notes
Record
Trumpet
Rattles
Handheld microphone
Guitar
Electric guitar

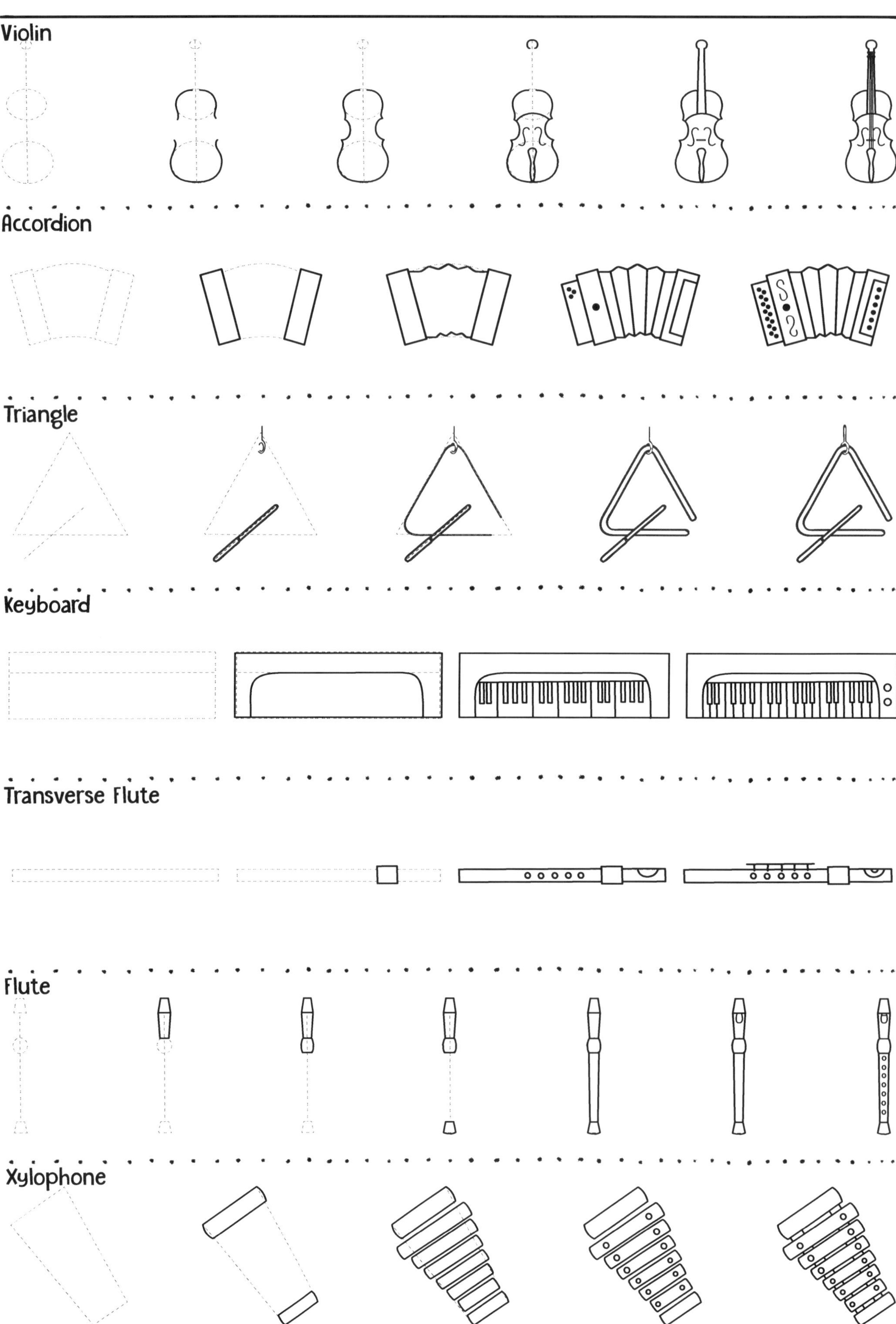
Violin
Accordion
Triangle
Keyboard
Transverse Flute
Flute
Xylophone

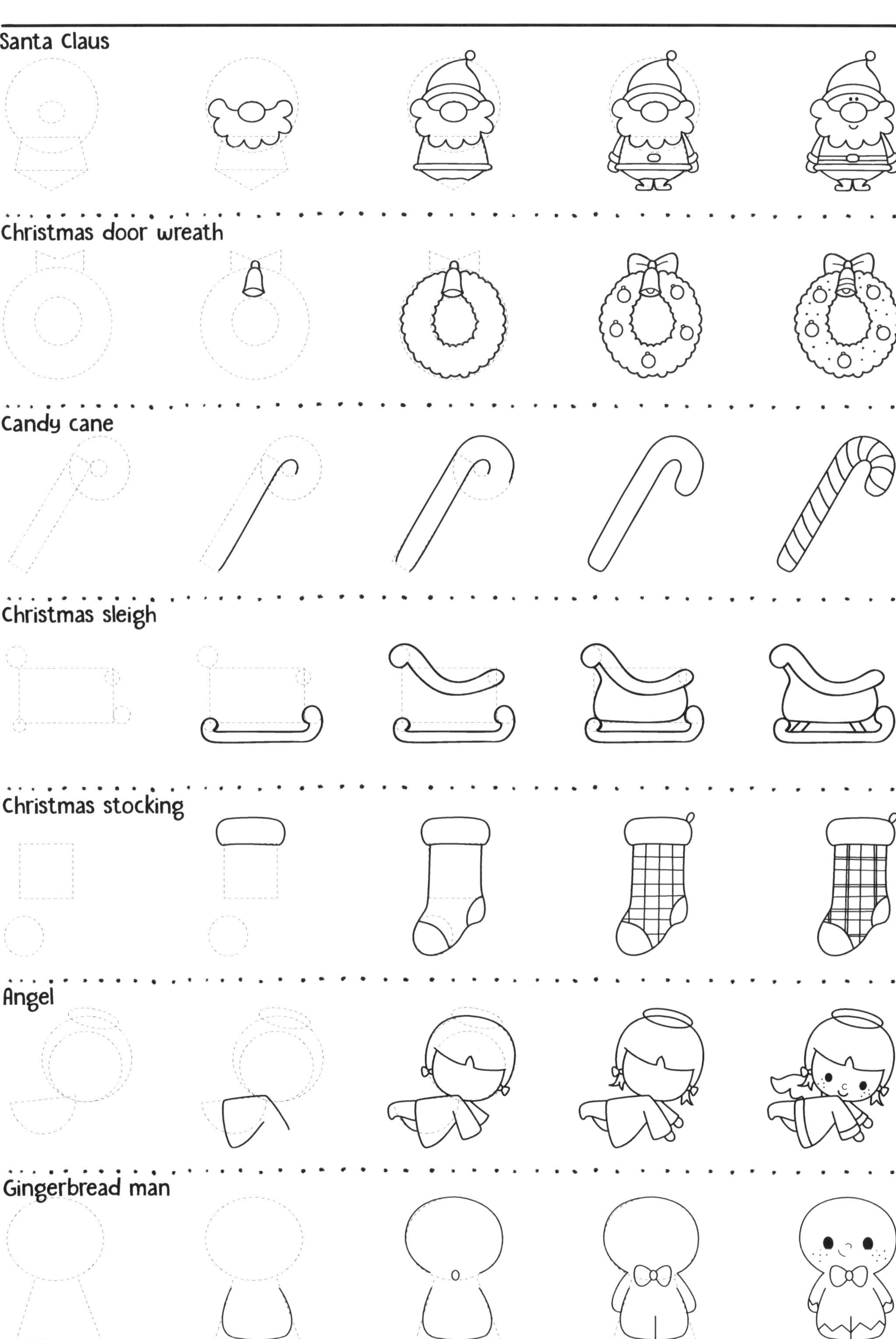
Santa Claus
Christmas door wreath
Candy cane
Christmas sleigh
Christmas stocking
Angel
Gingerbread man

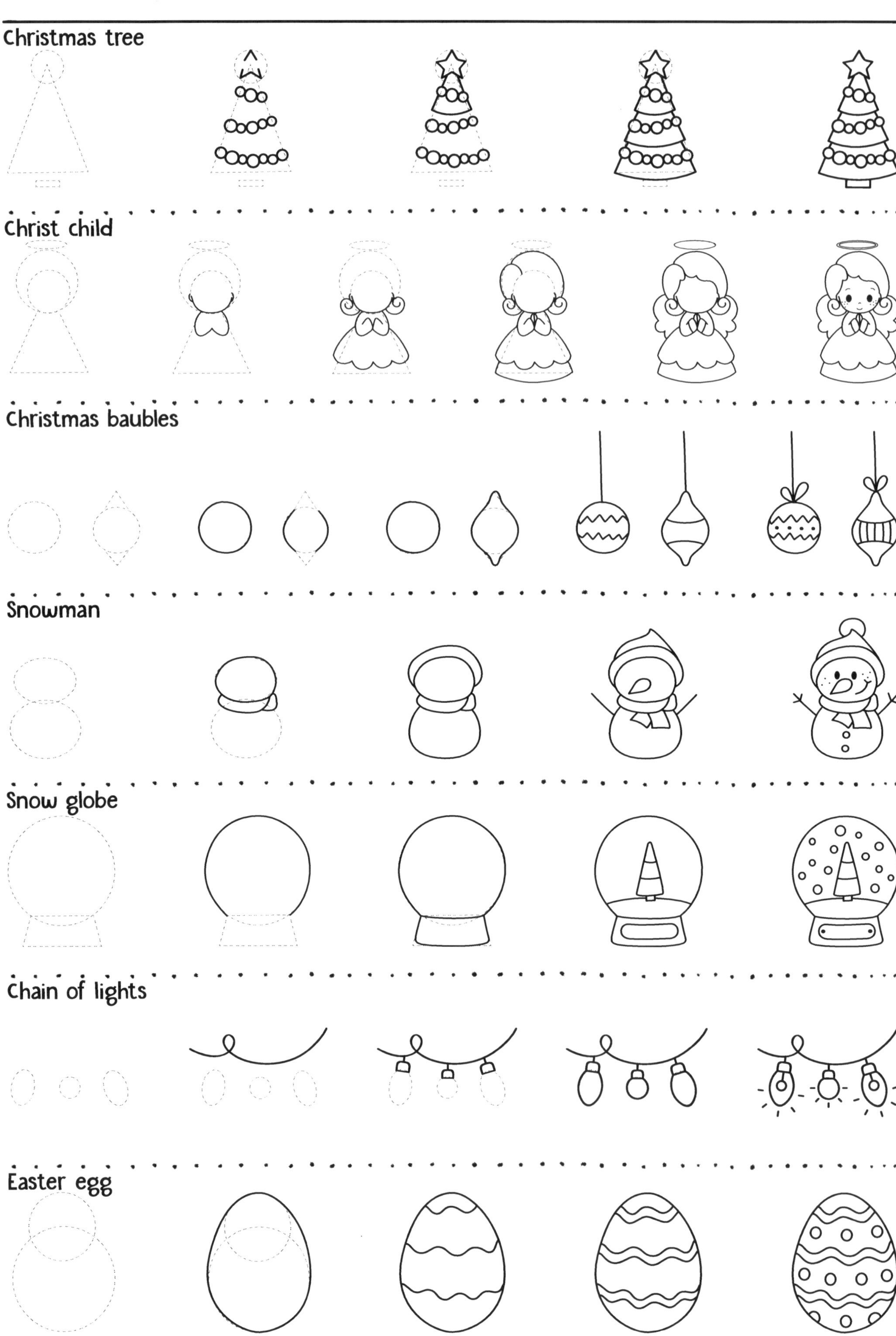
Christmas tree
Christ child
Christmas baubles
Snowman
Snow globe
Chain of lights
Easter egg

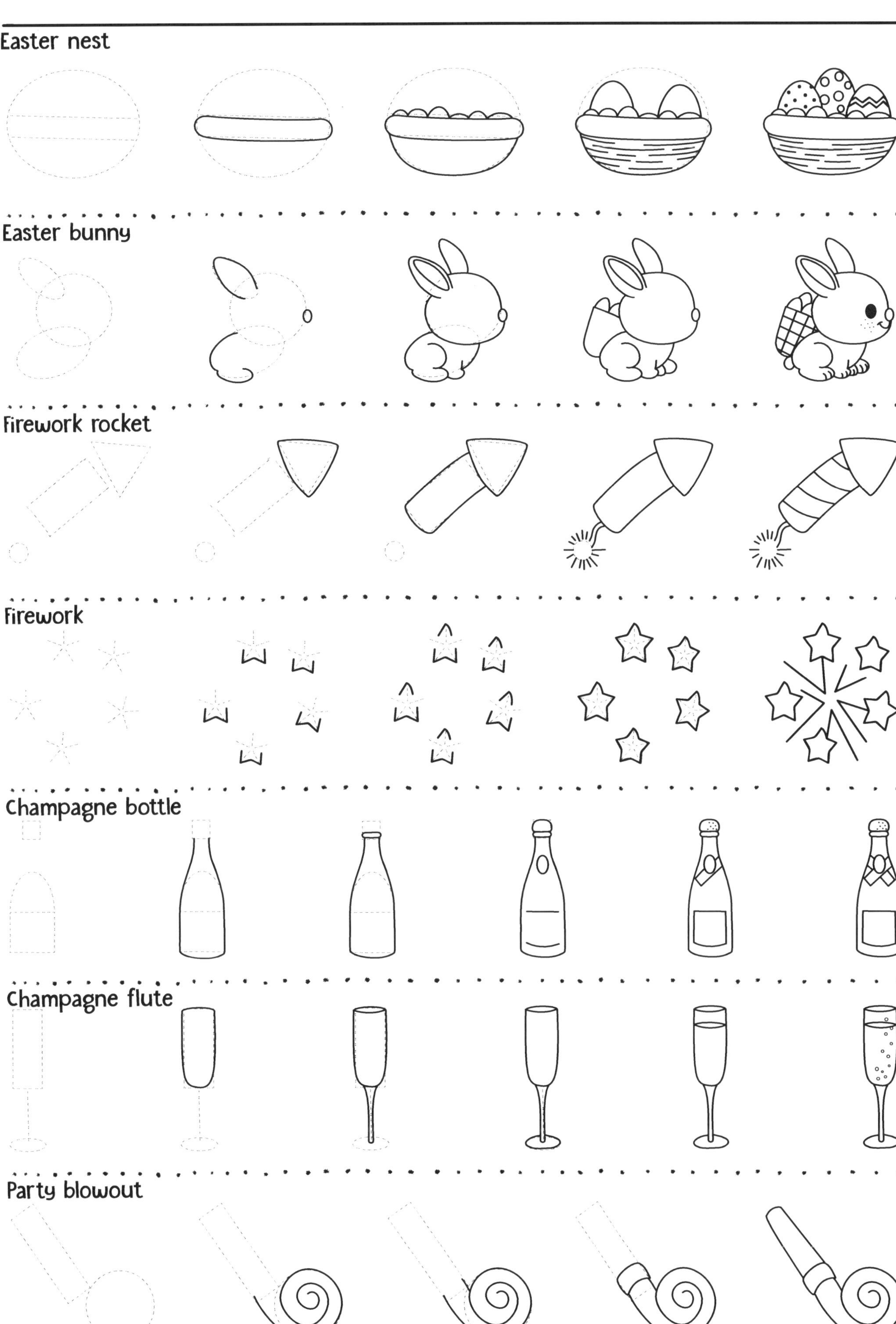
Easter nest
Easter bunny
Firework rocket
Firework
Champagne bottle
Champagne flute
Party blowout

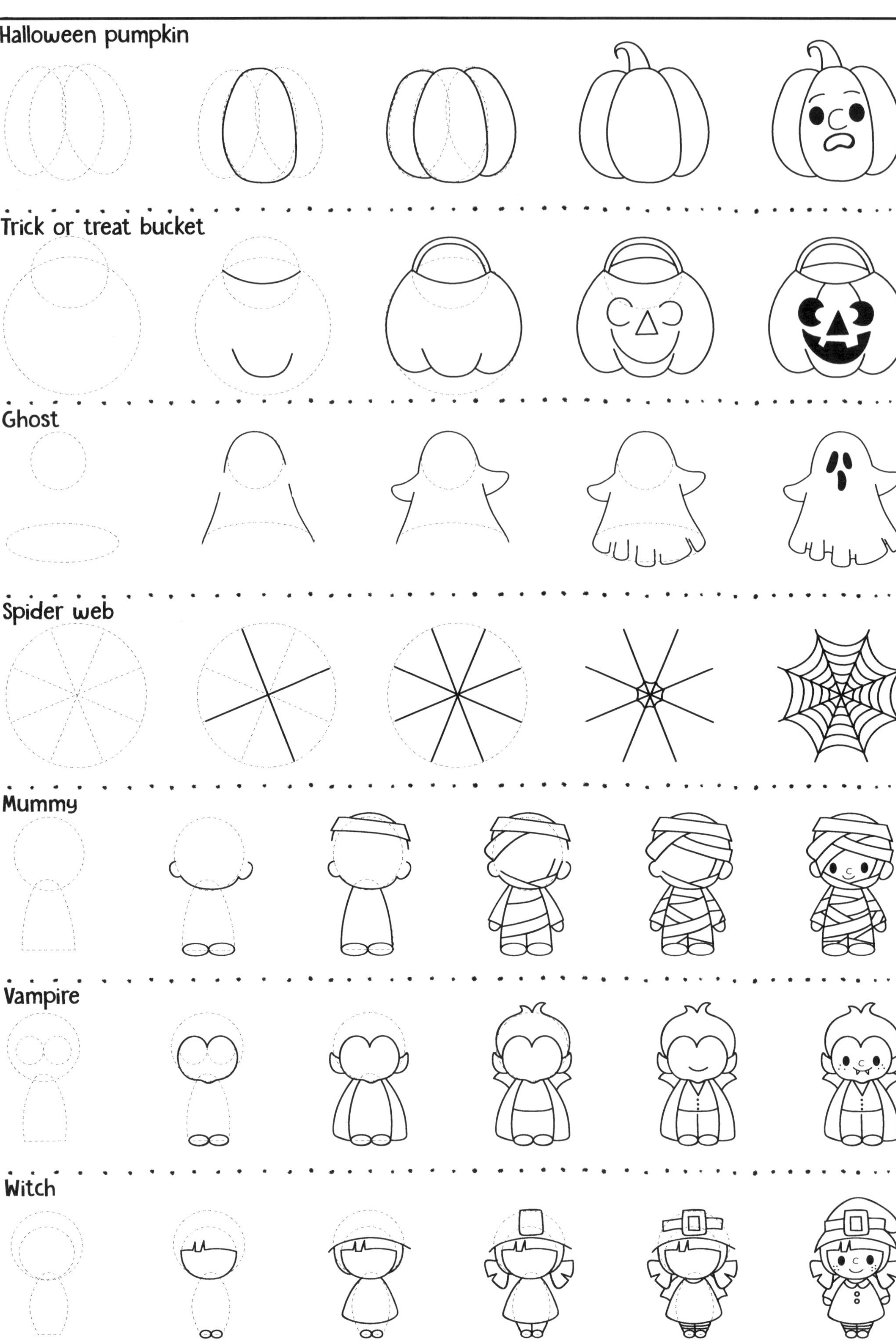
Halloween pumpkin
Trick or treat bucket
Ghost
Spider web
Mummy
Vampire
Witch

Witch hat

Cauldron

Gift

Bouquet

Birthday cake

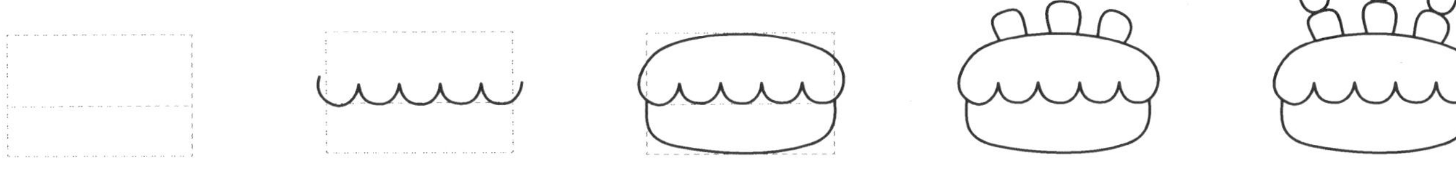

Garland

Party hat

Birthday card

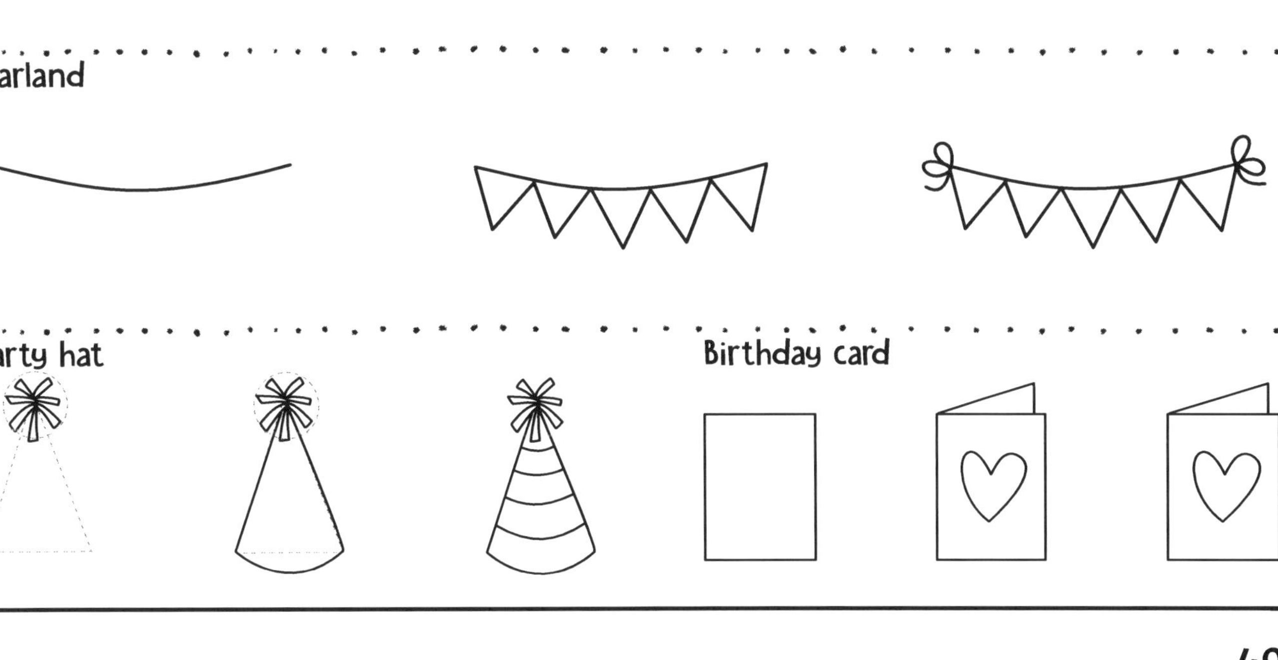

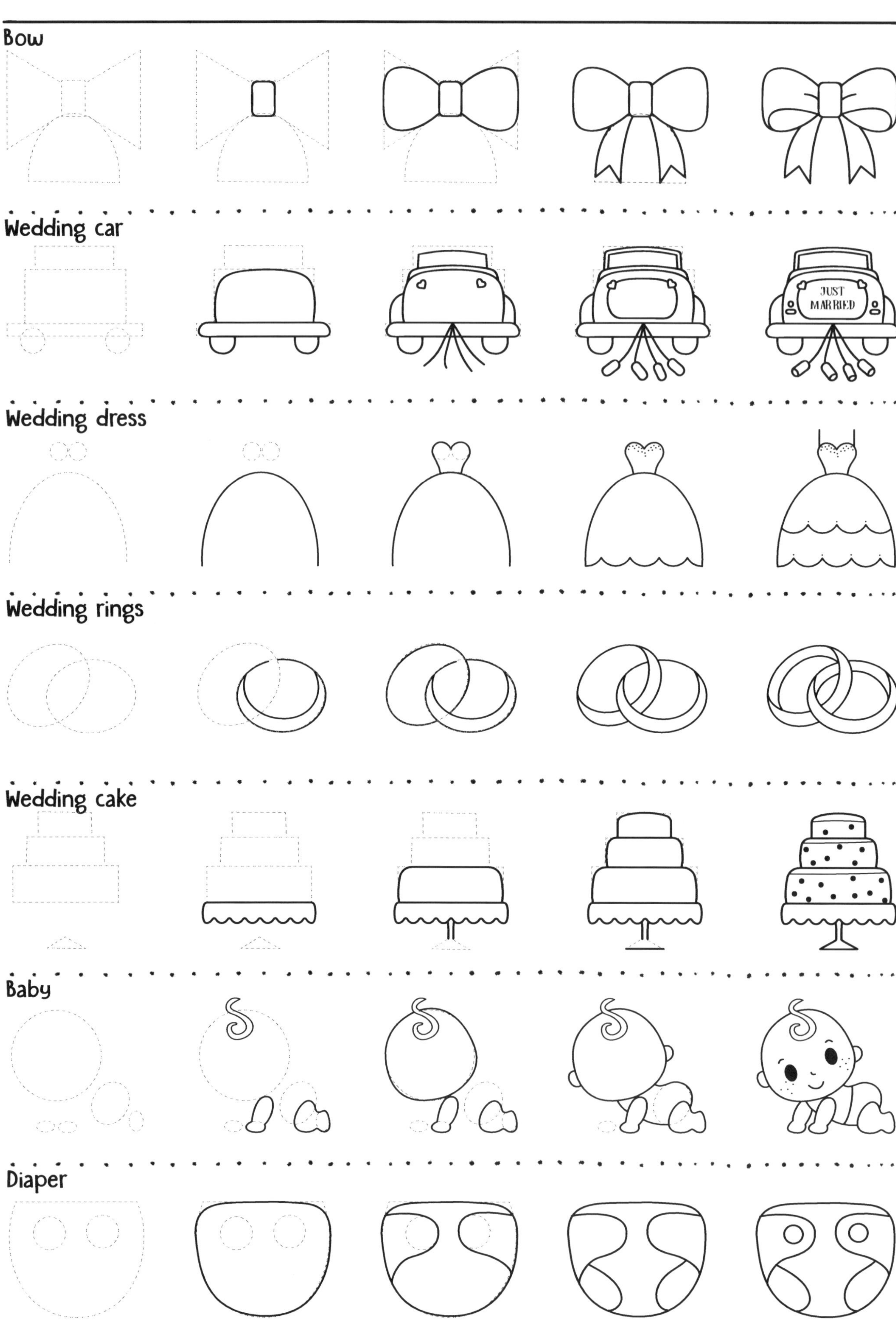
Bow
Wedding car
JUST MARRIED
Wedding dress
Wedding rings
Wedding cake
Baby
Diaper

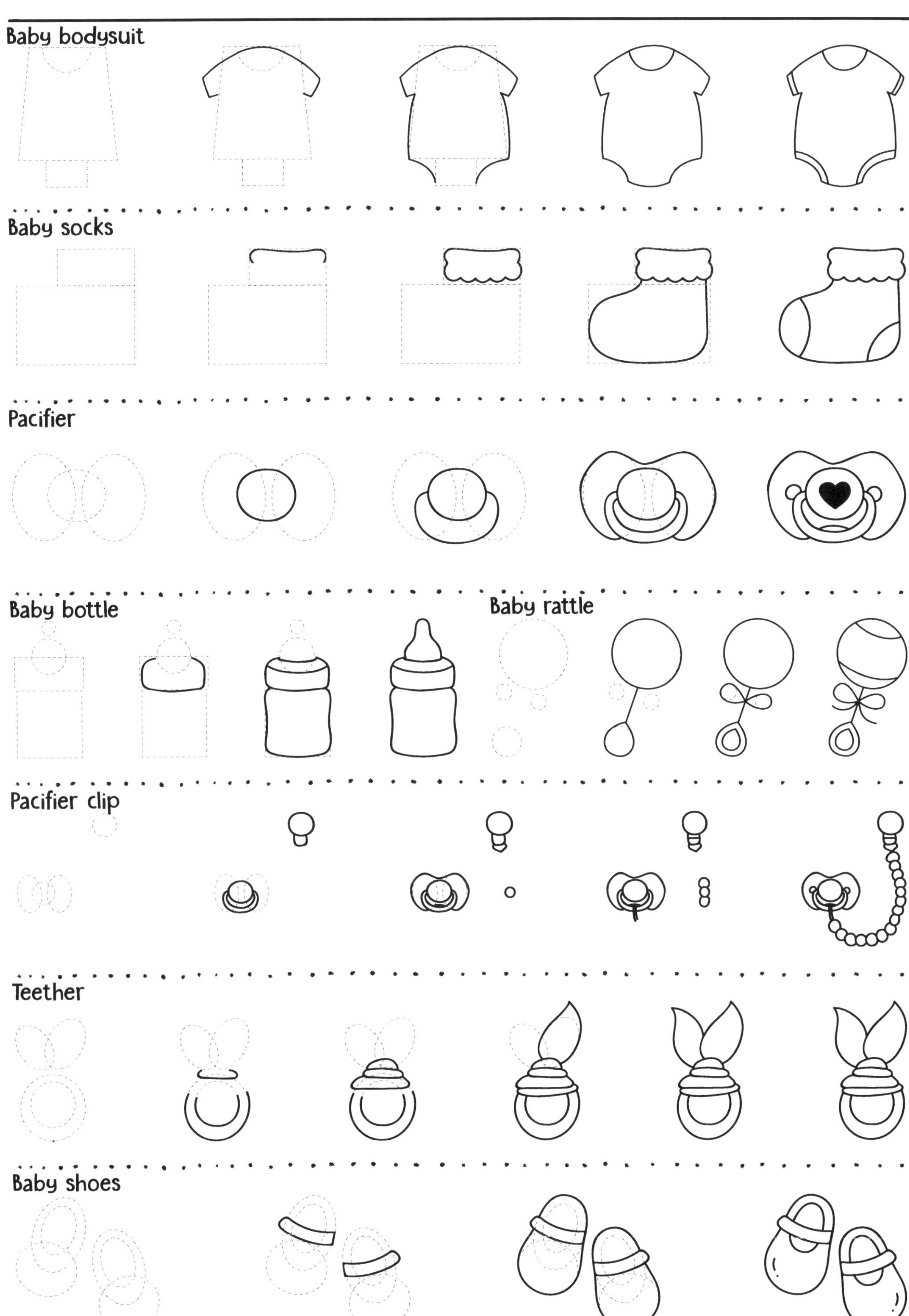
Baby bodysuit
Baby socks
Pacifier
Baby bottle
Baby rattle
Pacifier clip
Teether
Baby shoes

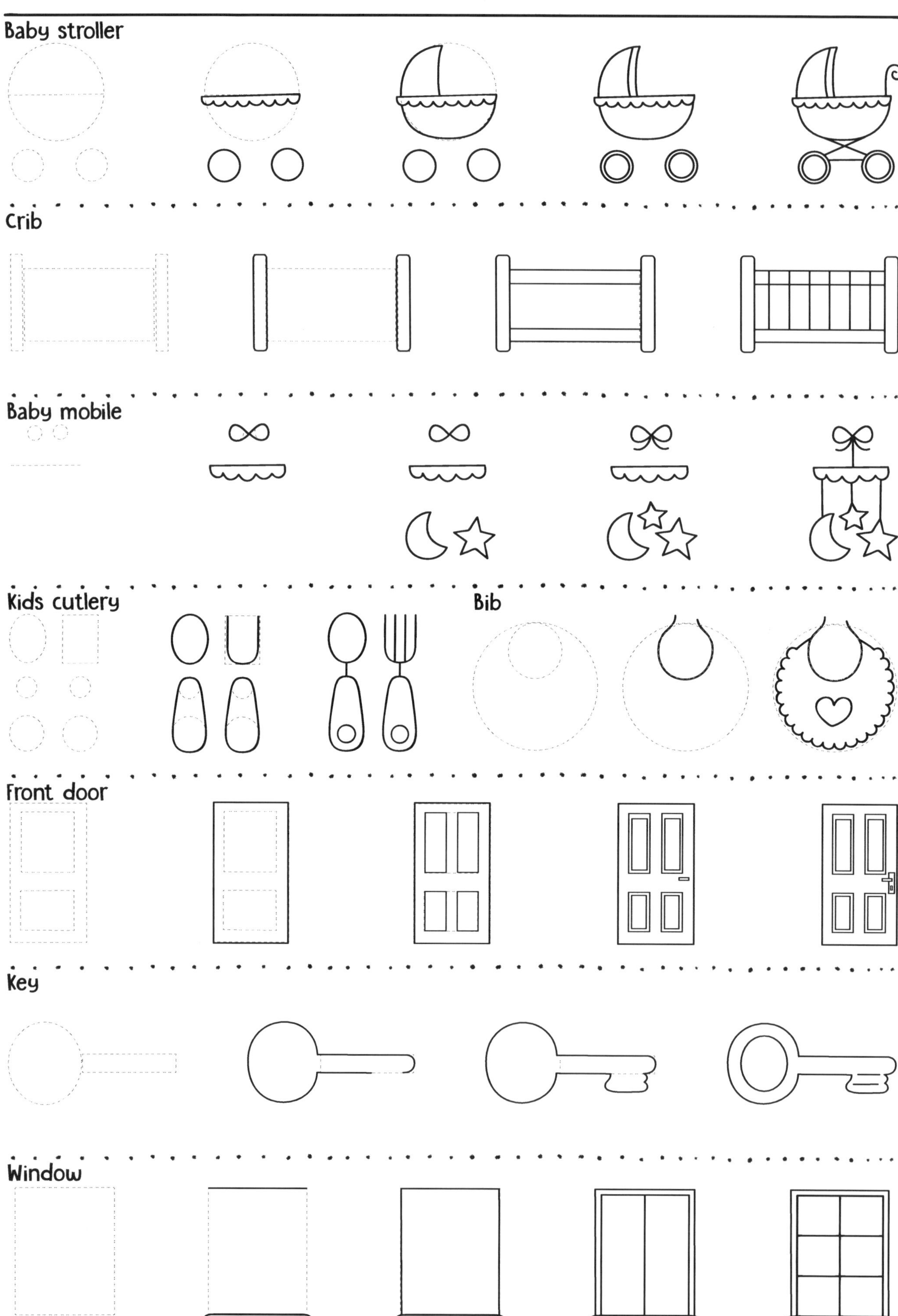
Baby stroller
Crib
Baby mobile
Kids cutlery
Bib
Front door
Key
Window

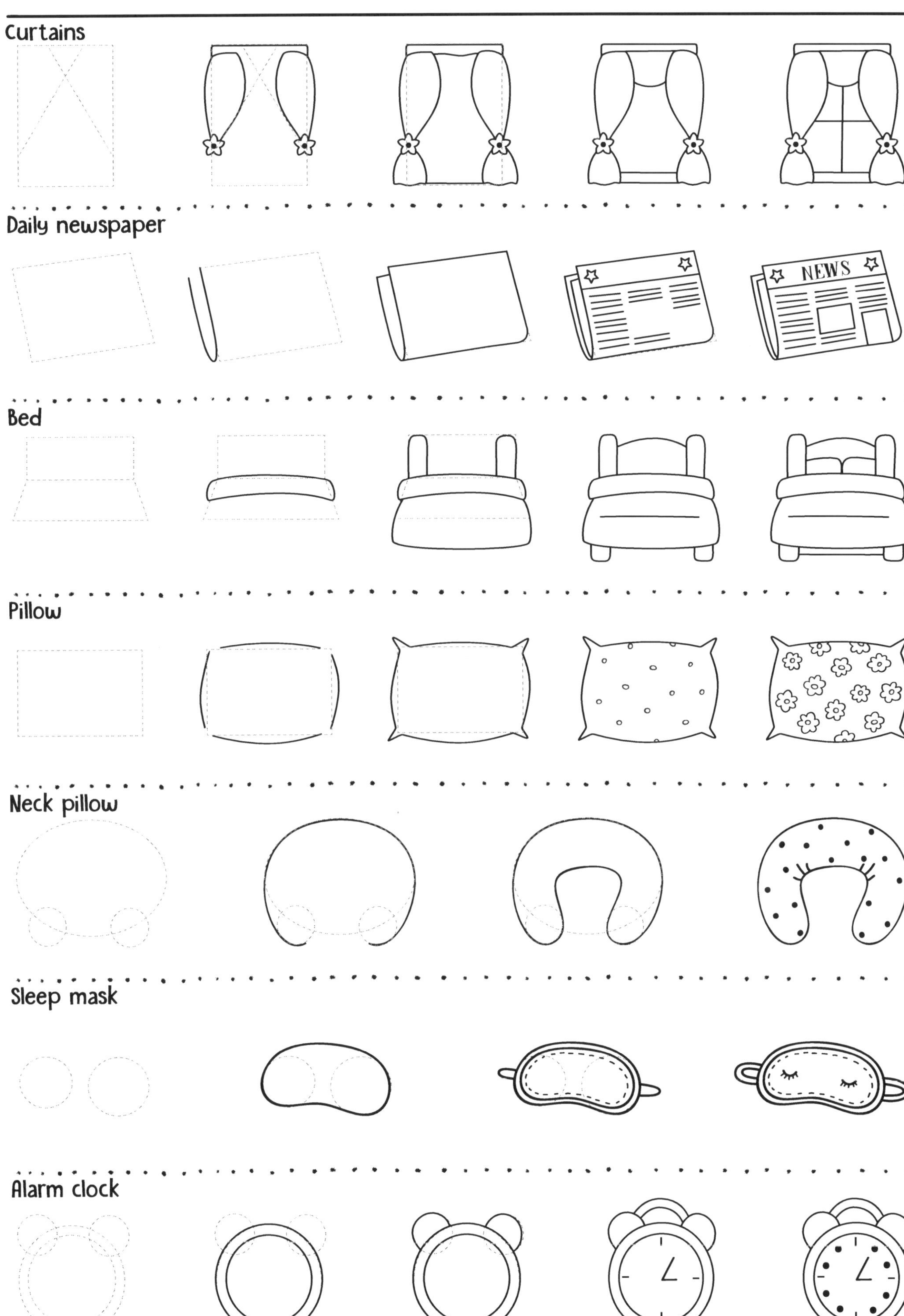
Curtains
Daily newspaper
NEWS
Bed
Pillow
Neck pillow
Sleep mask
Alarm clock

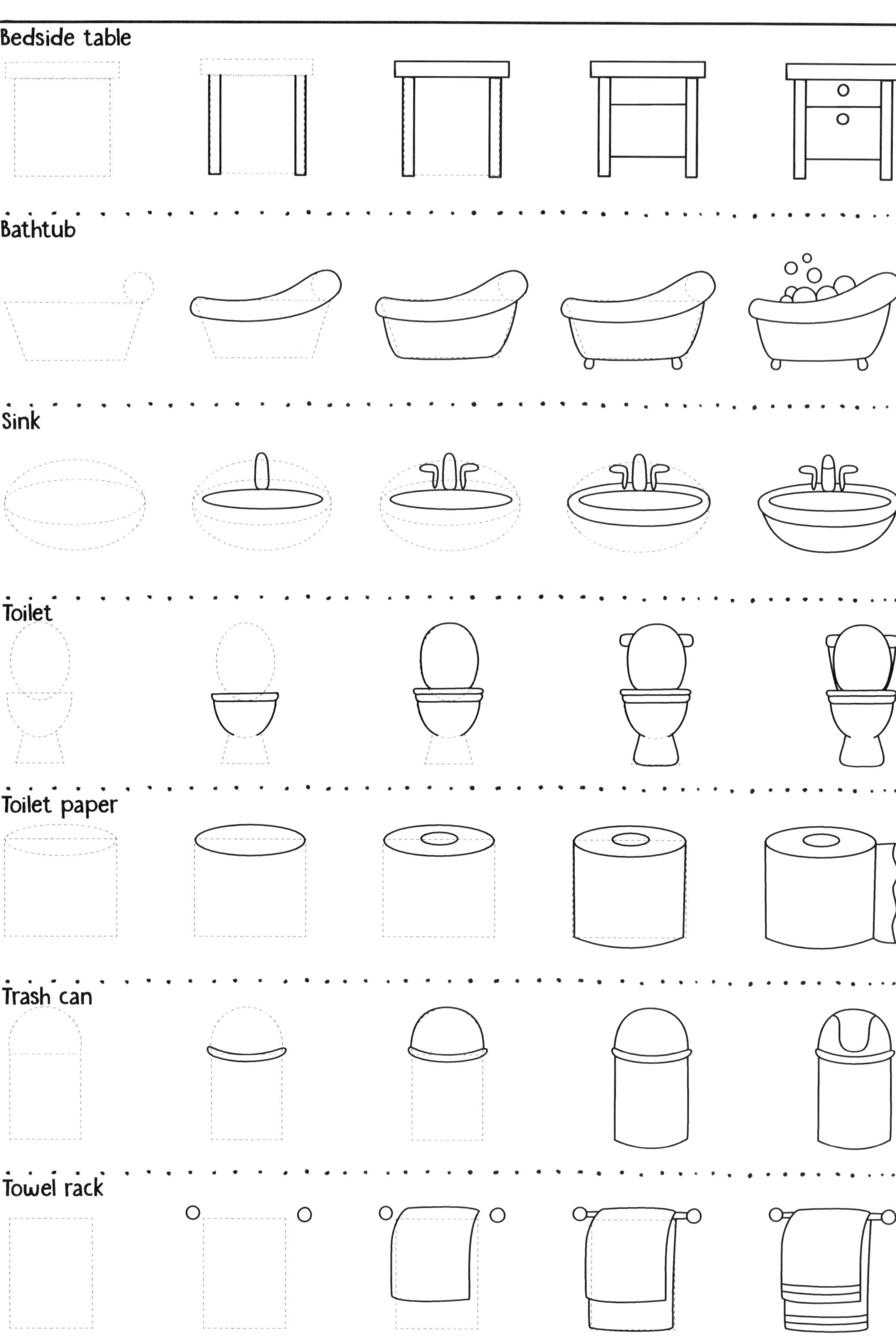
Bedside table
Bathtub
Sink
Toilet
Toilet paper
Trash can
Towel rack

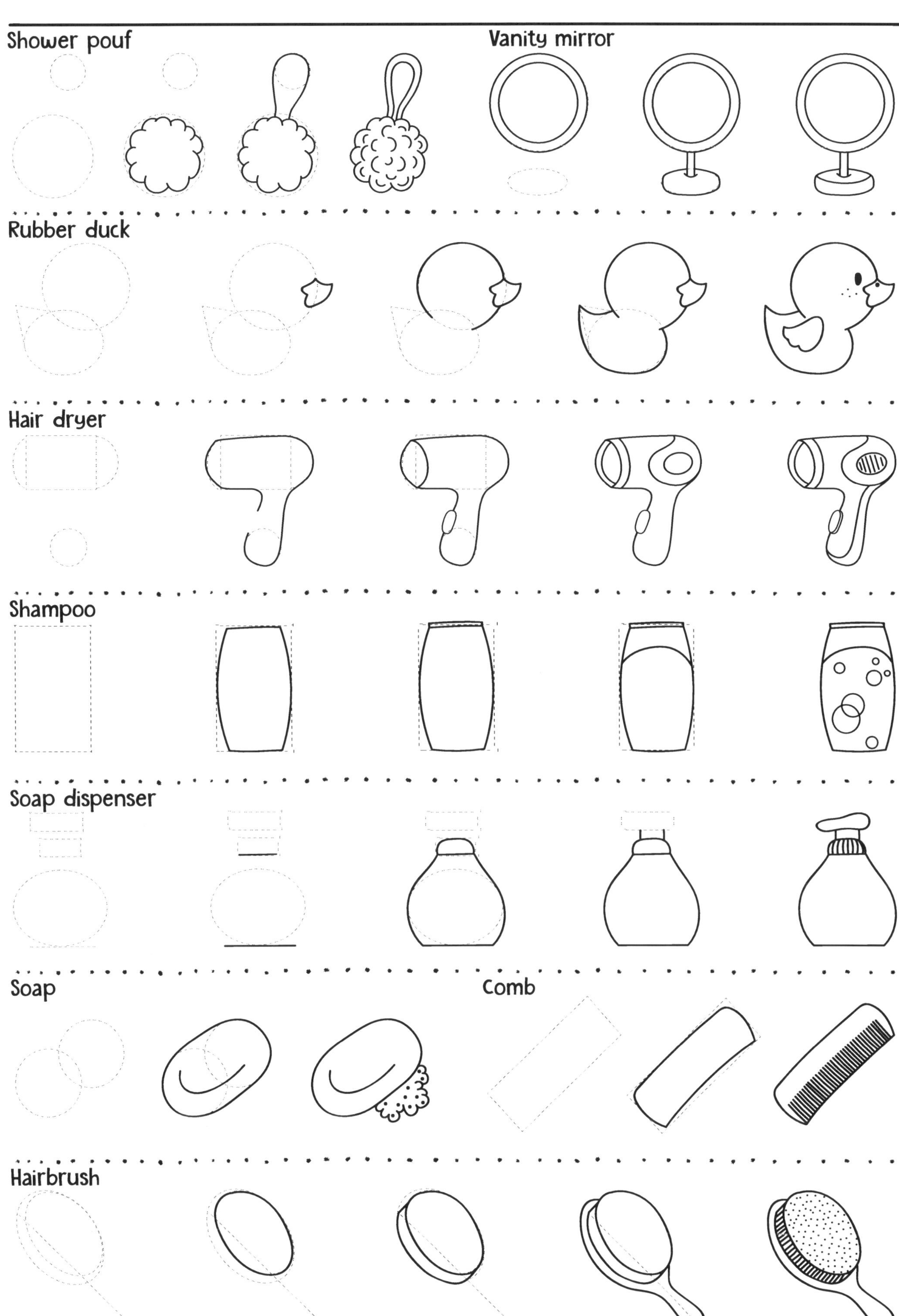
Shower pouf
Vanity mirror
Rubber duck
Hair dryer
Shampoo
Soap dispenser
Soap
Comb
Hairbrush

Toothbrush

Electric toothbrush

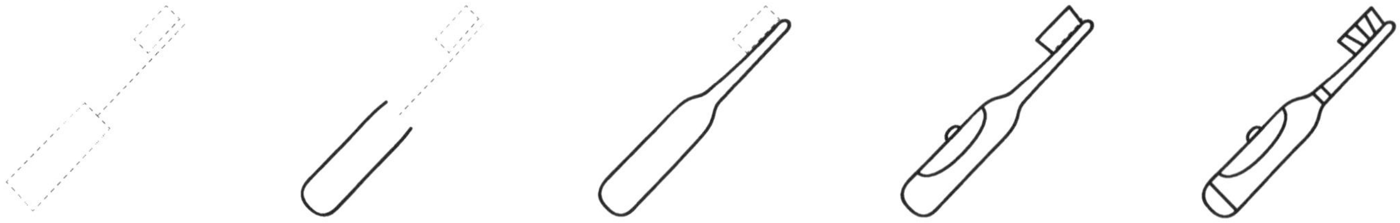

Toothpaste

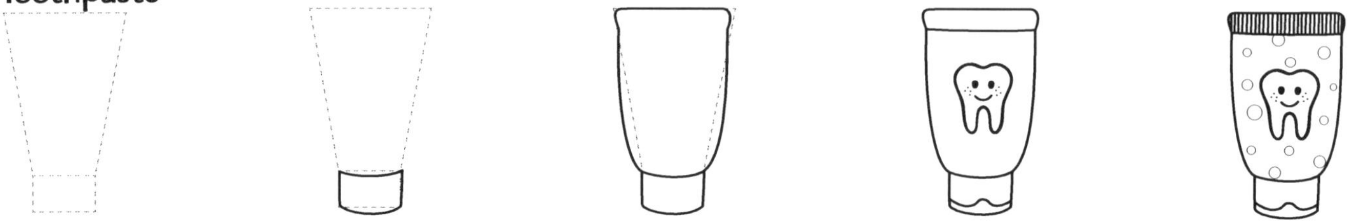

Sunscreen

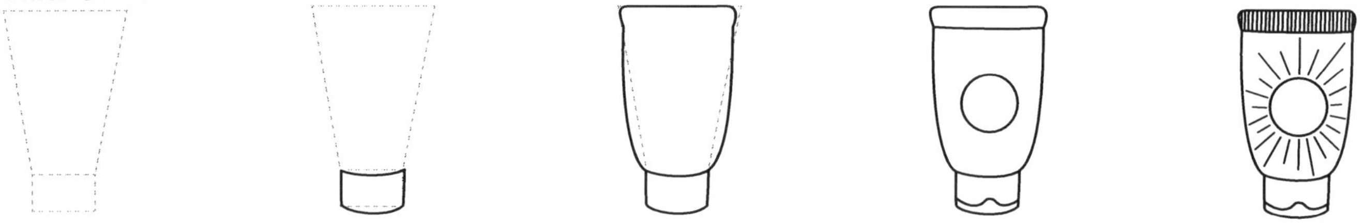

Make up brush

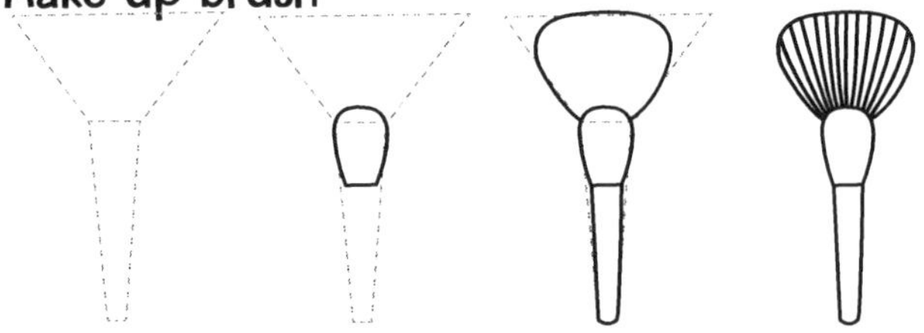

Lipstick

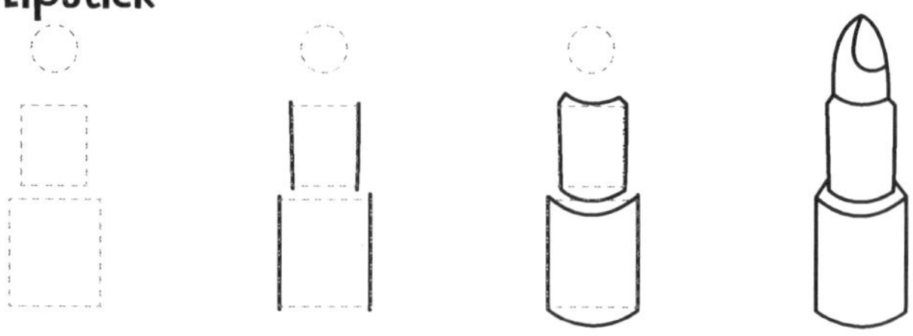

Hot-water bag

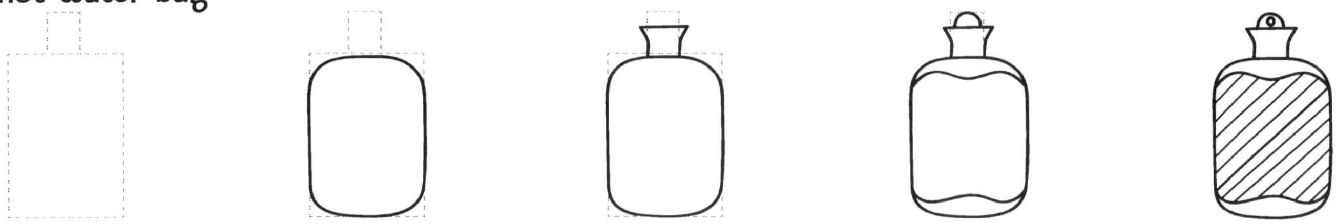

Detergent

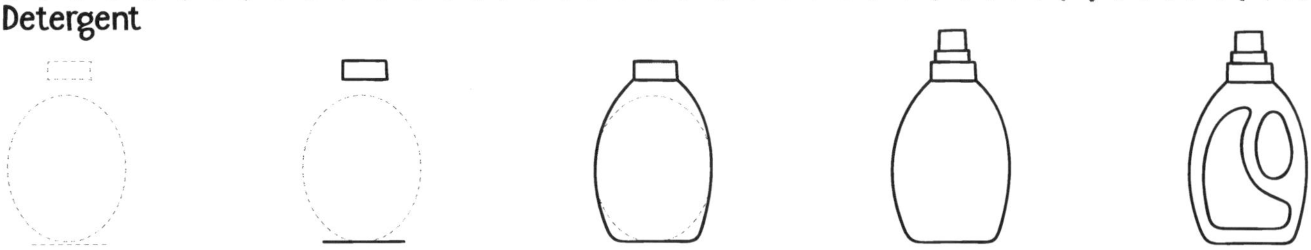

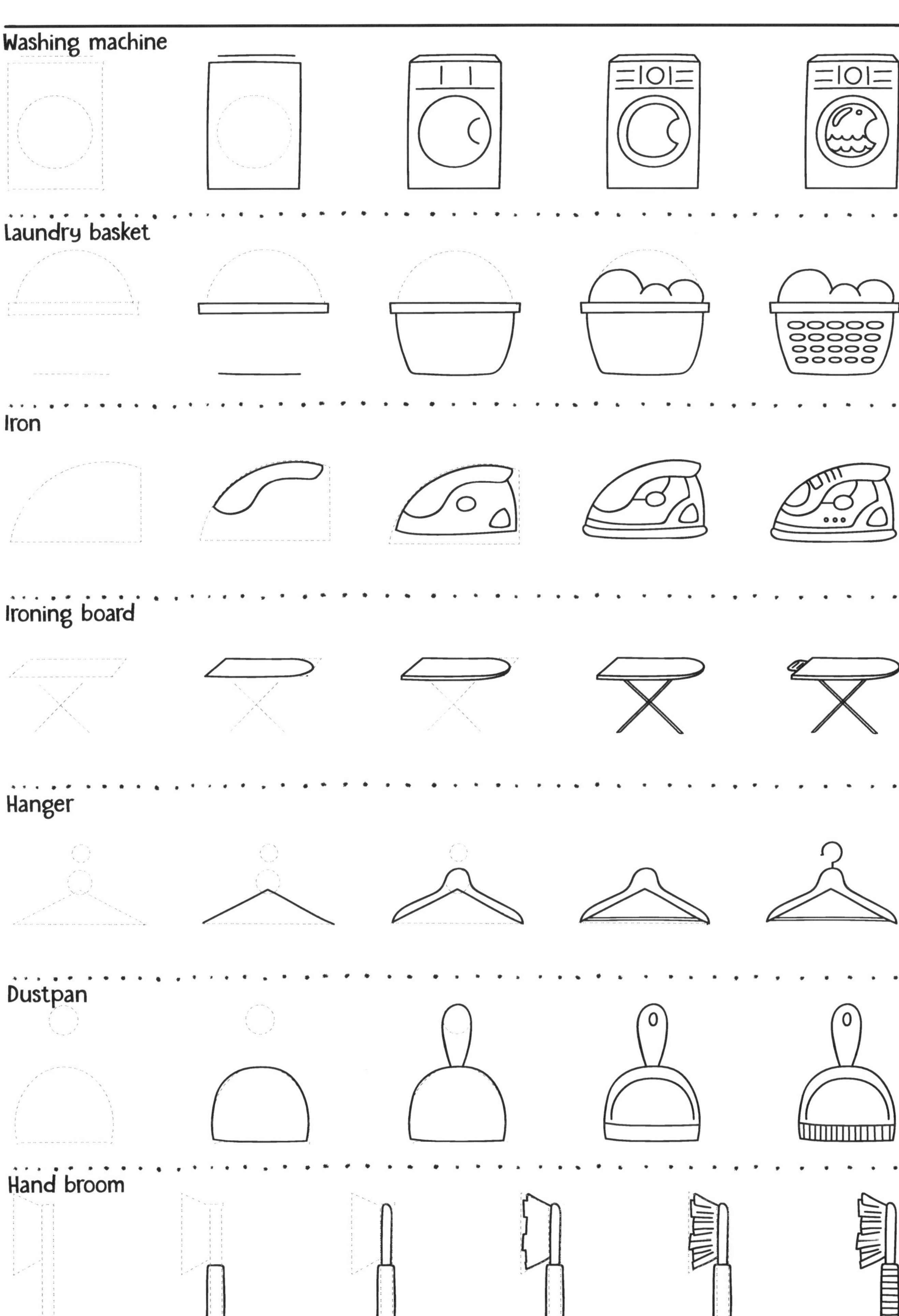
Washing machine
Laundry basket
Iron
Ironing board
Hanger
Dustpan
Hand broom

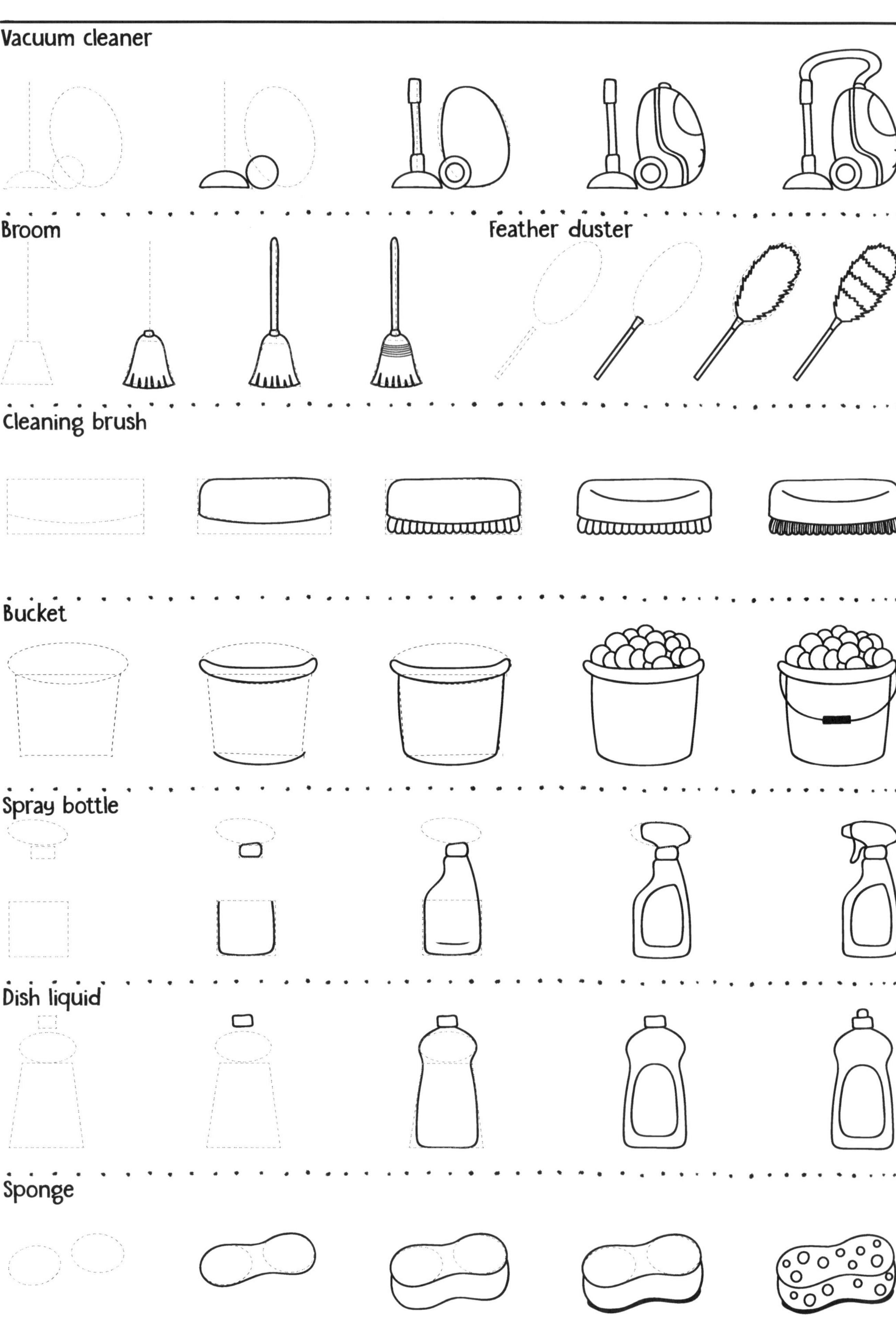
Vacuum cleaner
Broom
Feather duster
Cleaning brush
Bucket
Spray bottle
Dish liquid
Sponge

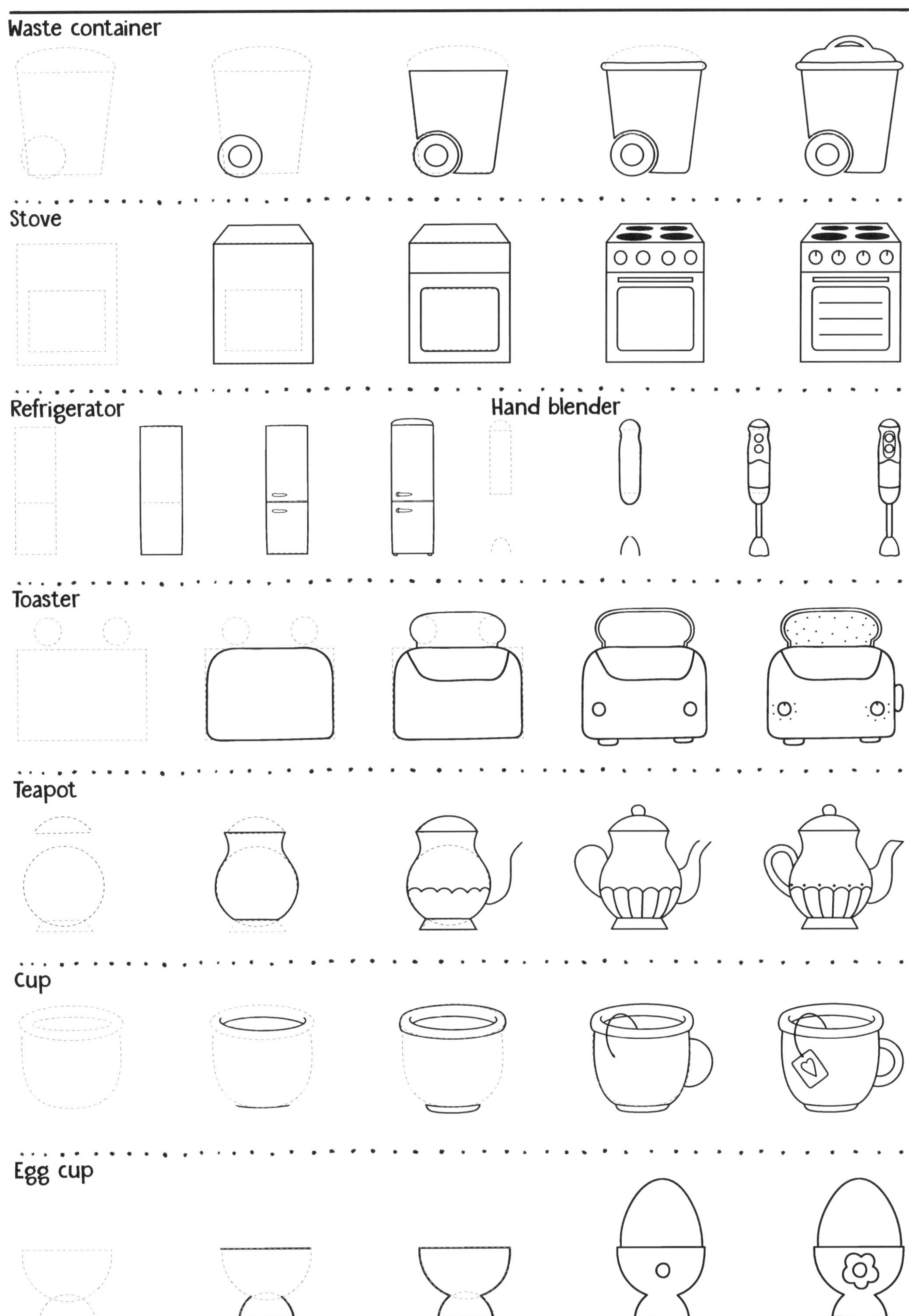
Waste container
Stove
Refrigerator
Hand blender
Toaster
Teapot
Cup
Egg cup

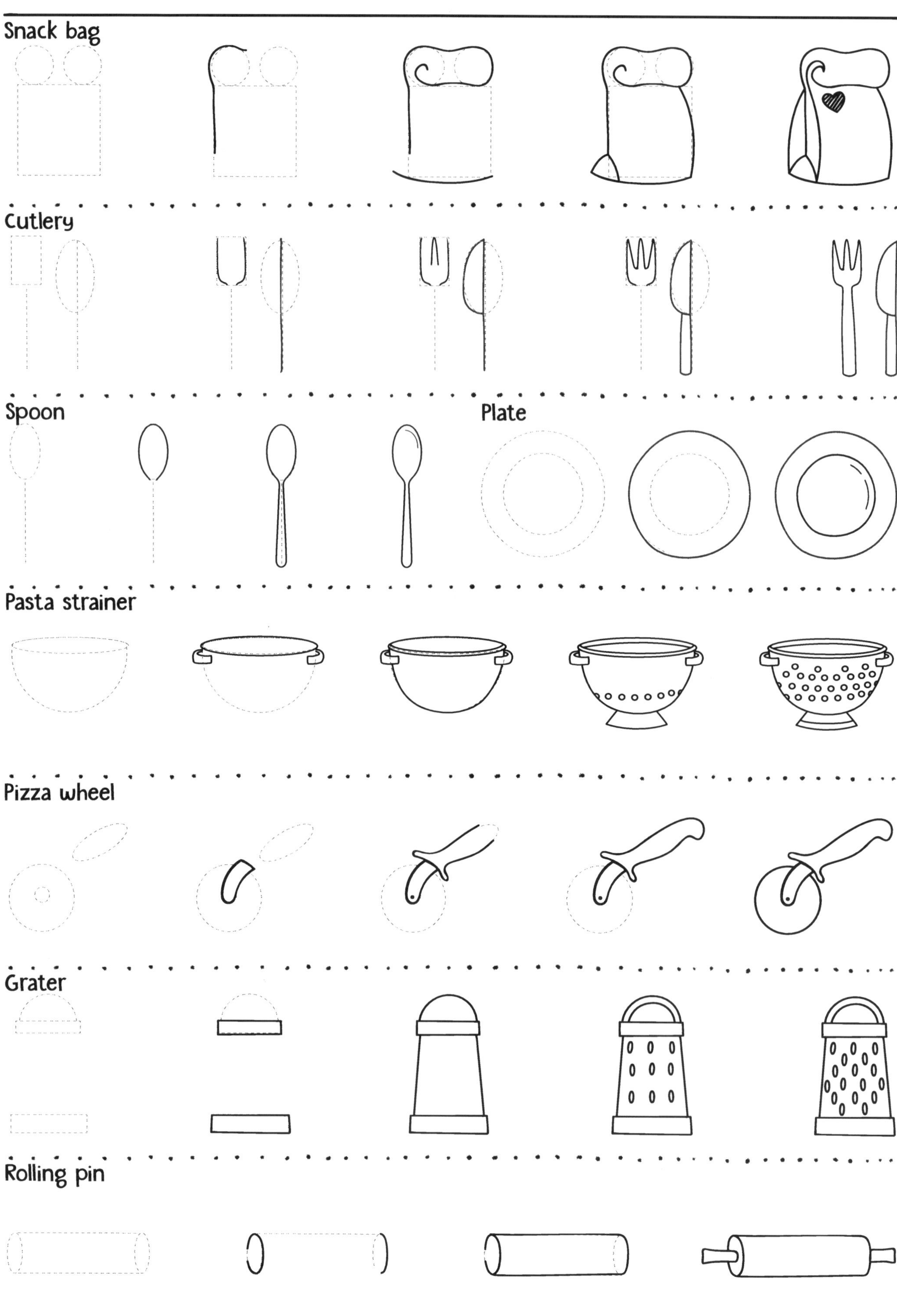
Snack bag
Cutlery
Spoon
Plate
Pasta strainer
Pizza wheel
Grater
Rolling pin

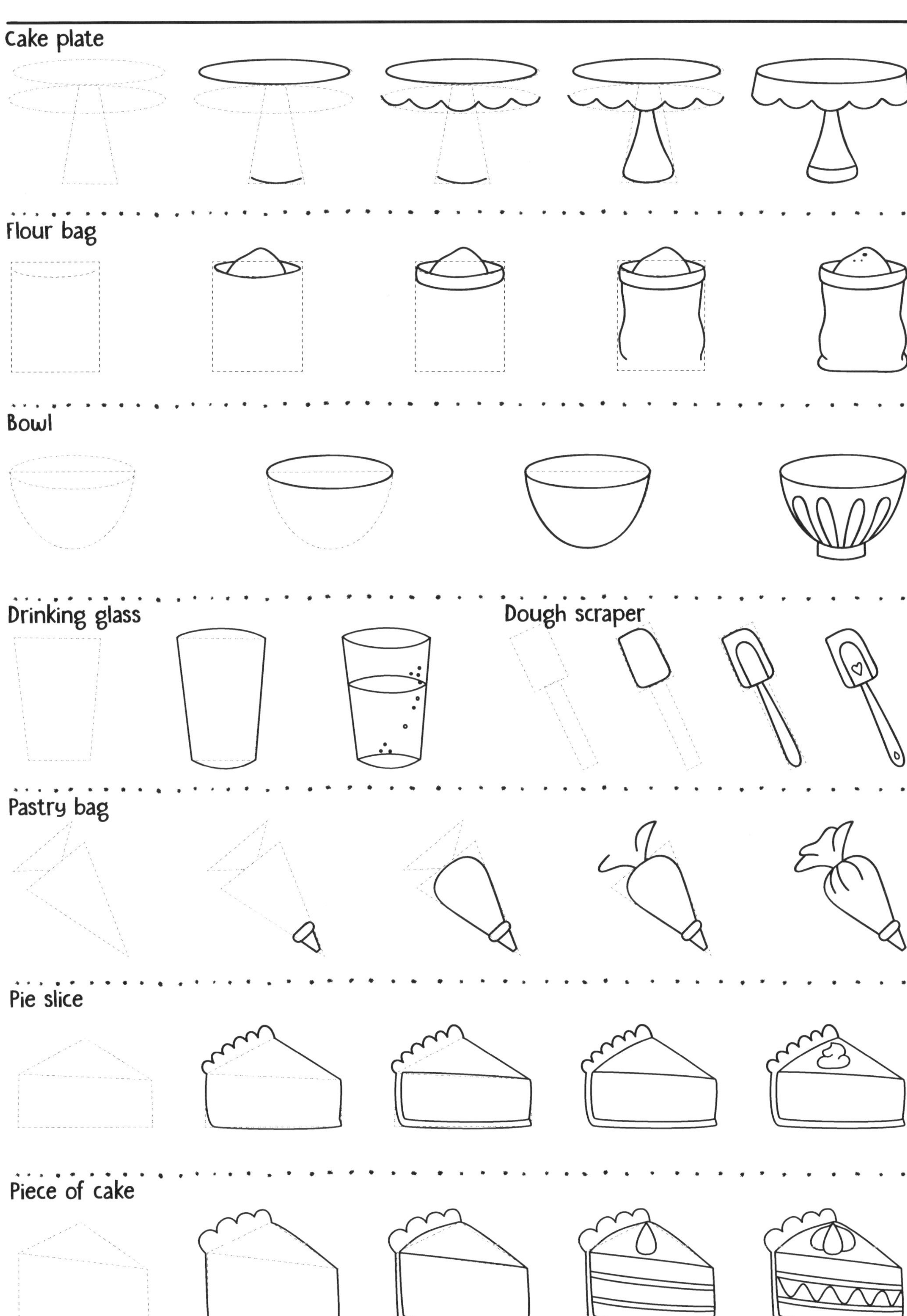
Cake plate
Flour bag
Bowl
Drinking glass
Dough scraper
Pastry bag
Pie slice
Piece of cake

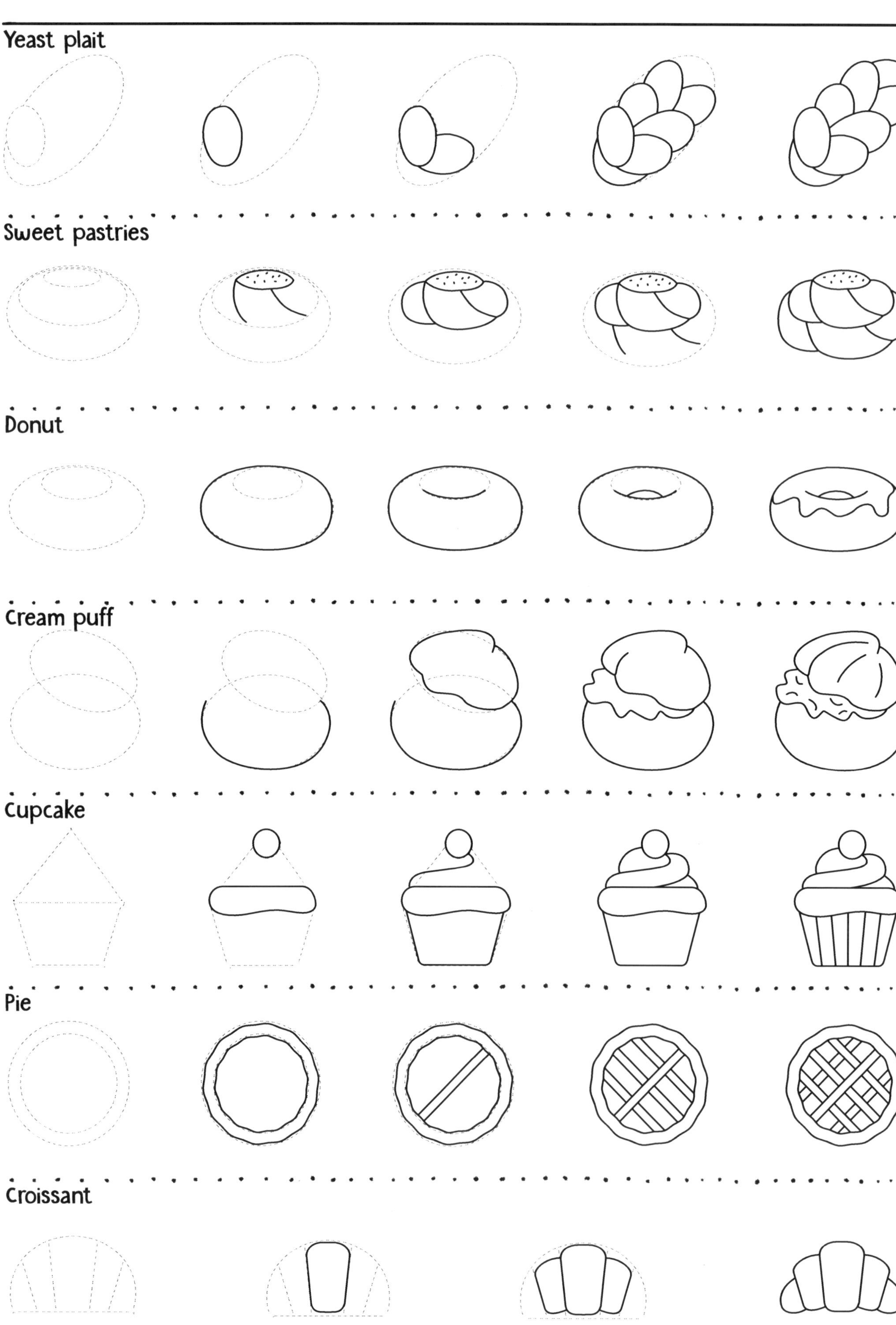
Yeast plait
Sweet pastries
Donut
Cream puff
Cupcake
Pie
Croissant

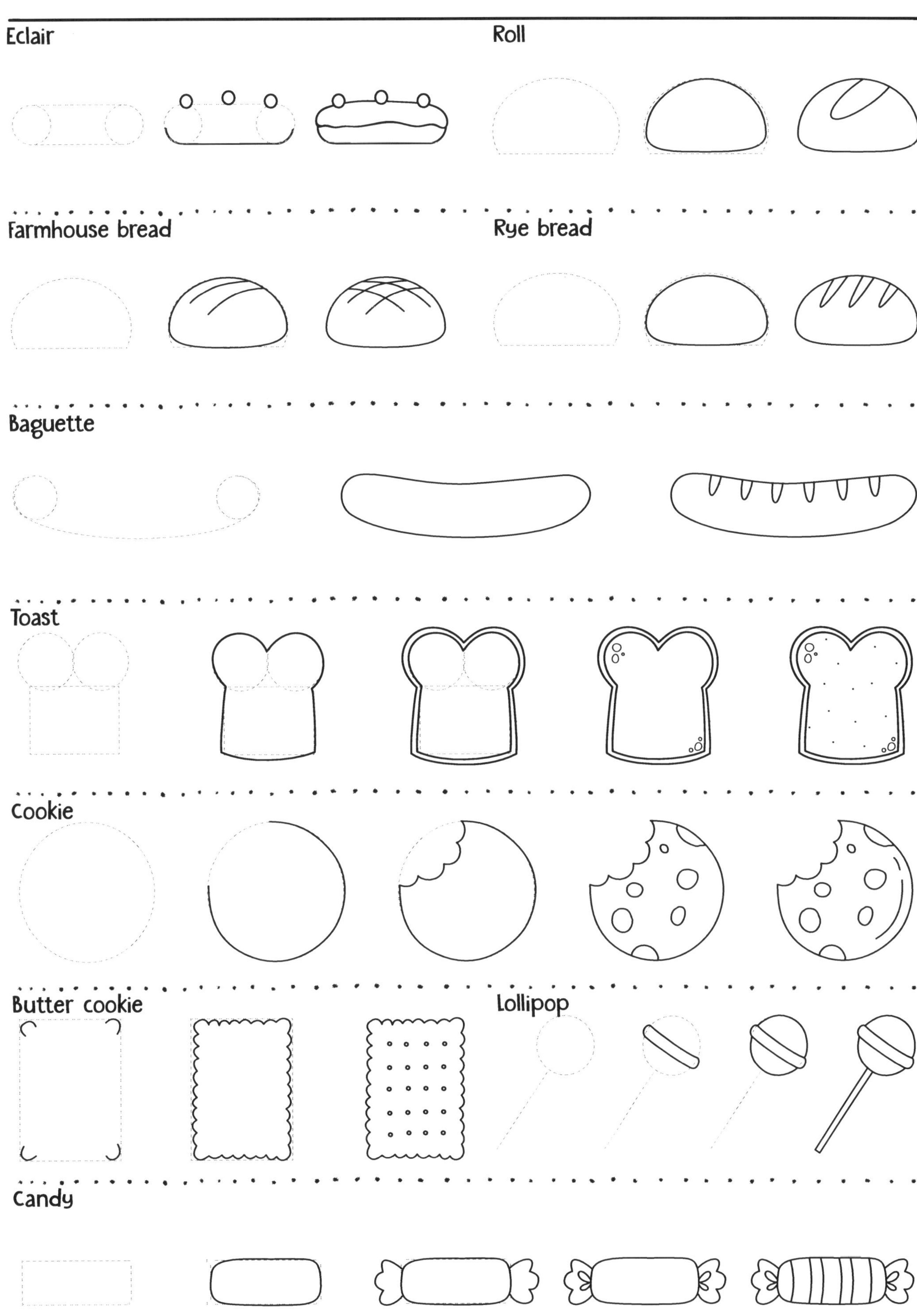
Eclair
Roll
Farmhouse bread
Rye bread
Baguette
Toast
Cookie
Butter cookie
Lollipop
Candy

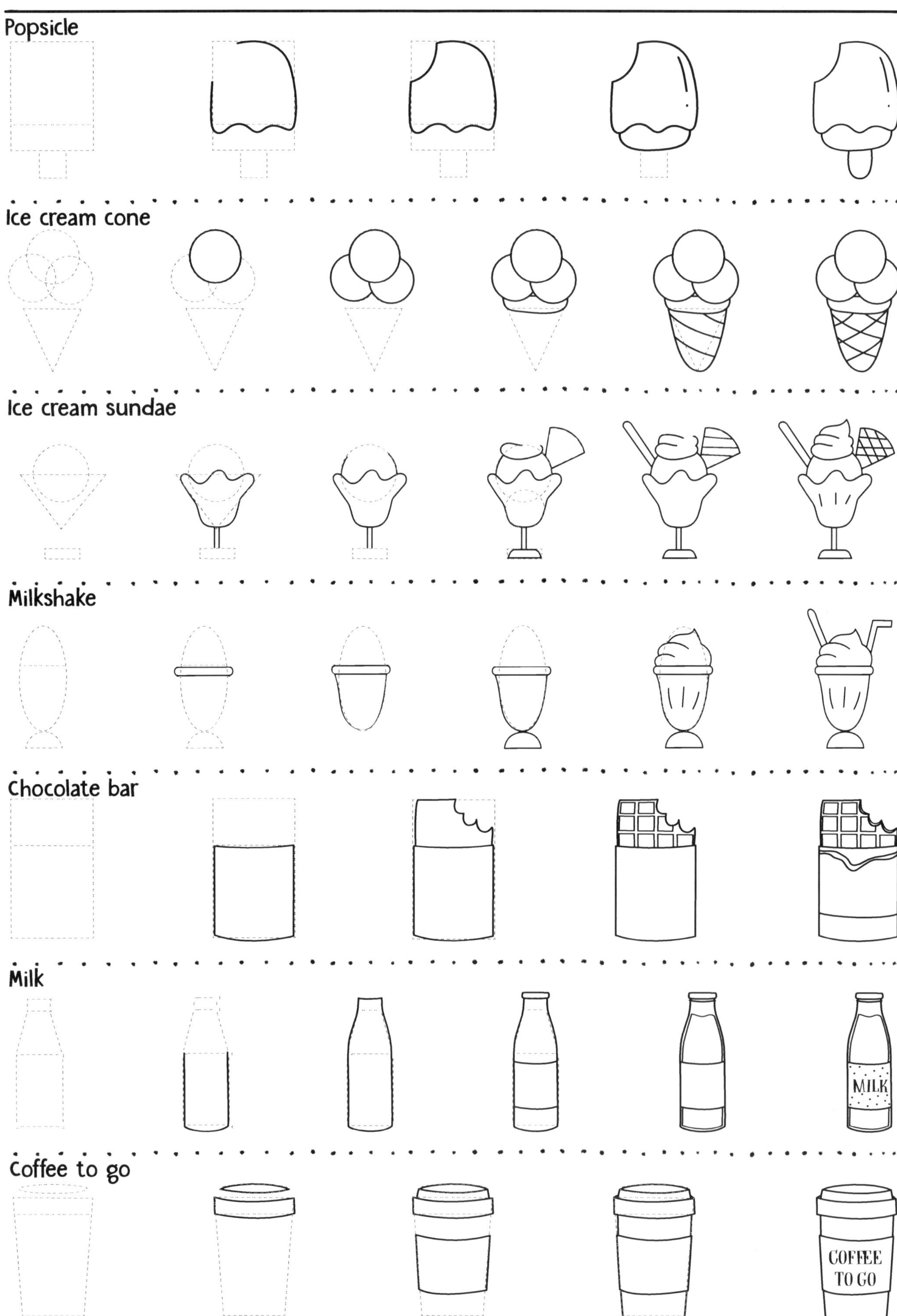
Popsicle
Ice cream cone
Ice cream sundae
Milkshake
Chocolate bar
Milk
MILK
Coffee to go
COFFEE
TO GO

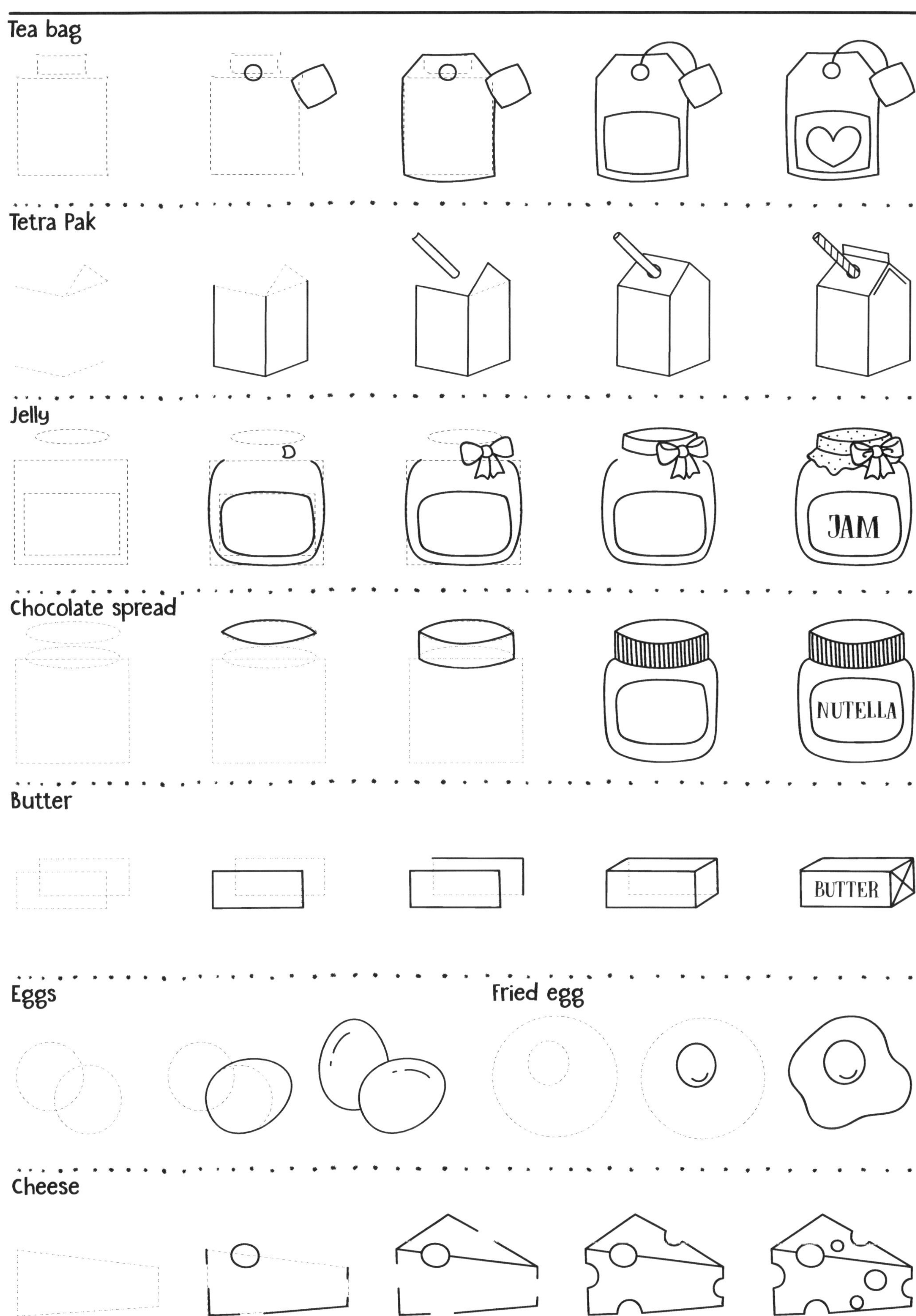
Tea bag
Tetra Pak
Jelly
JAM
Chocolate spread
NUTELLA
Butter
BUTTER
Eggs
Fried egg
Cheese

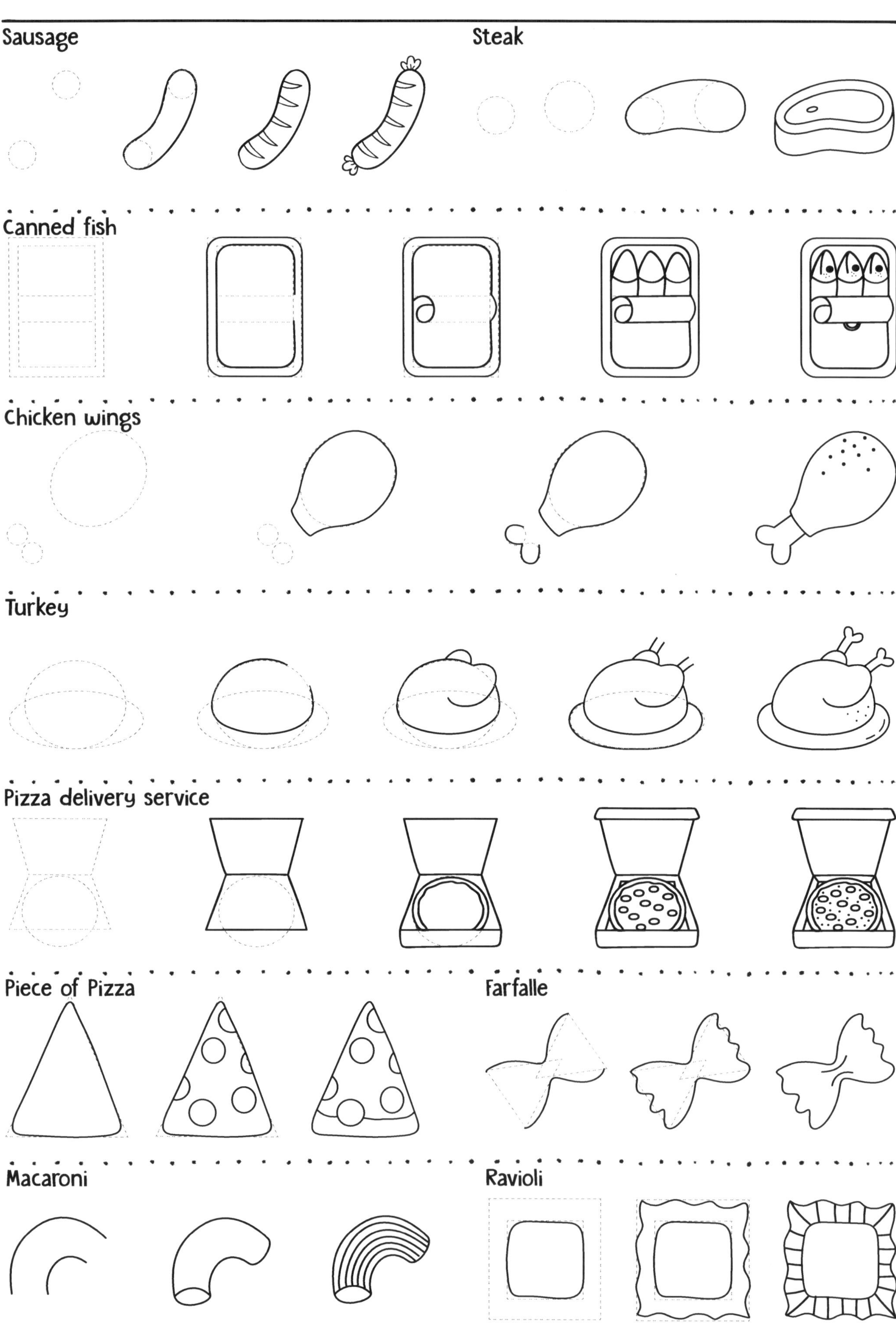
Sausage
Steak
Canned fish
Chicken wings
Turkey
Pizza delivery service
Piece of Pizza
Farfalle
Macaroni
Ravioli

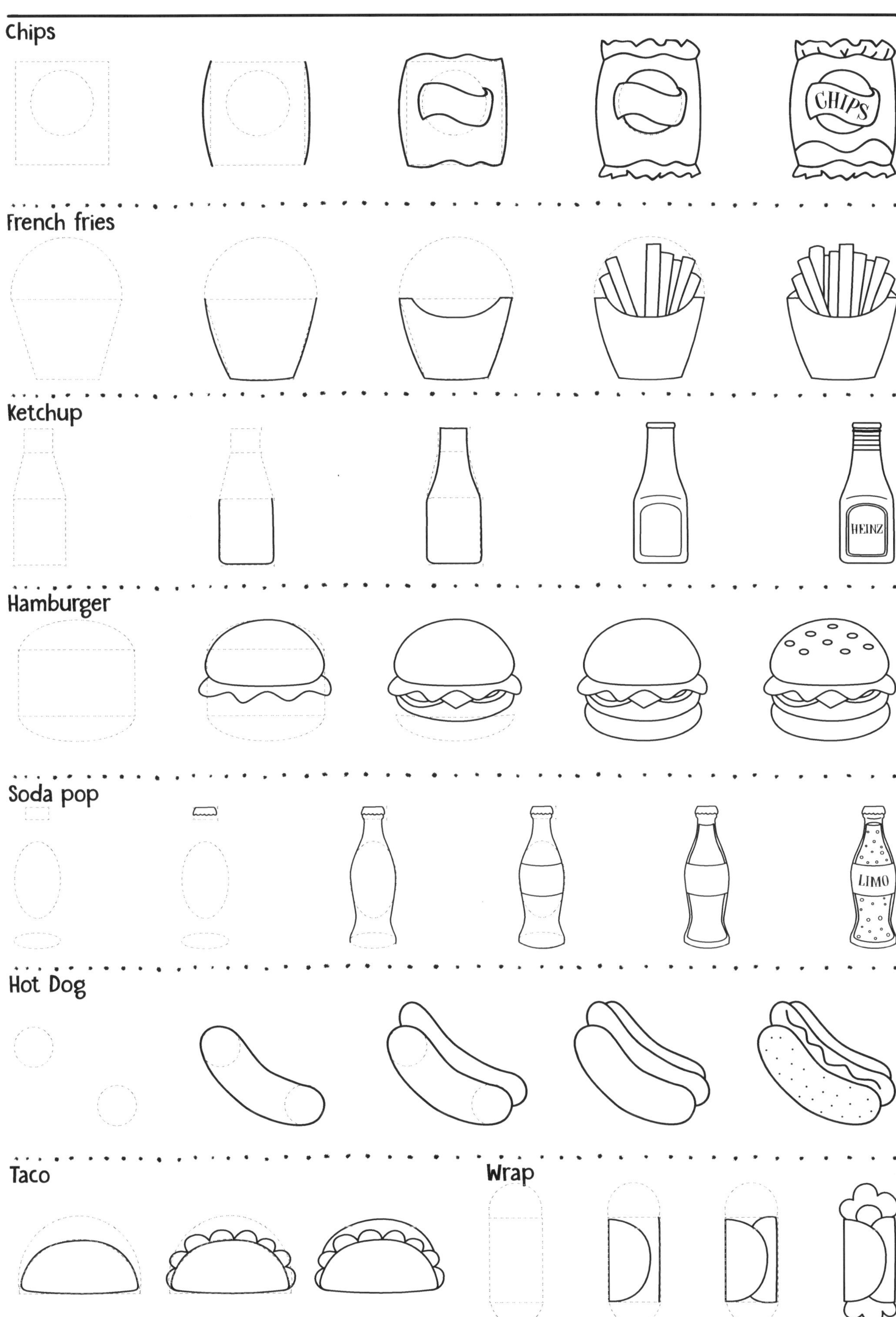
Chips
CHIPS
French fries
Ketchup
HEINZ
Hamburger
Soda pop
LIMO
Hot Dog
Taco
Wrap

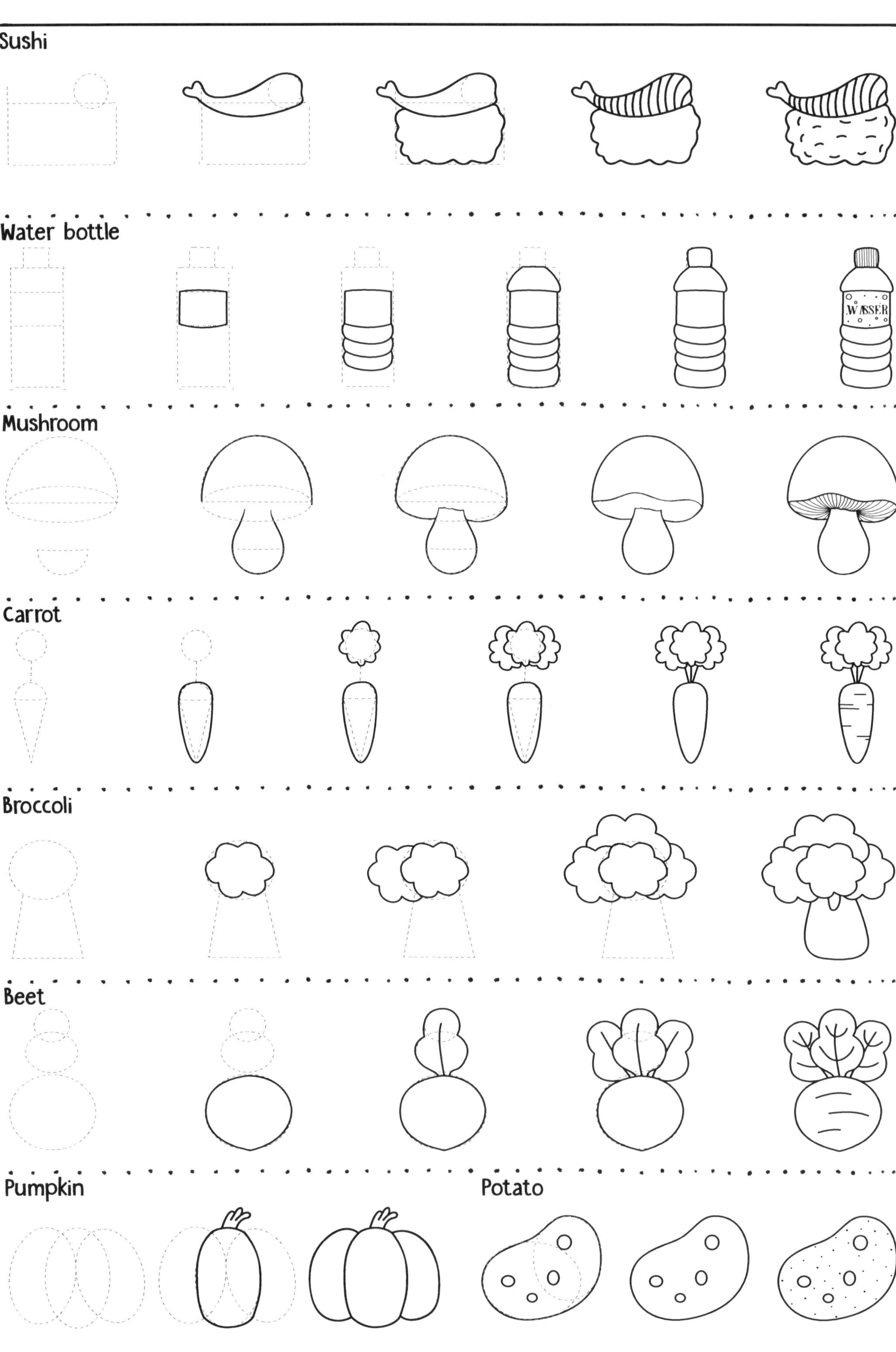
Sushi
Water bottle
WASSER
Mushroom
Carrot
Broccoli
Beet
Pumpkin
Potato

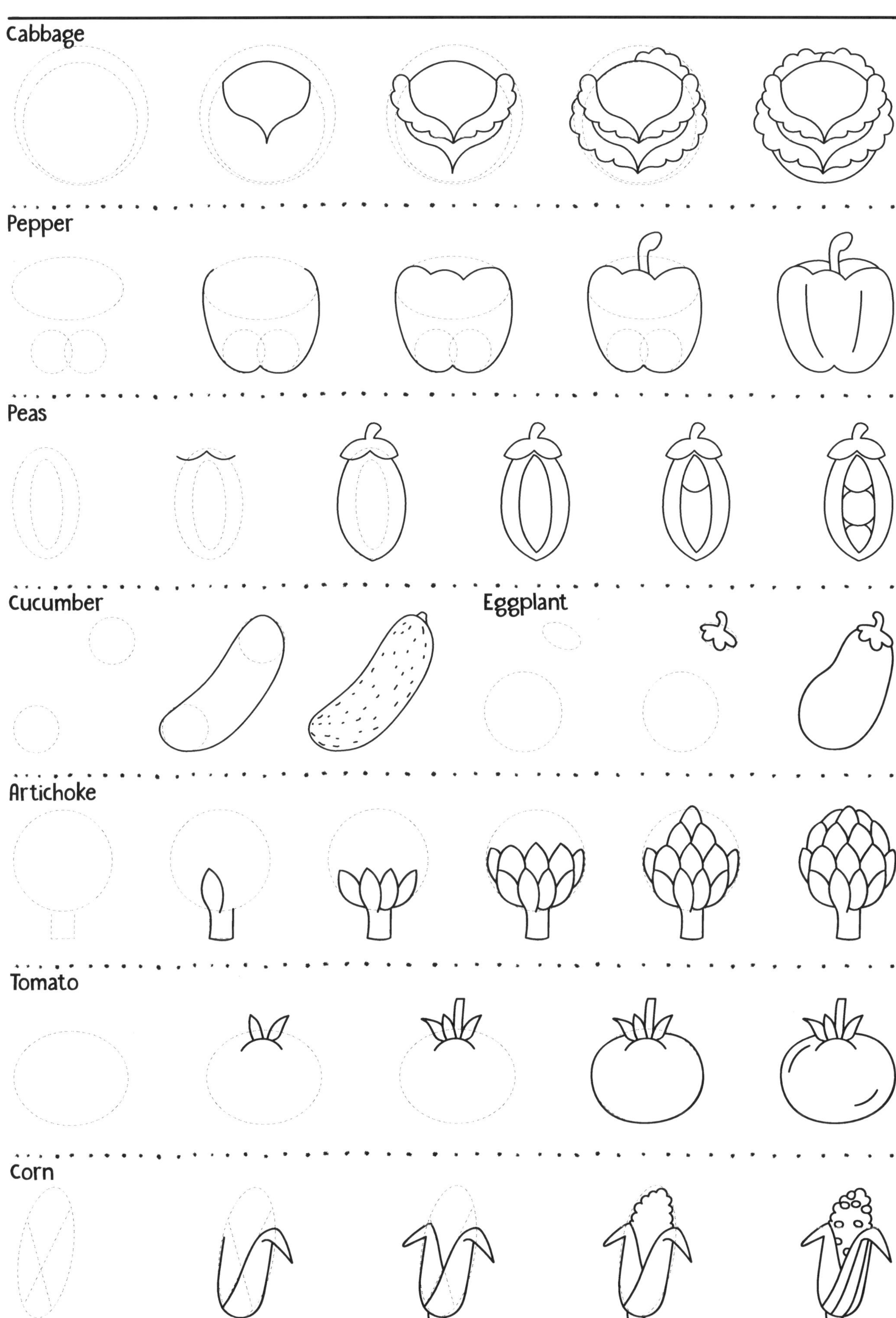
Cabbage
Pepper
Peas
Cucumber
Eggplant
Artichoke
Tomato
Corn

Cauliflower

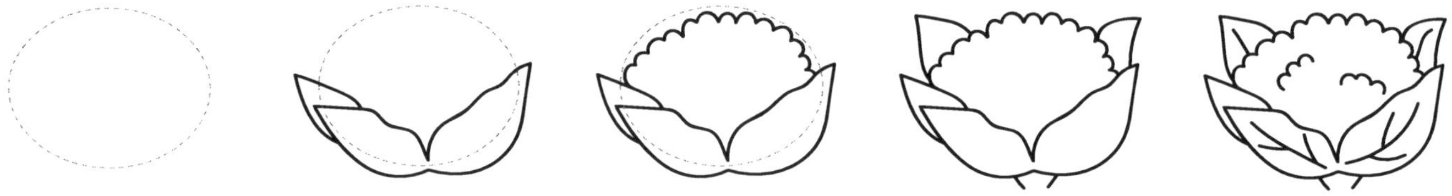

Lettuce

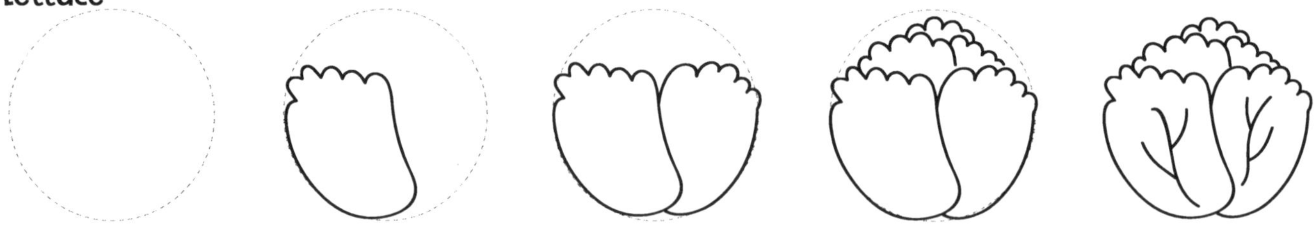

Bean

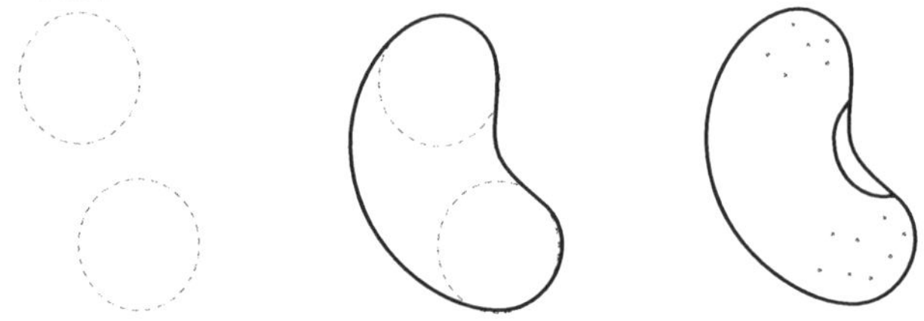

Orange slice

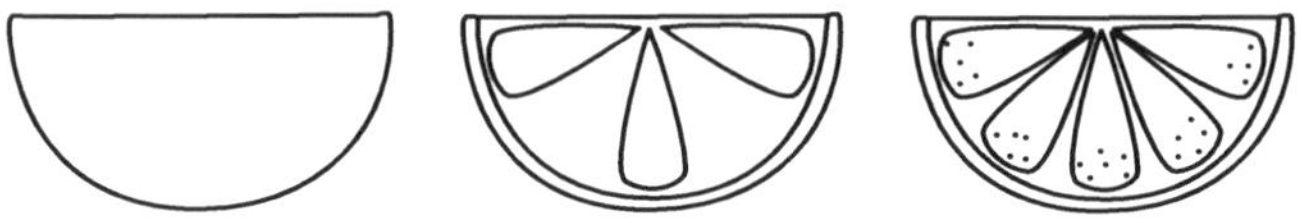

Apple

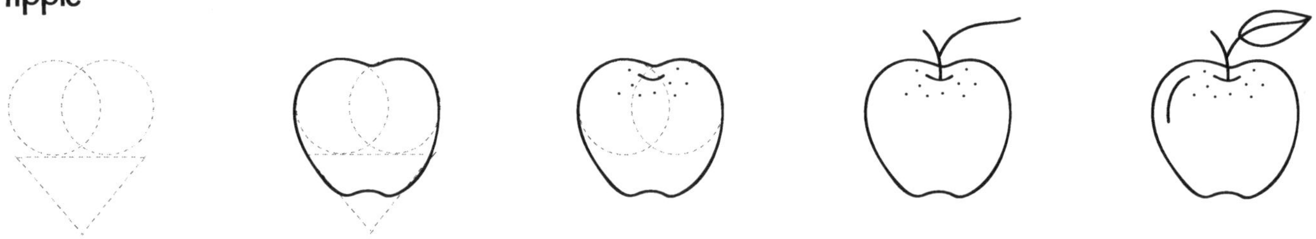

Banana

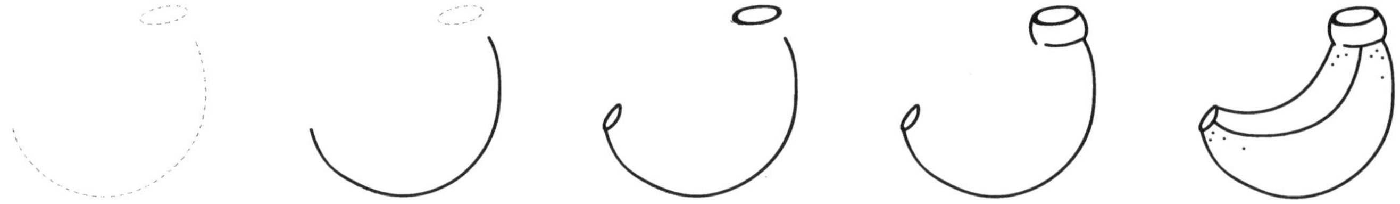

Pear

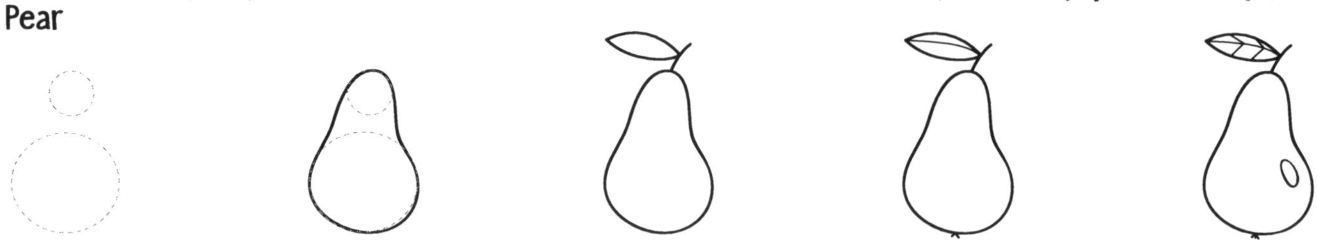

Pineapple

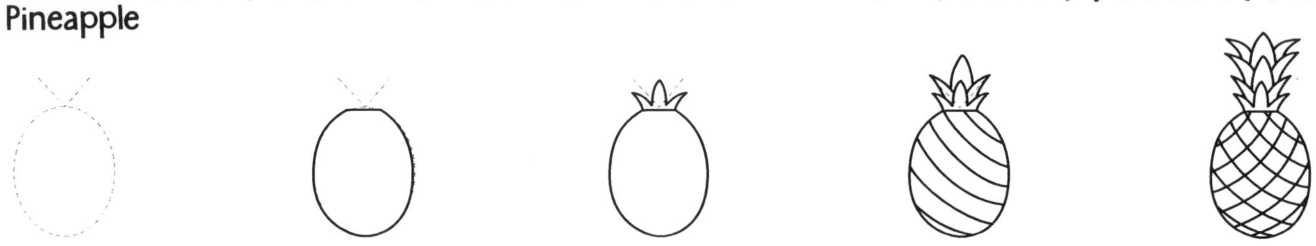

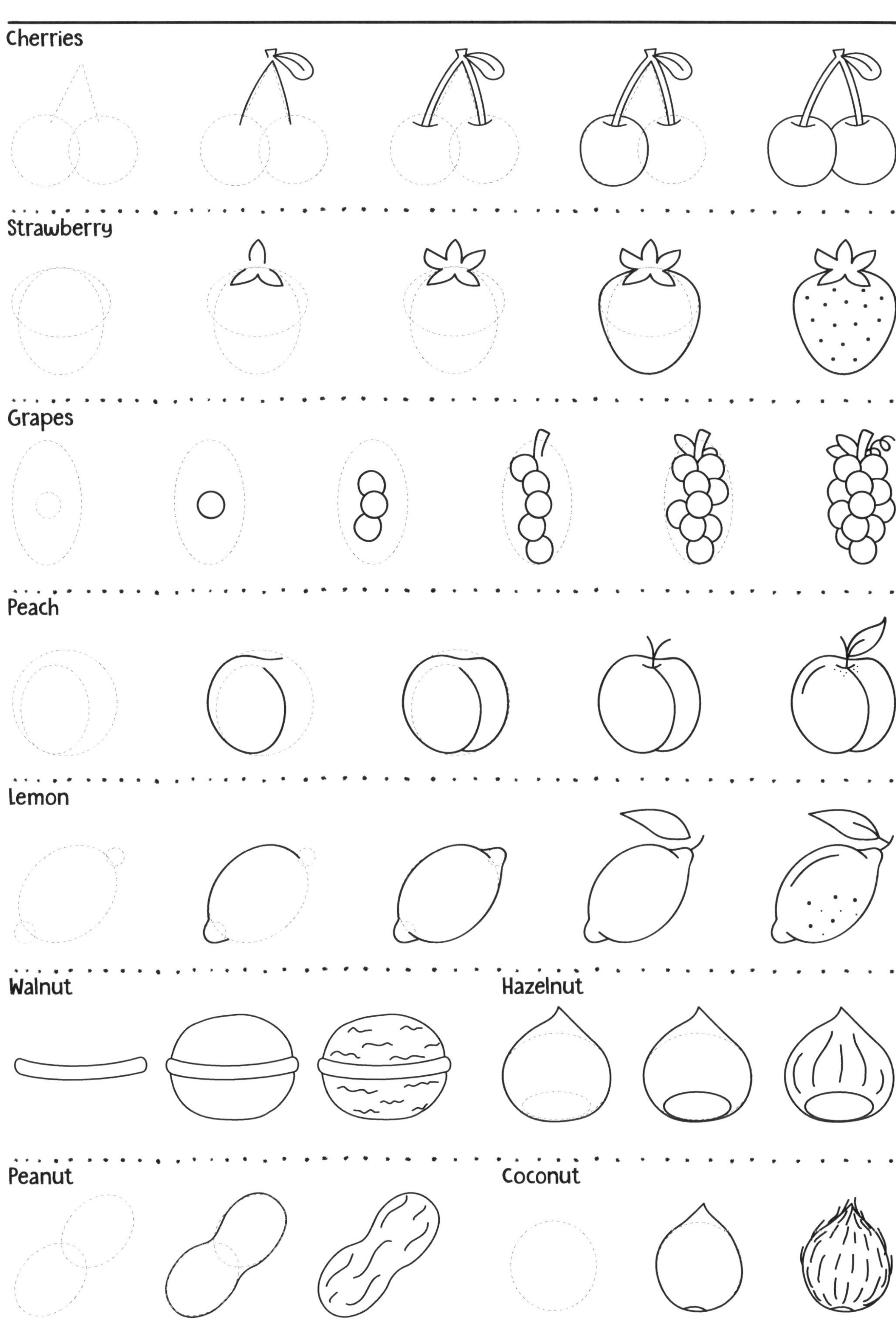
Cherries
Strawberry
Grapes
Peach
Lemon
Walnut
Hazelnut
Peanut
Coconut

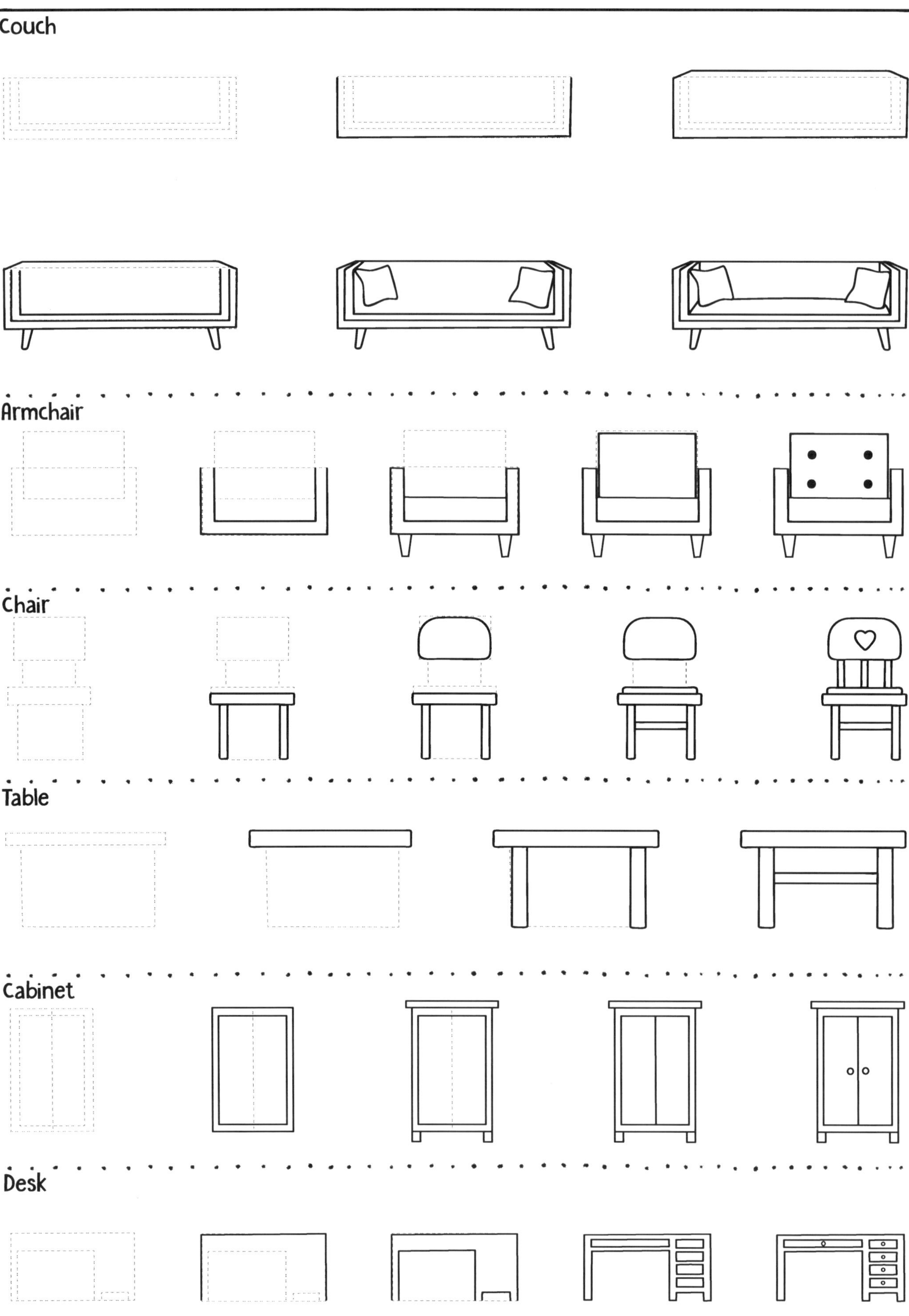
Couch
Armchair
Chair
Table
Cabinet
Desk

Wall shelf

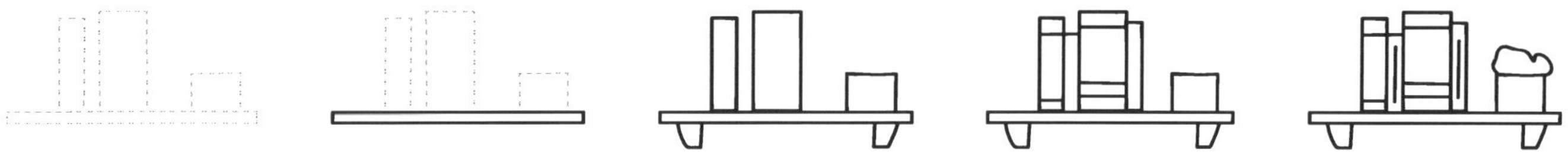

Painting

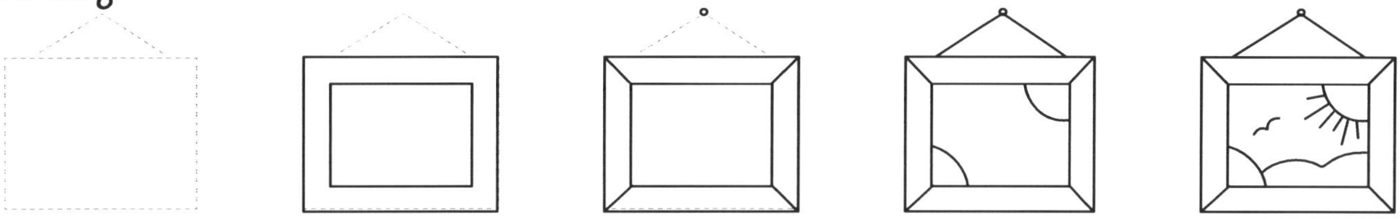

Goldfish bowl

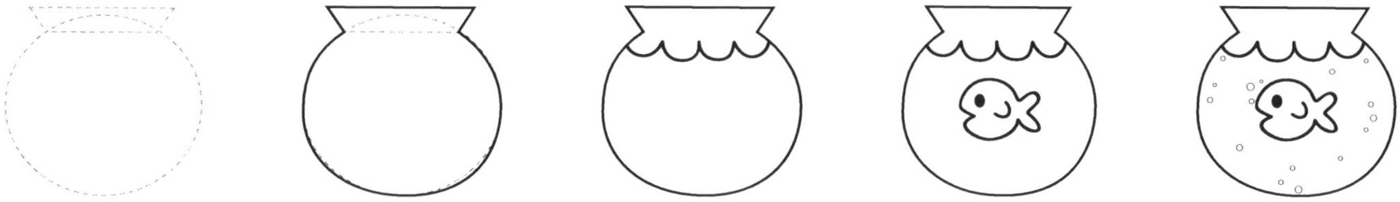

Aquarium

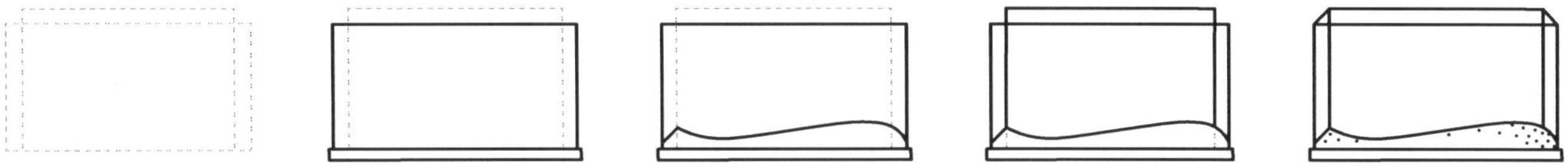

Bird cage

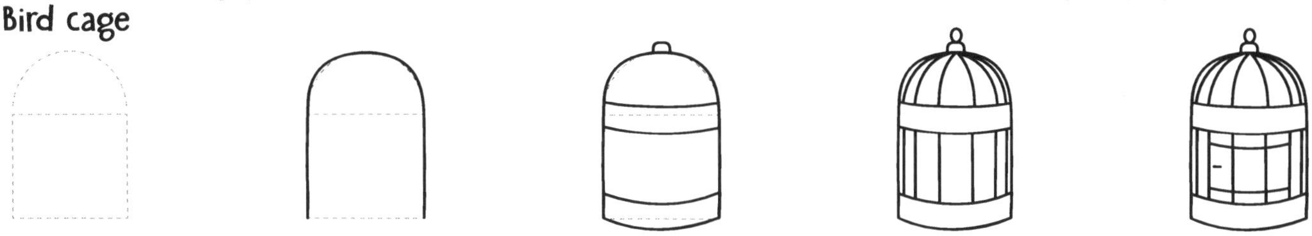

Dog basket

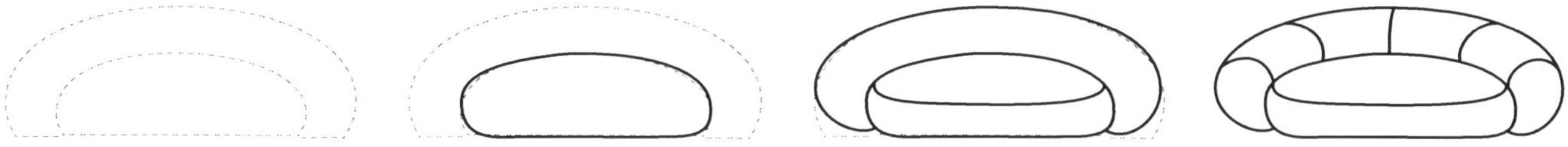

Food bowl

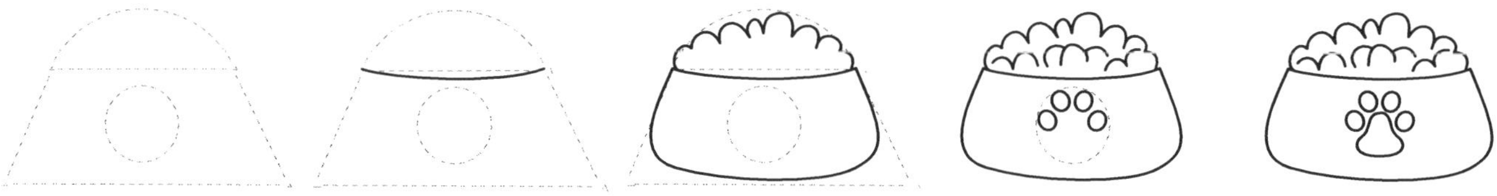

Bone

Doghouse

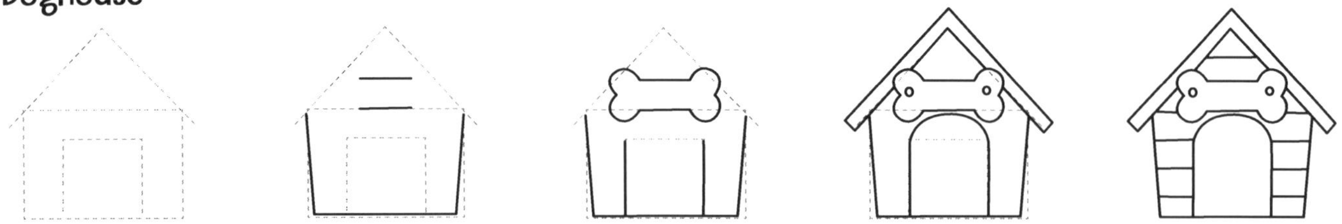

Birdfeeder

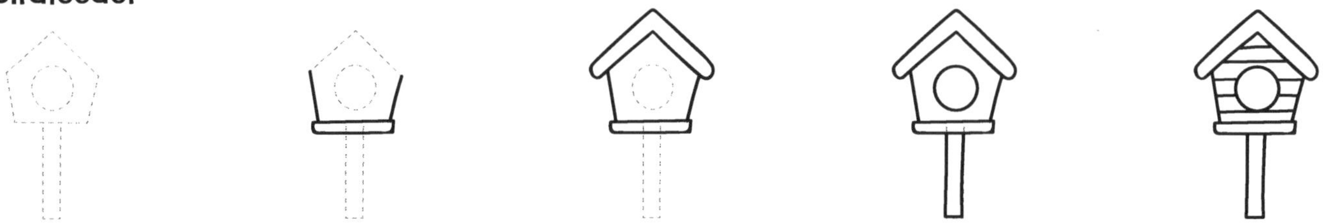

Fence

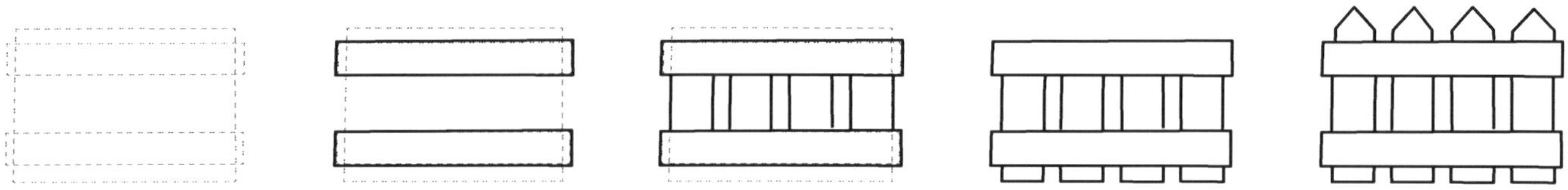

Ladder

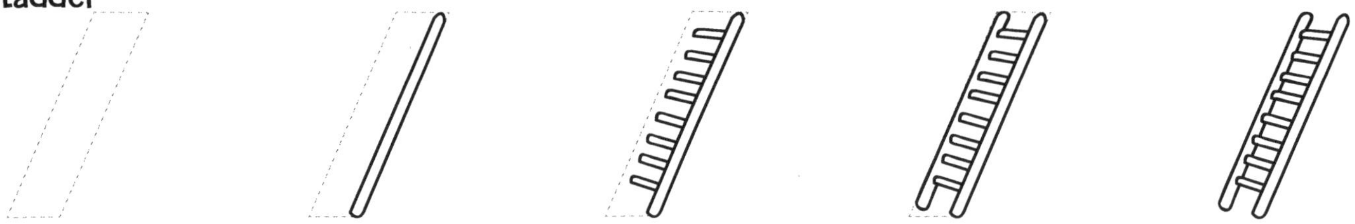

Kettle barbecue

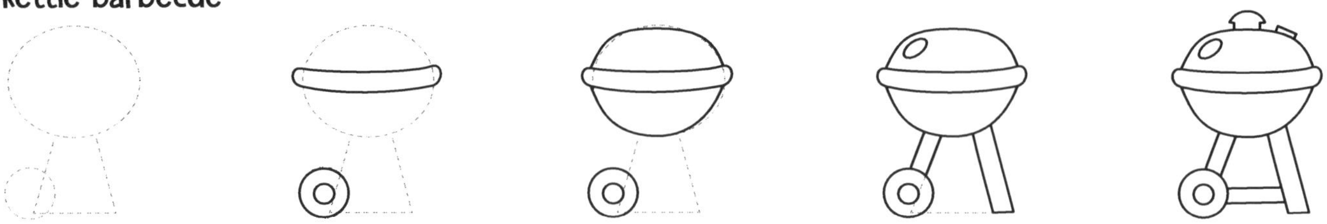

Deck chair

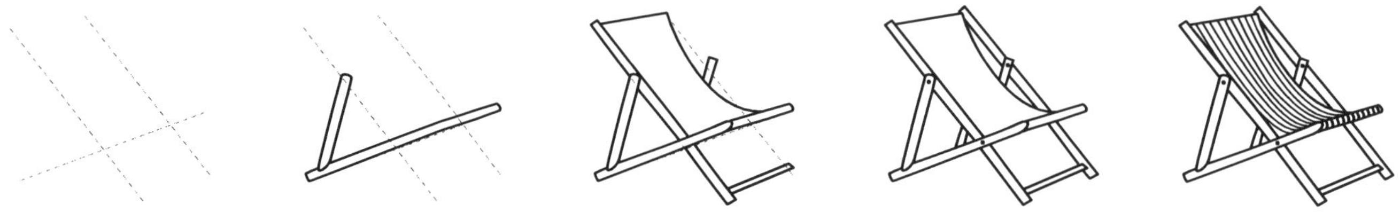

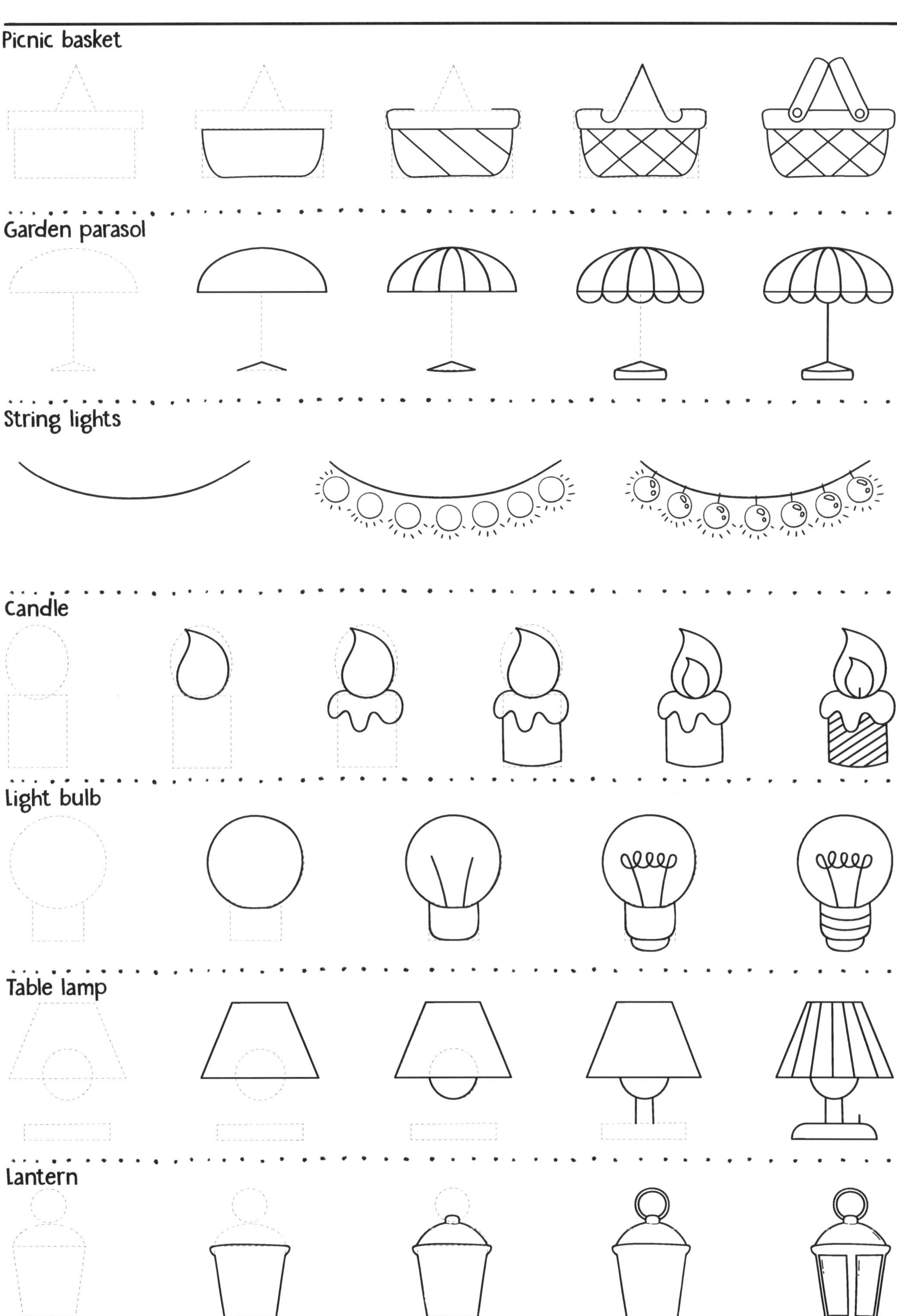
Picnic basket
Garden parasol
String lights
Candle
Light bulb
Table lamp
Lantern

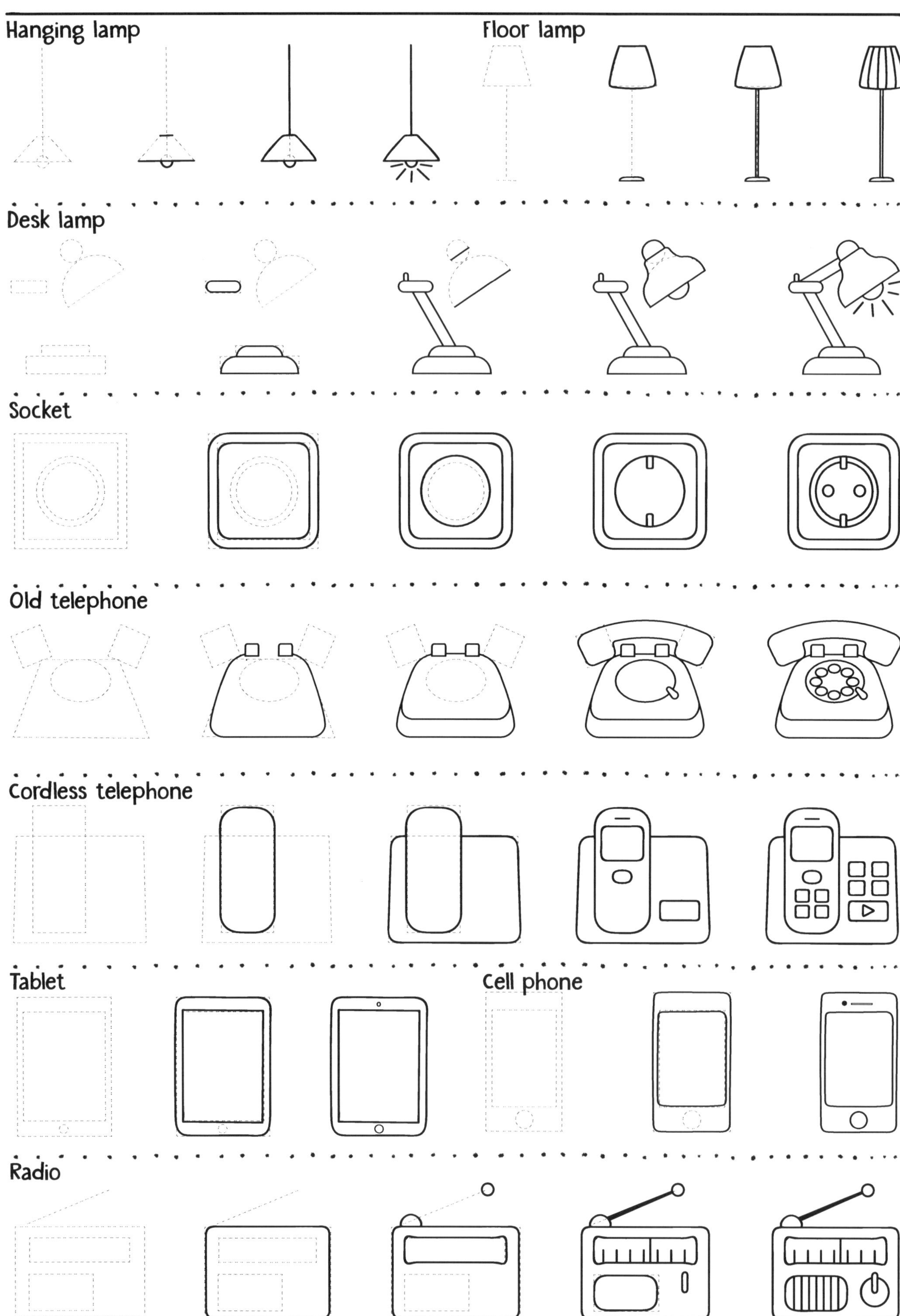
Hanging lamp
Floor lamp
Desk lamp
Socket
Old telephone
Cordless telephone
Tablet
Cell phone
Radio

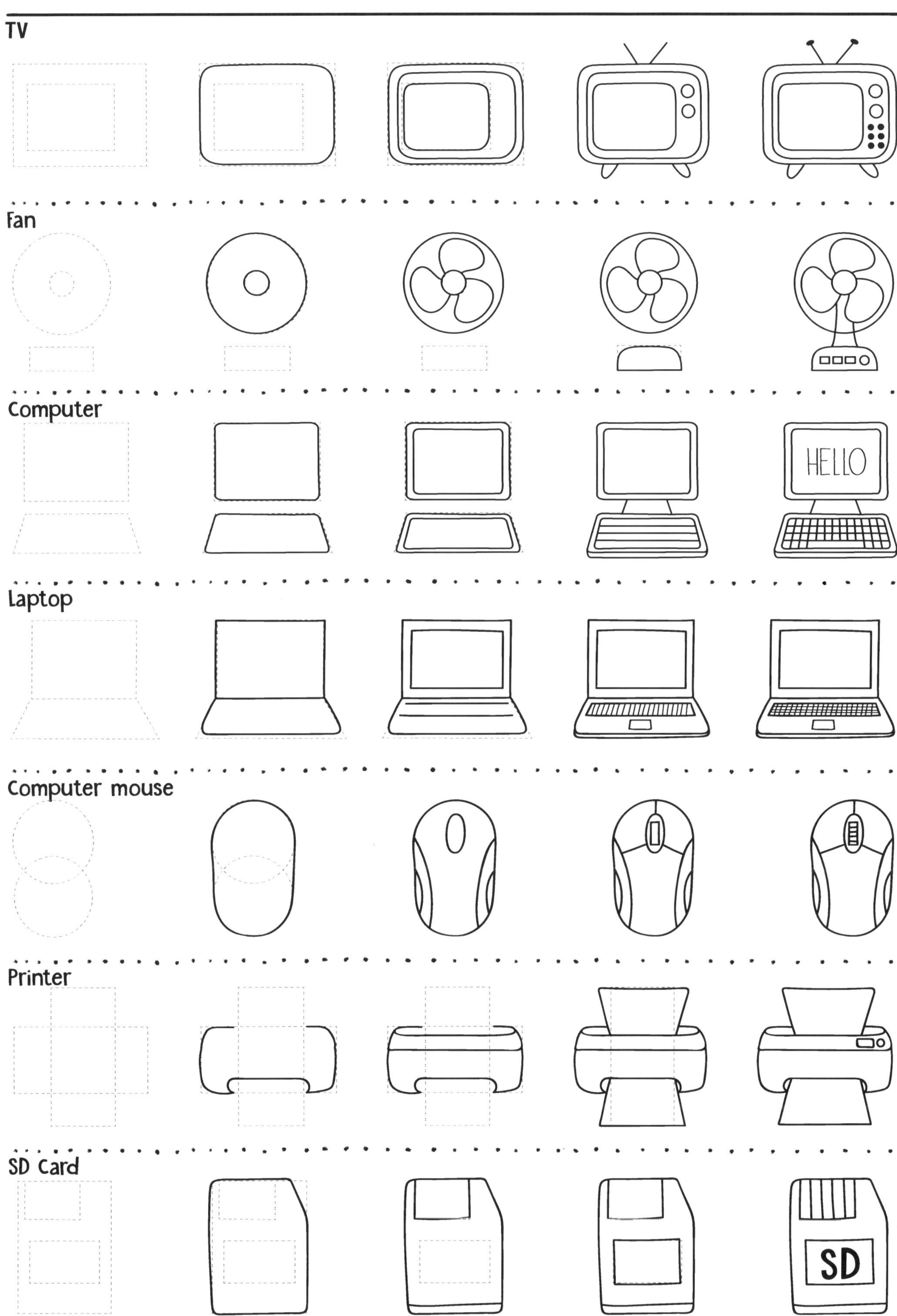
TV
Fan
Computer
HELLO
Laptop
Computer mouse
Printer
SD Card
SD

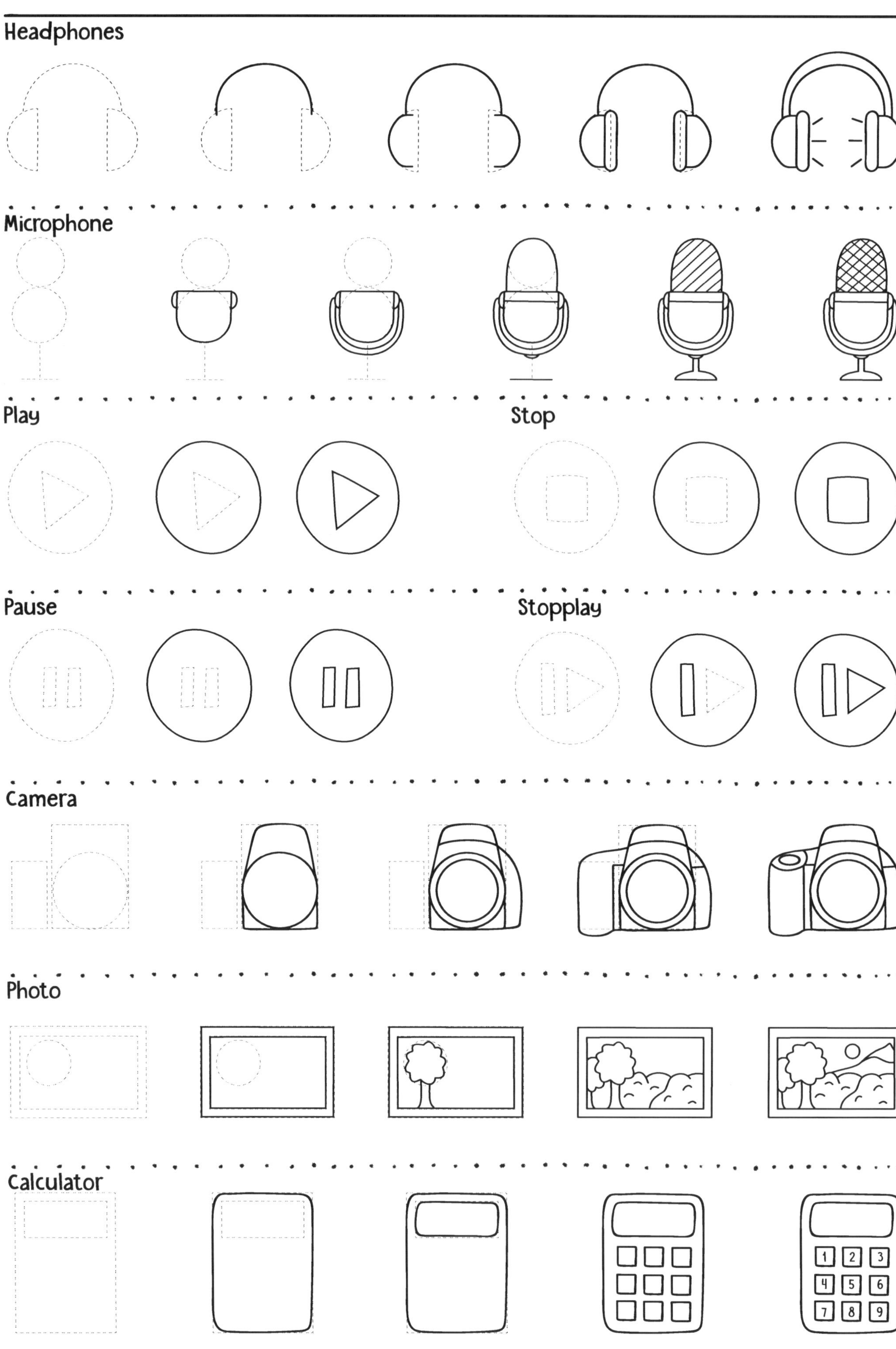
Headphones
Microphone
Play
Stop
Pause
Stopplay
Camera
Photo
Calculator
1 2 3
4 5 6
7 8 9

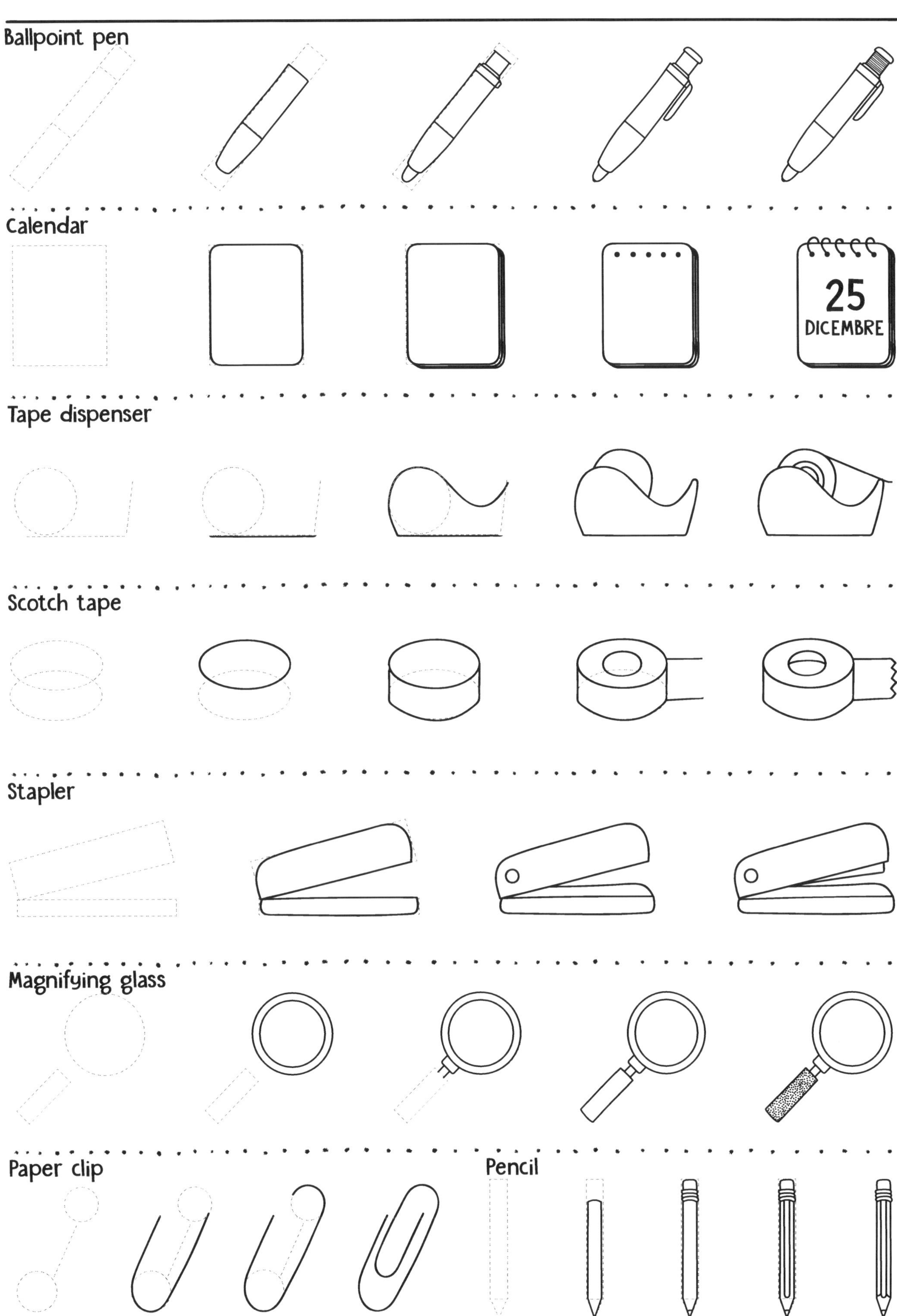
Ballpoint pen
Calendar
25
DICEMBRE
Tape dispenser
Scotch tape
Stapler
Magnifying glass
Paper clip
Pencil

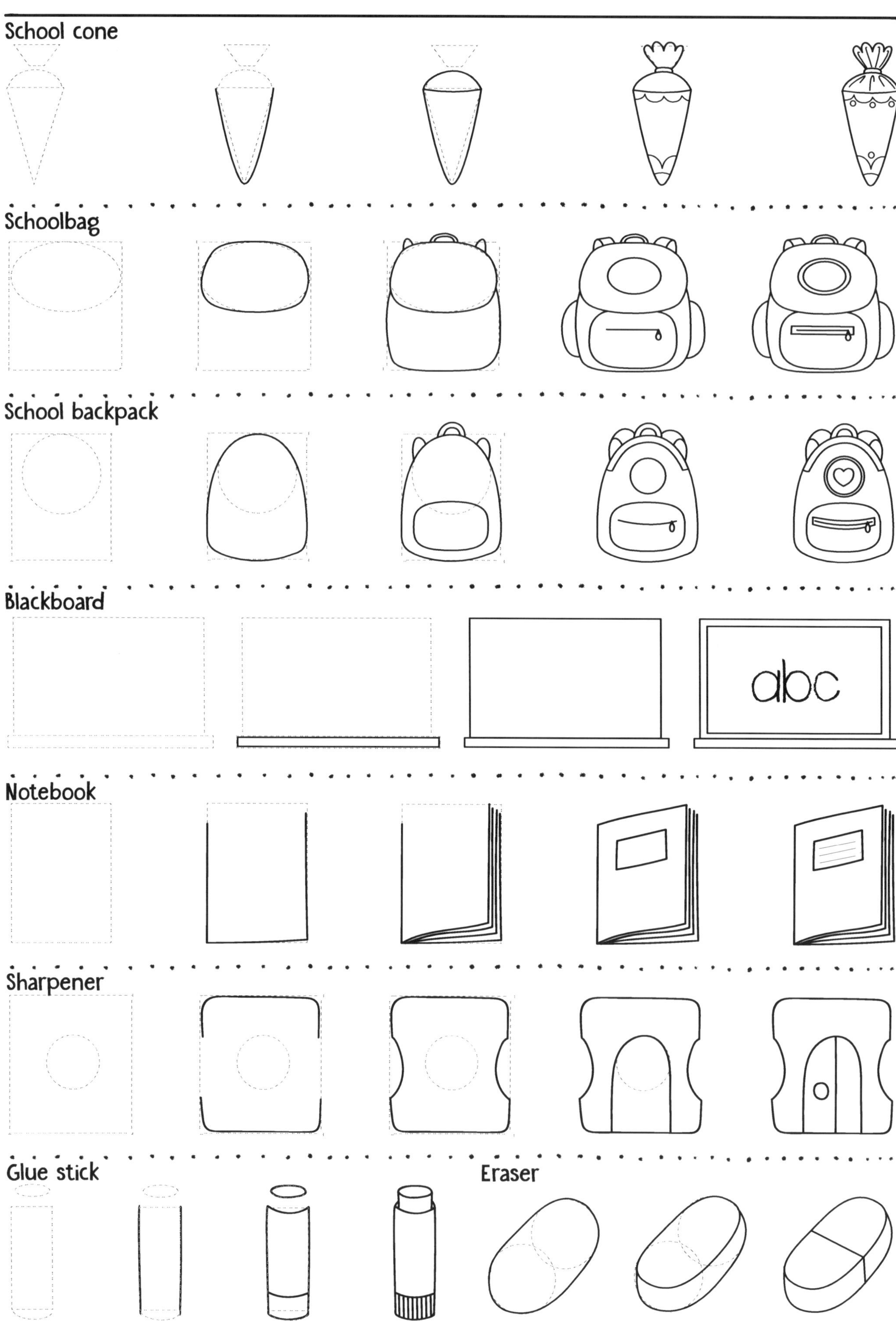
School cone
Schoolbag
School backpack
Blackboard
abc
Notebook
Sharpener
Glue stick
Eraser

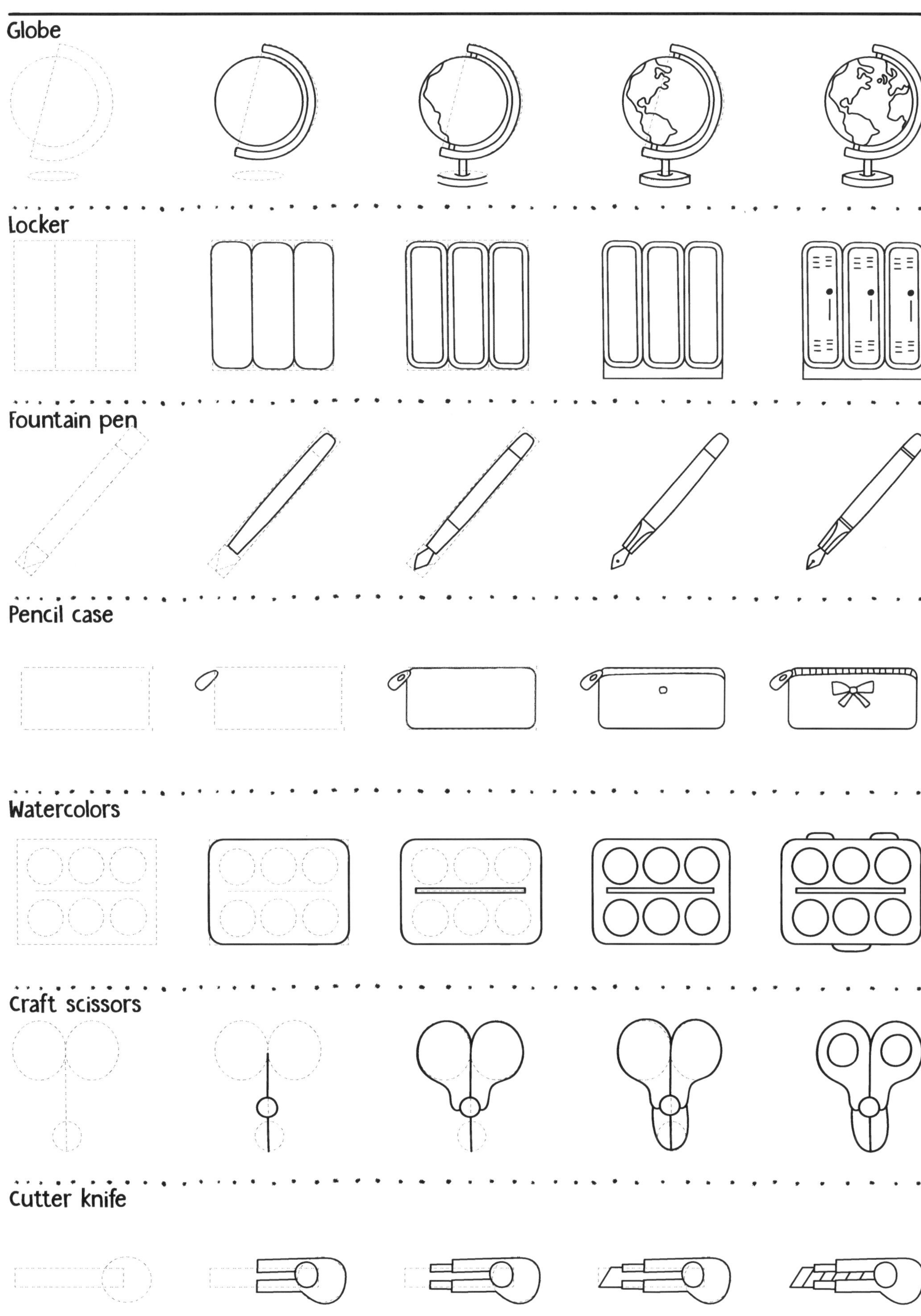
Globe
Locker
Fountain pen
Pencil case
Watercolors
Craft scissors
Cutter knife

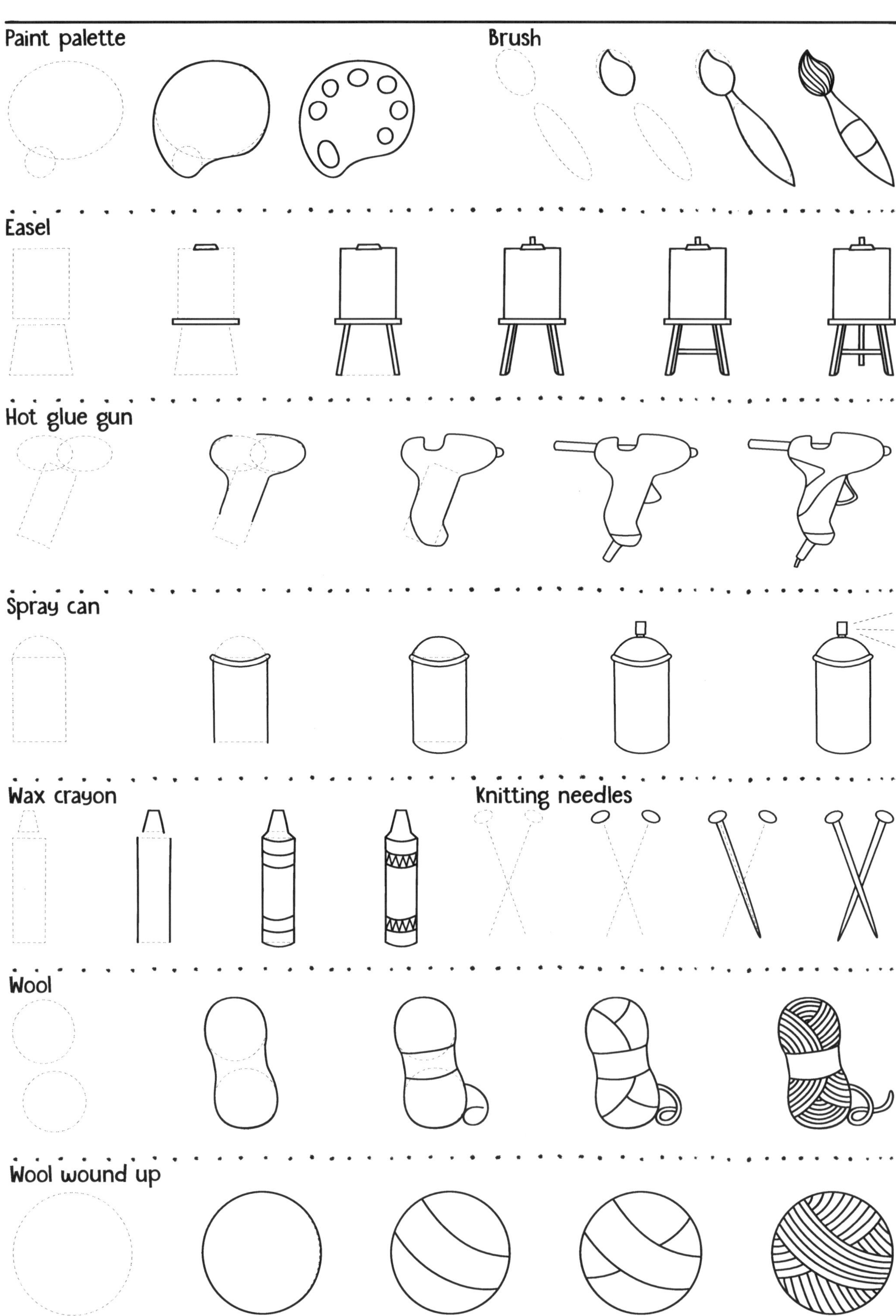
Paint palette
Brush
Easel
Hot glue gun
Spray can
Wax crayon
Knitting needles
Wool
Wool wound up

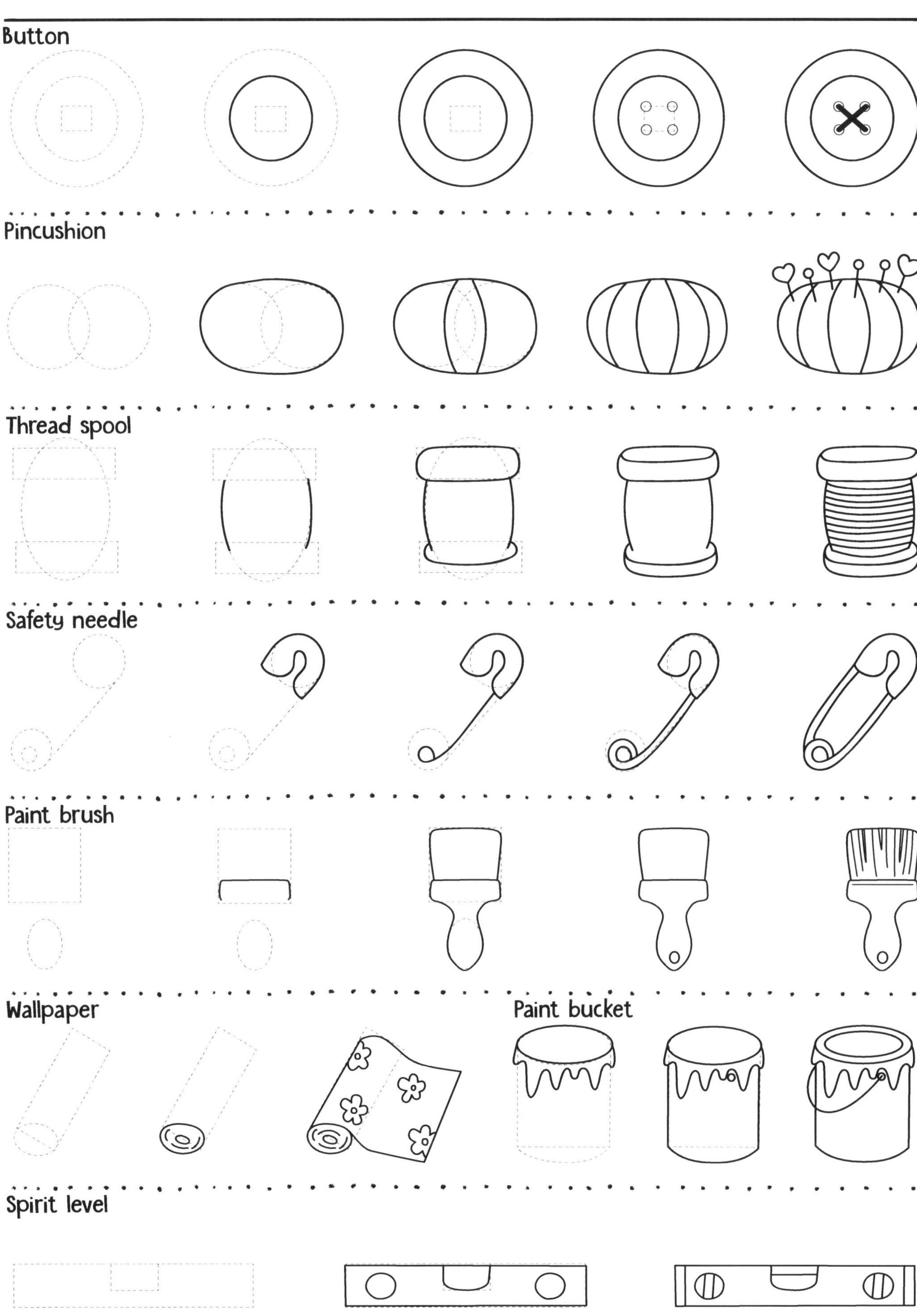
Button
Pincushion
Thread spool
Safety needle
Paint brush
Wallpaper
Paint bucket
Spirit level

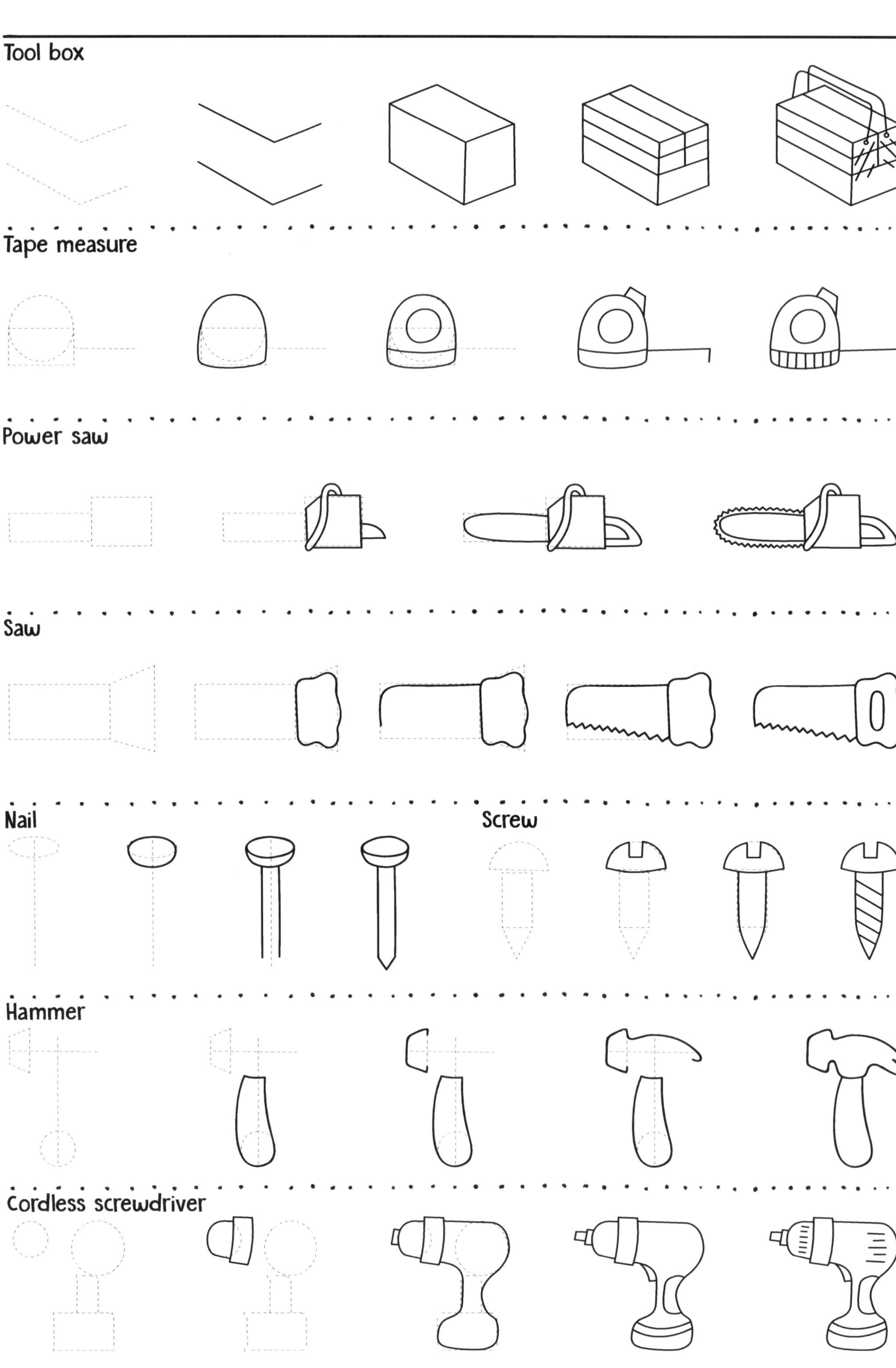
Tool box
Tape measure
Power saw
Saw
Nail
Screw
Hammer
Cordless screwdriver

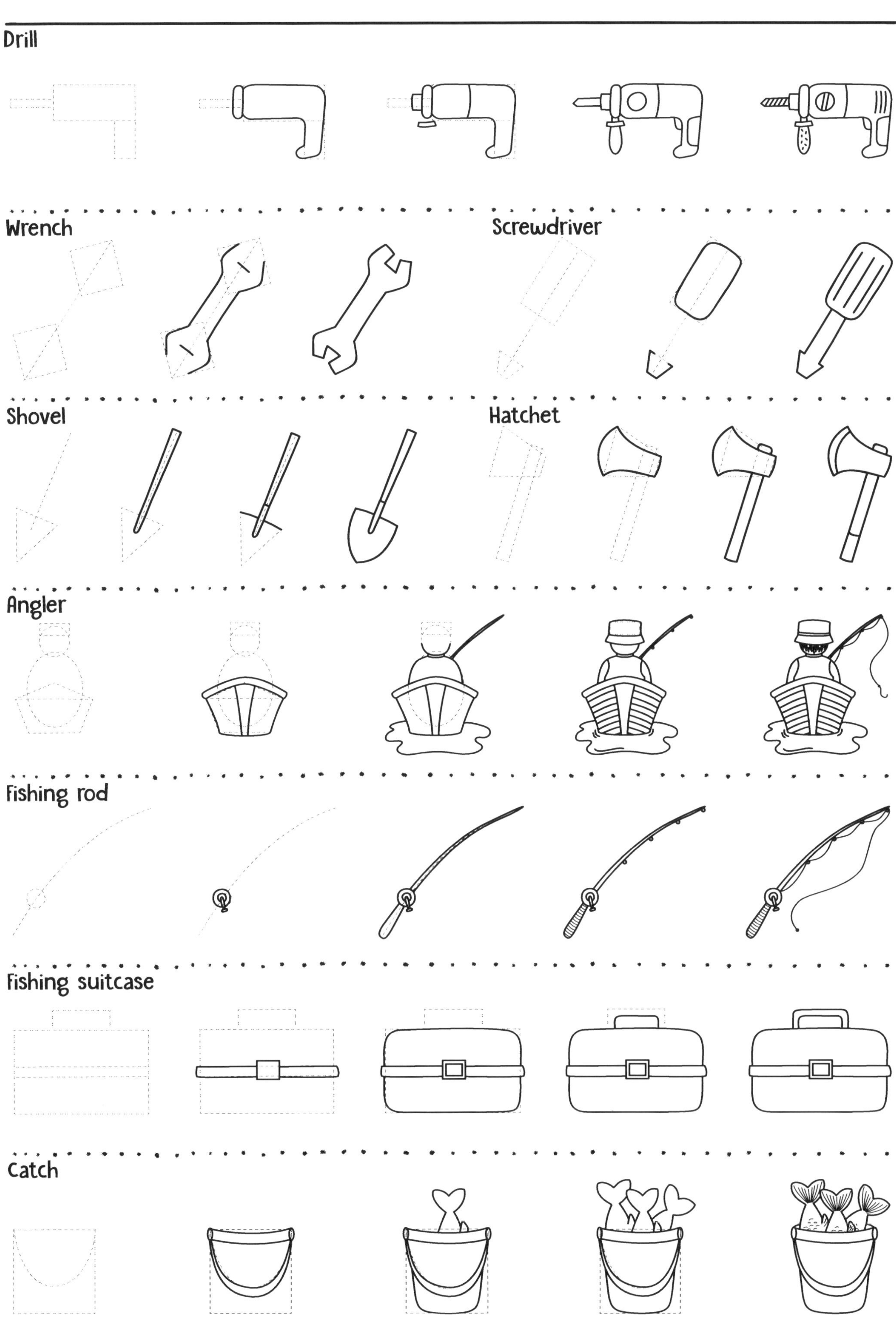
Drill
Wrench
Screwdriver
Shovel
Hatchet
Angler
Fishing rod
Fishing suitcase
Catch

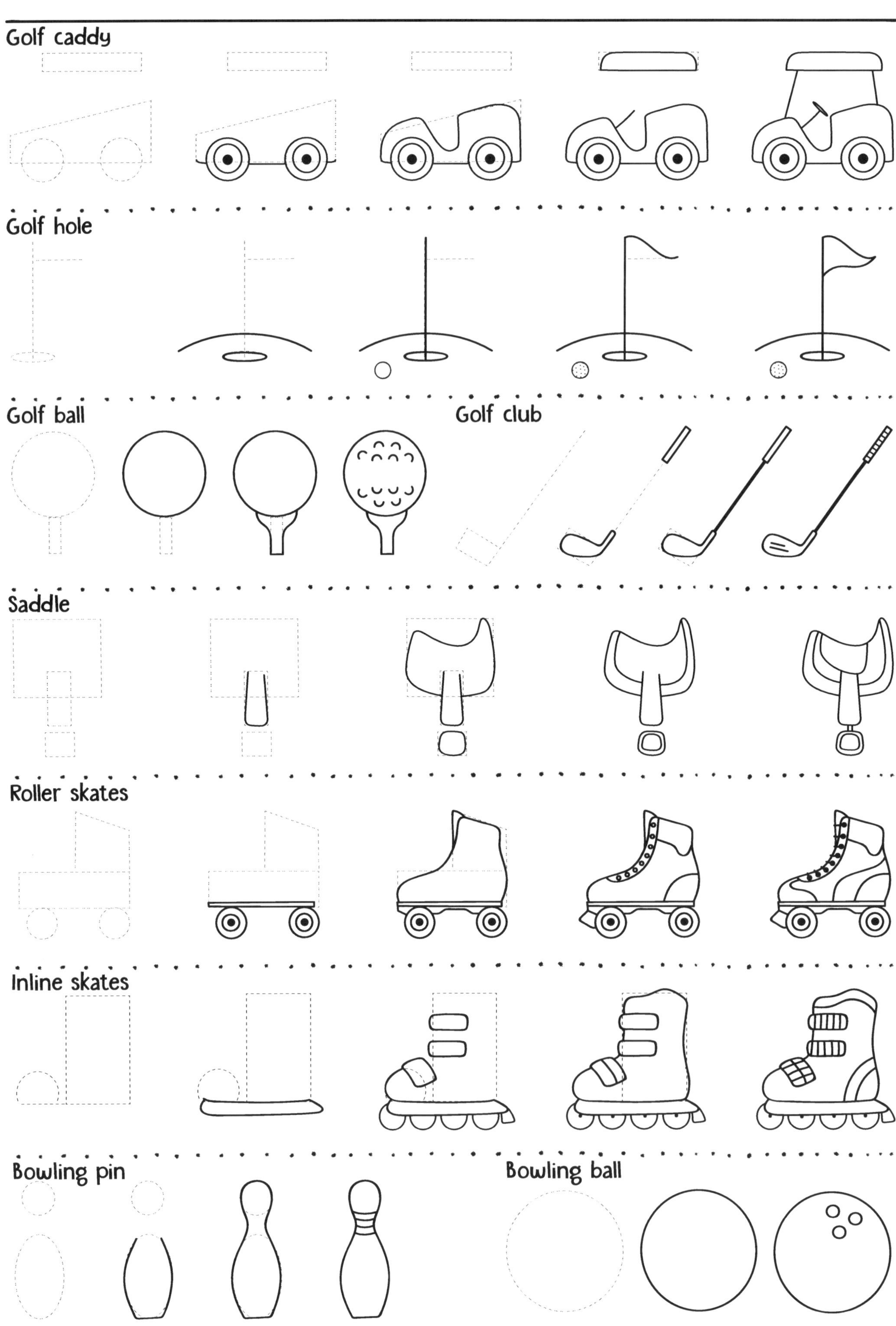
Golf caddy
Golf hole
Golf ball
Golf club
Saddle
Roller skates
Inline skates
Bowling pin
Bowling ball

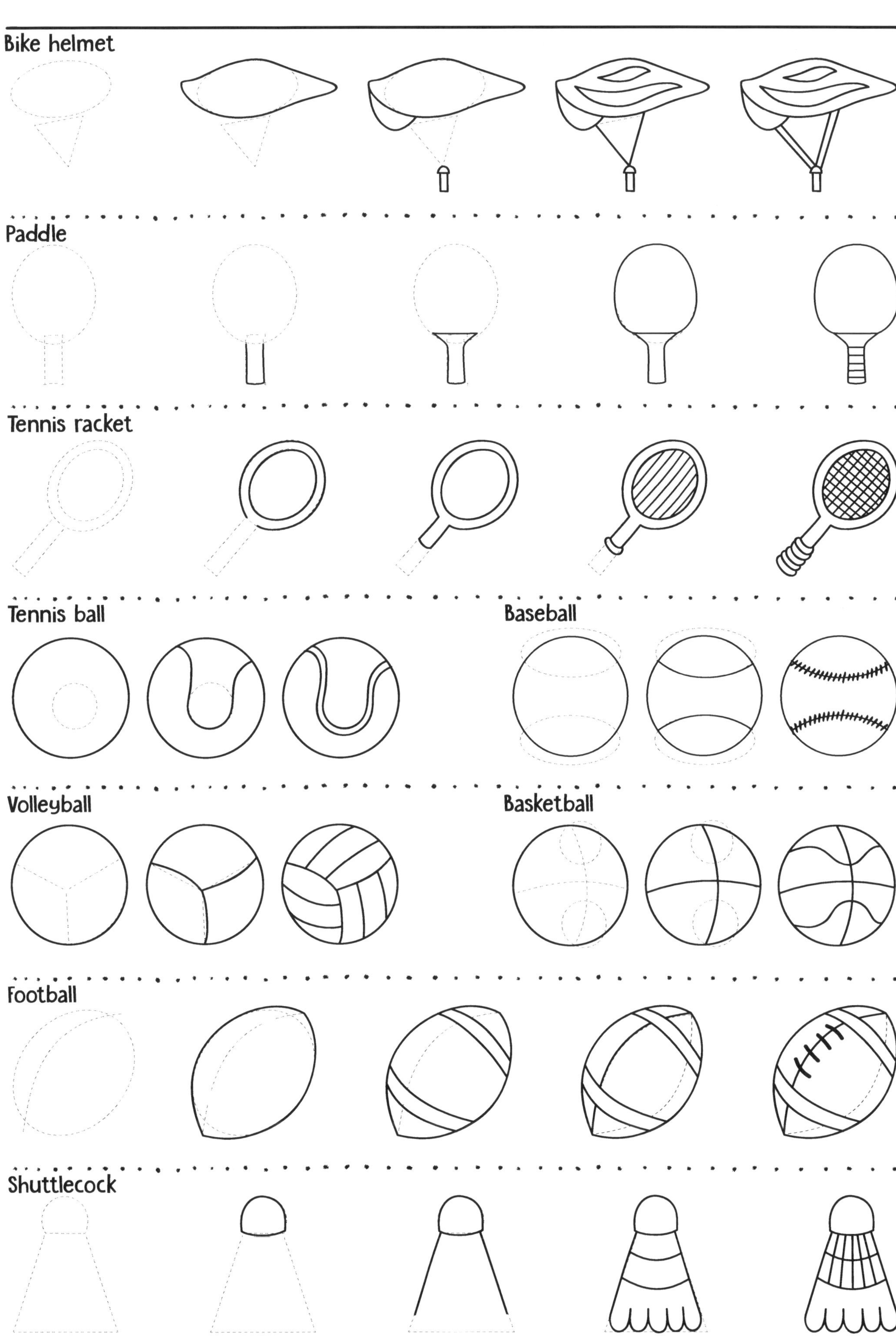
Bike helmet
Paddle
Tennis racket
Tennis ball
Baseball
Volleyball
Basketball
Football
Shuttlecock

Soccer ball

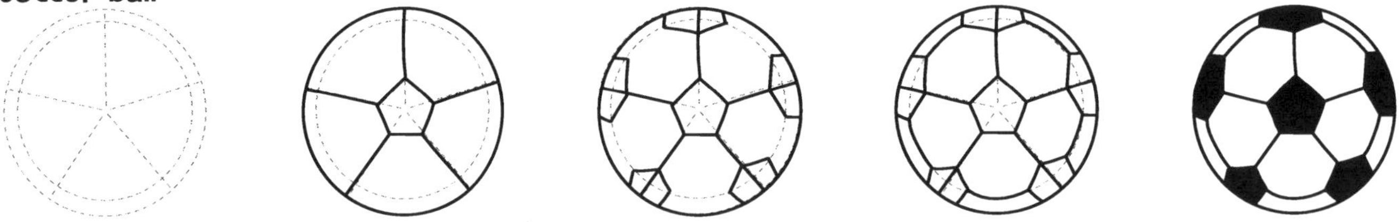

Soccer goal

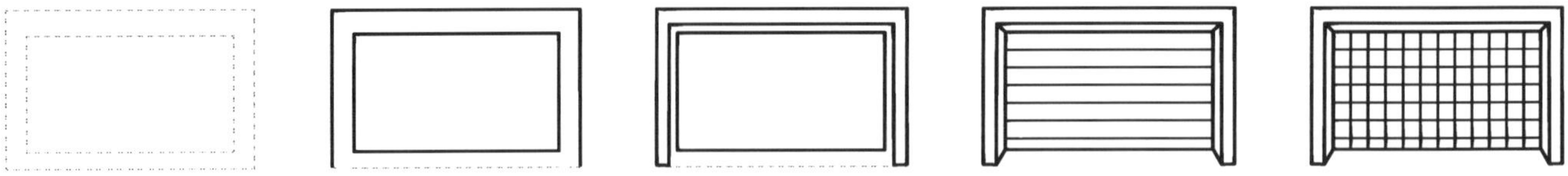

Soccer field

Soccer shoes

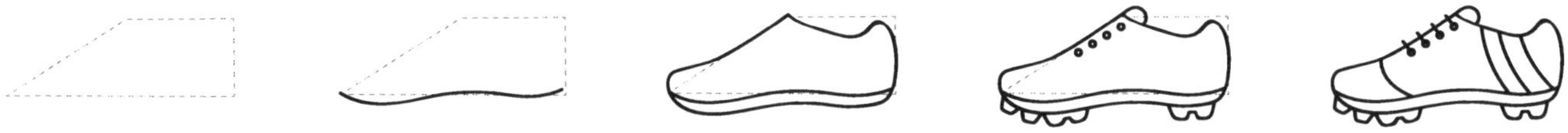

Whistle

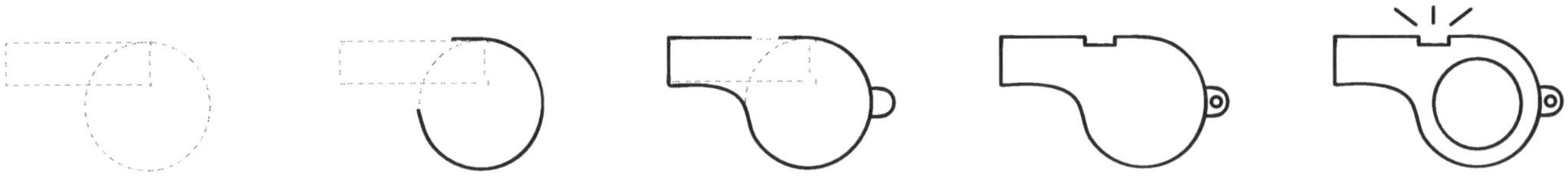

Soccer stadium

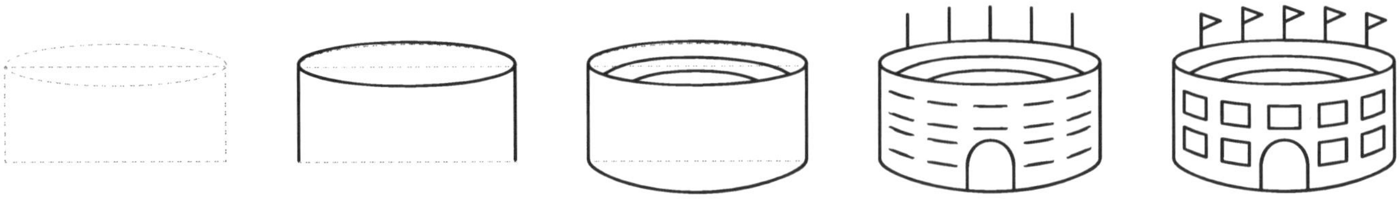

Cup

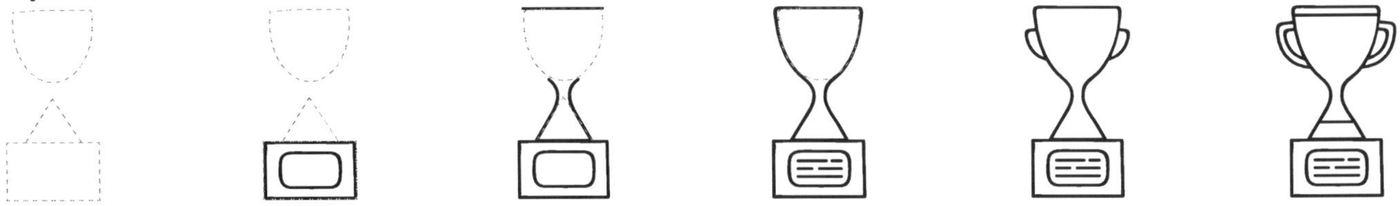

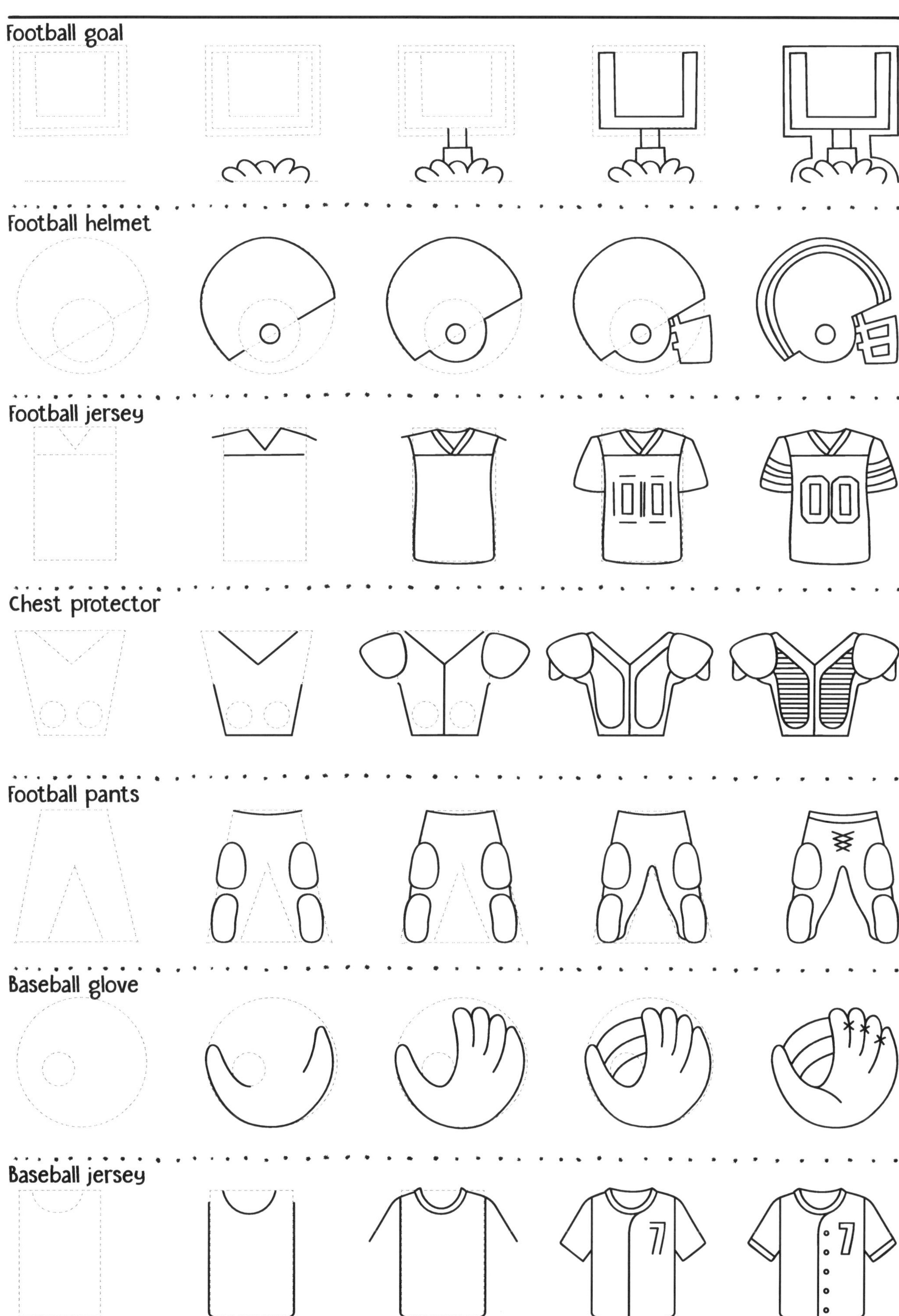
Football goal
Football helmet
Football jersey
Chest protector
Football pants
Baseball glove
Baseball jersey

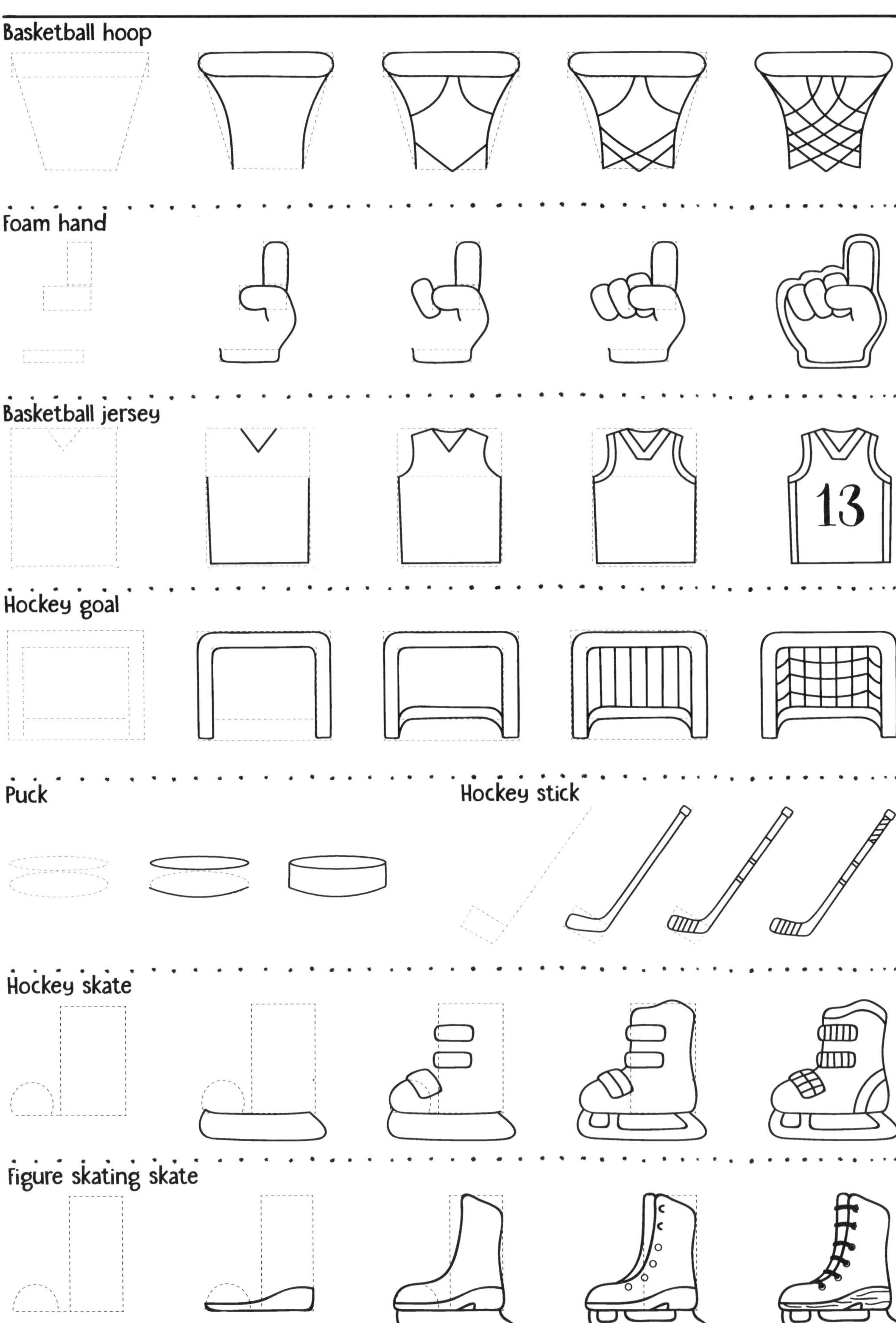
Basketball hoop
Foam hand
Basketball jersey
13
Hockey goal
Puck
Hockey stick
Hockey skate
Figure skating skate

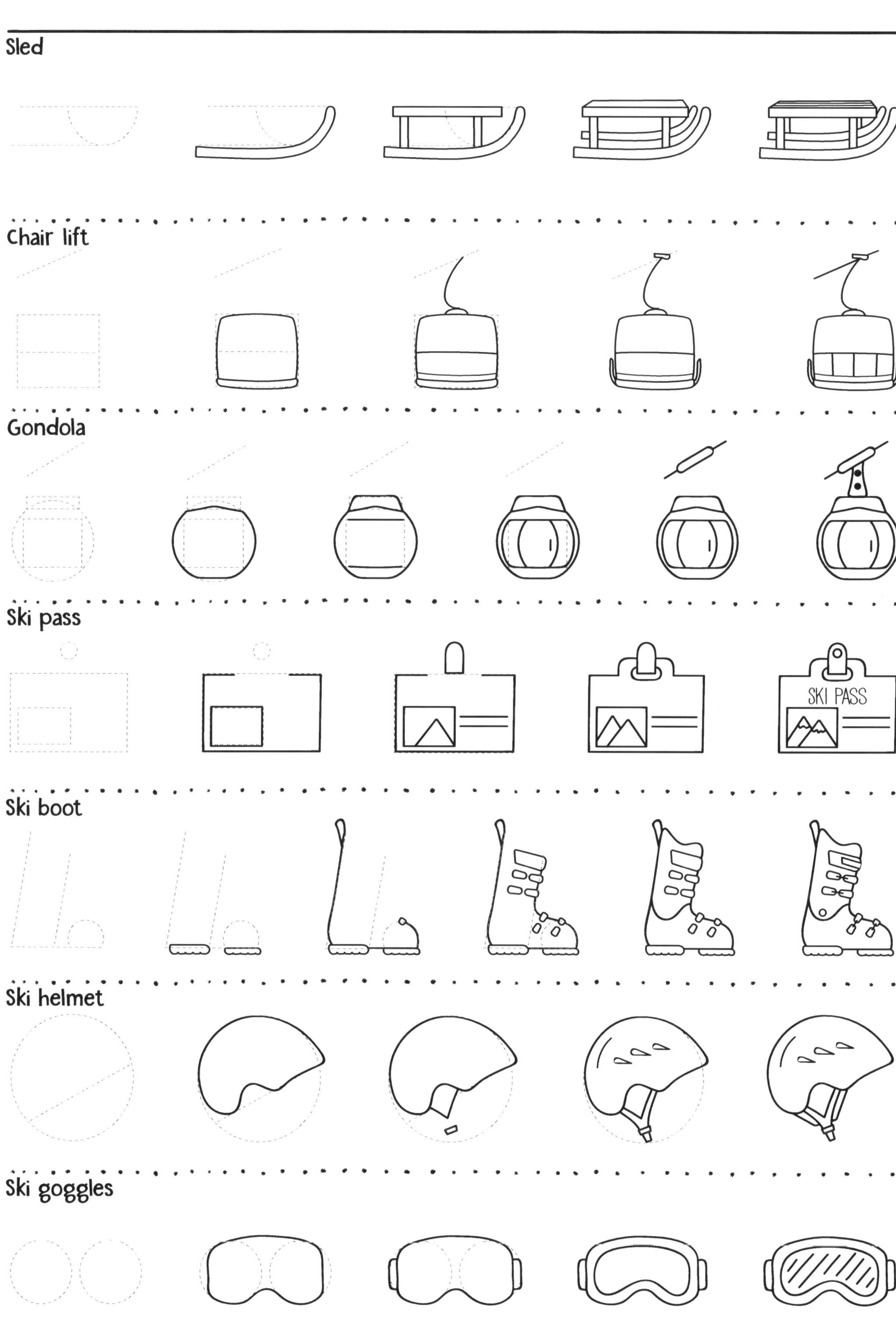
Sled
Chair lift
Gondola
Ski pass
SKI PASS
Ski boot
Ski helmet
Ski goggles

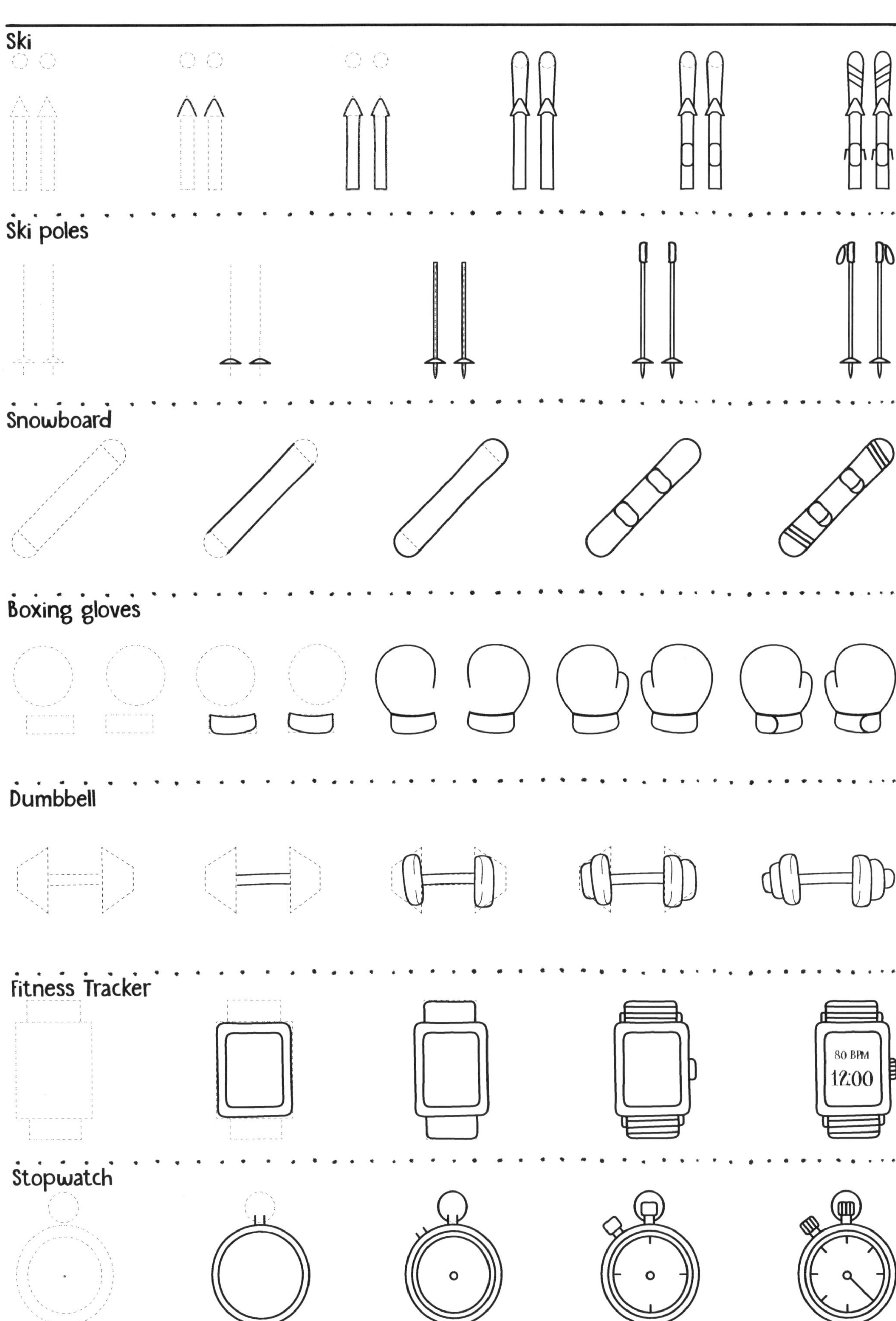
Ski
Ski poles
Snowboard
Boxing gloves
Dumbbell
Fitness Tracker
80 BPM
12:00
Stopwatch

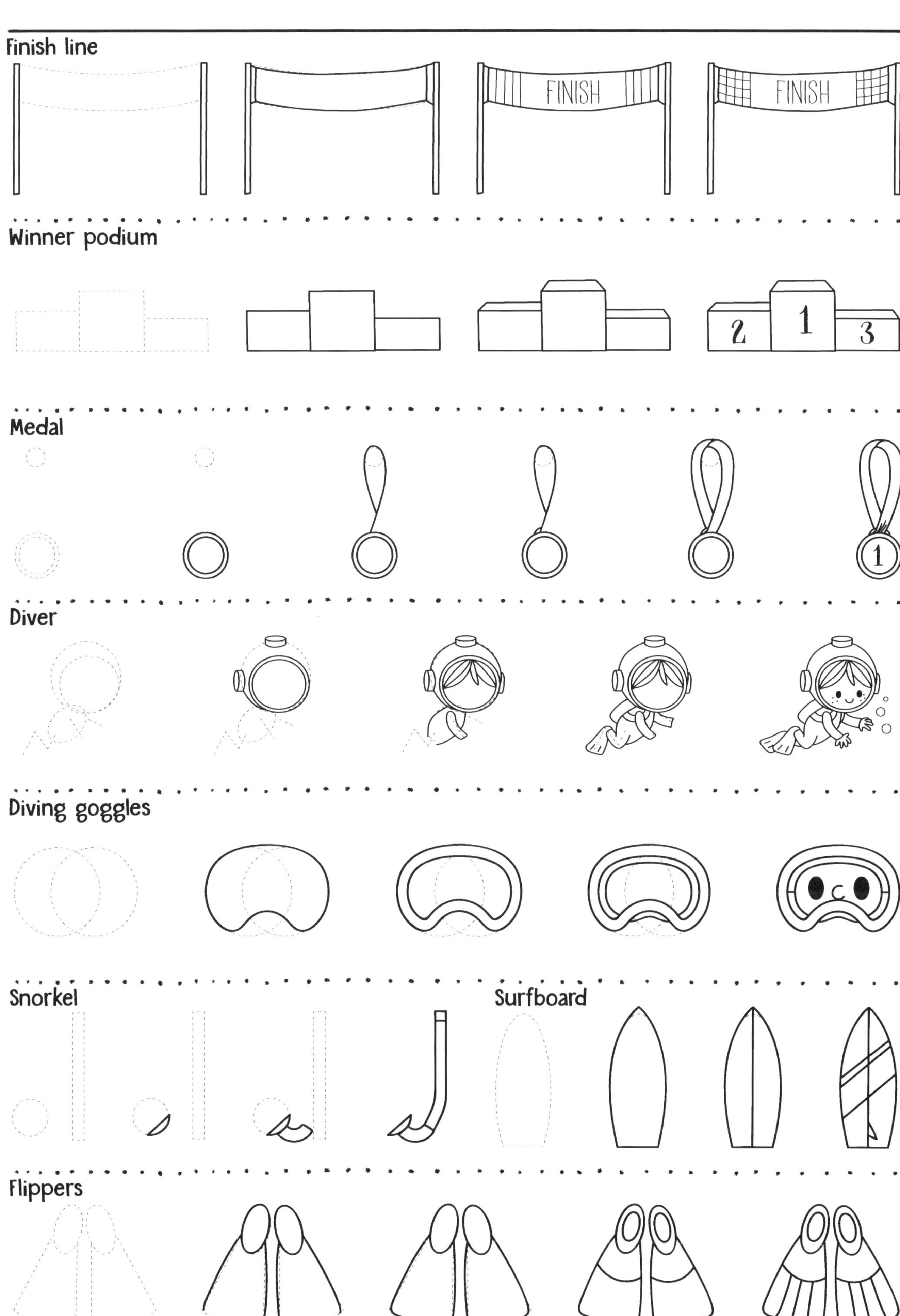
Finish line
FINISH
FINISH
Winner podium
2
1
3
Medal
1
Diver
Diving goggles
Snorkel
Surfboard
Flippers

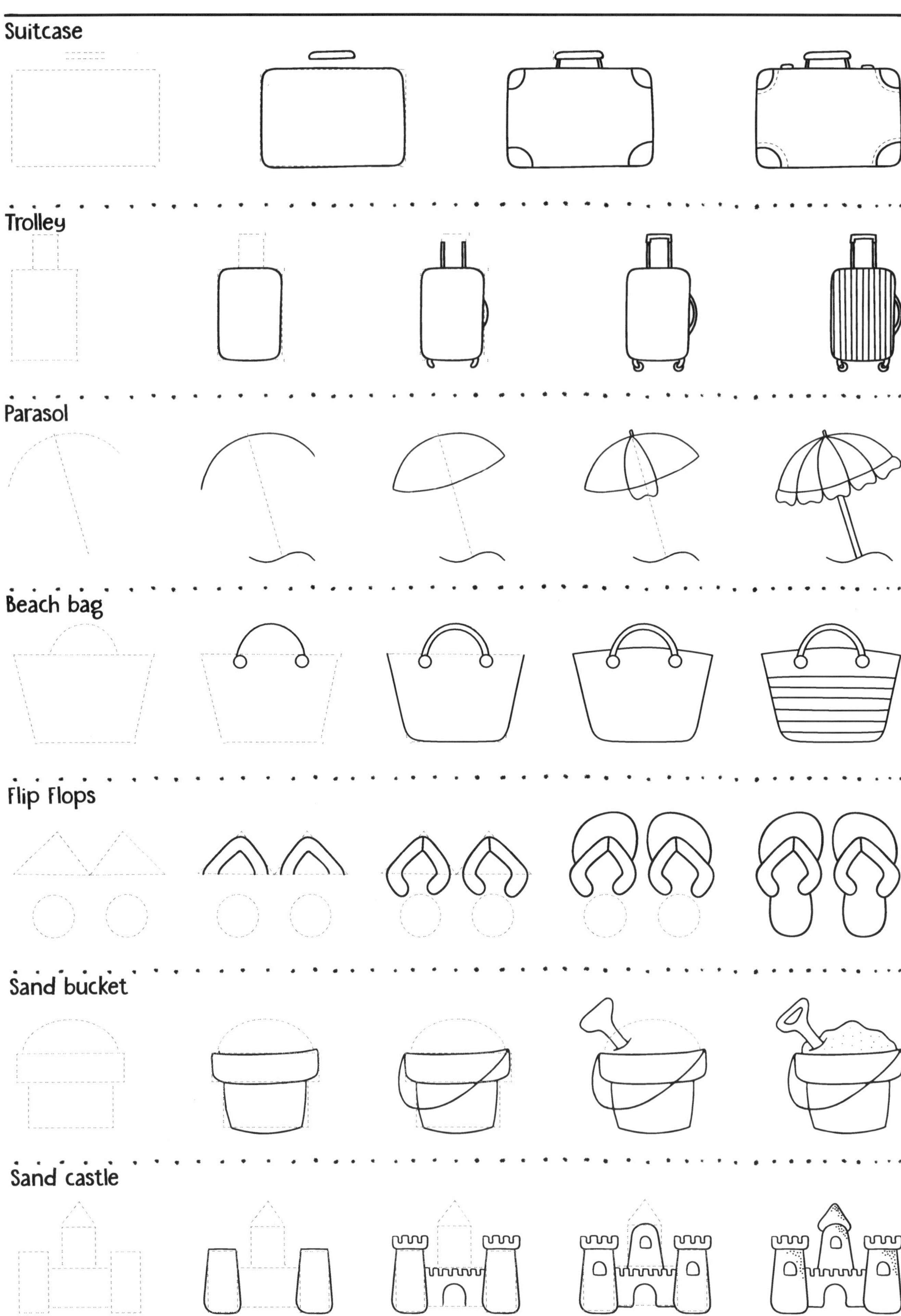
Suitcase
Trolley
Parasol
Beach bag
Flip Flops
Sand bucket
Sand castle

Swimming ring

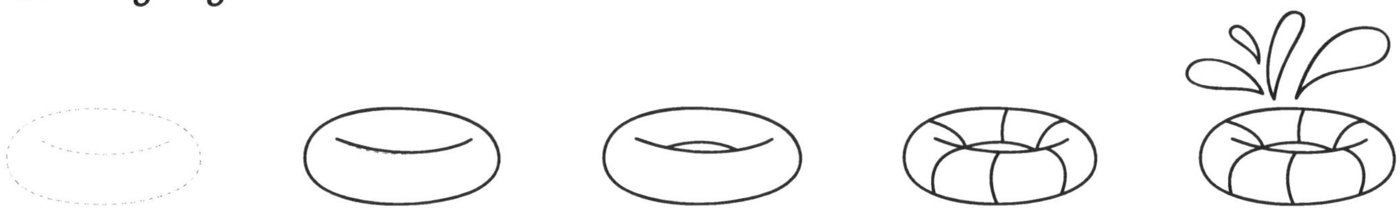

Hammock

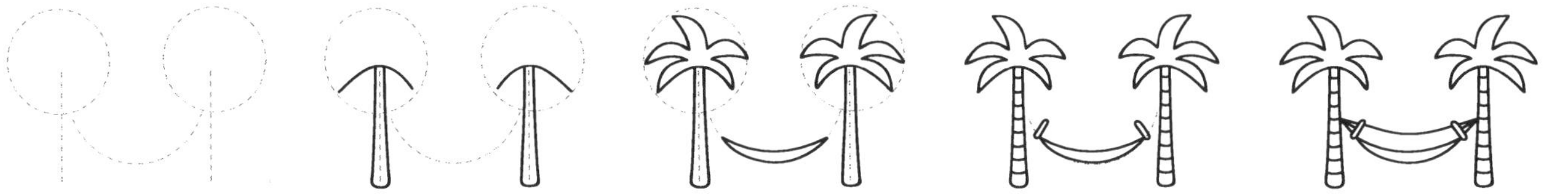

Life ring

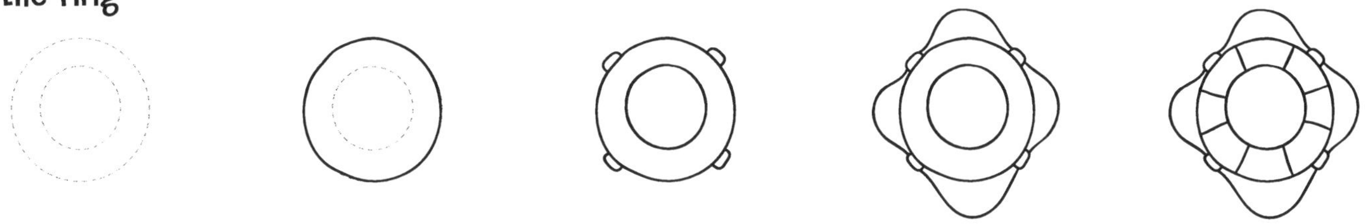

Anchor

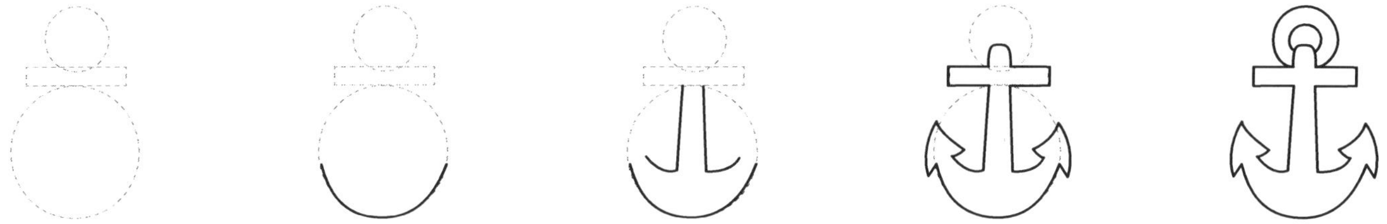

Lighthouse

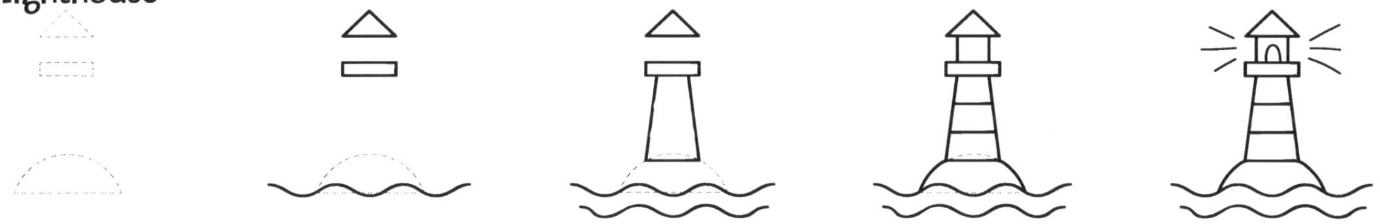

Captain´s cap

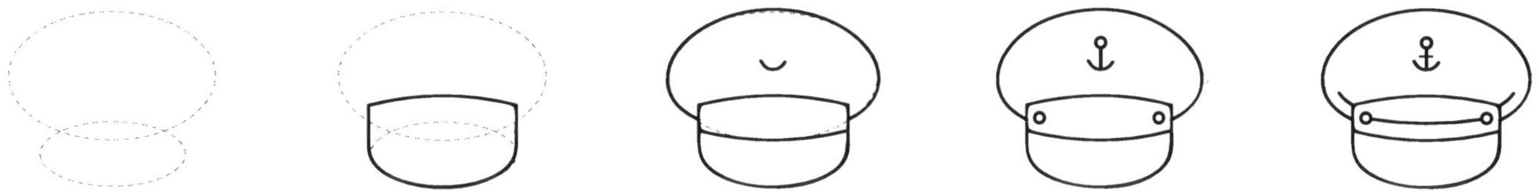

Bull´s eye

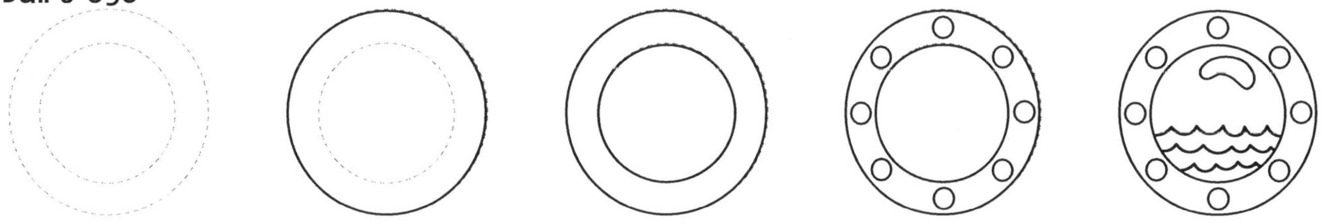

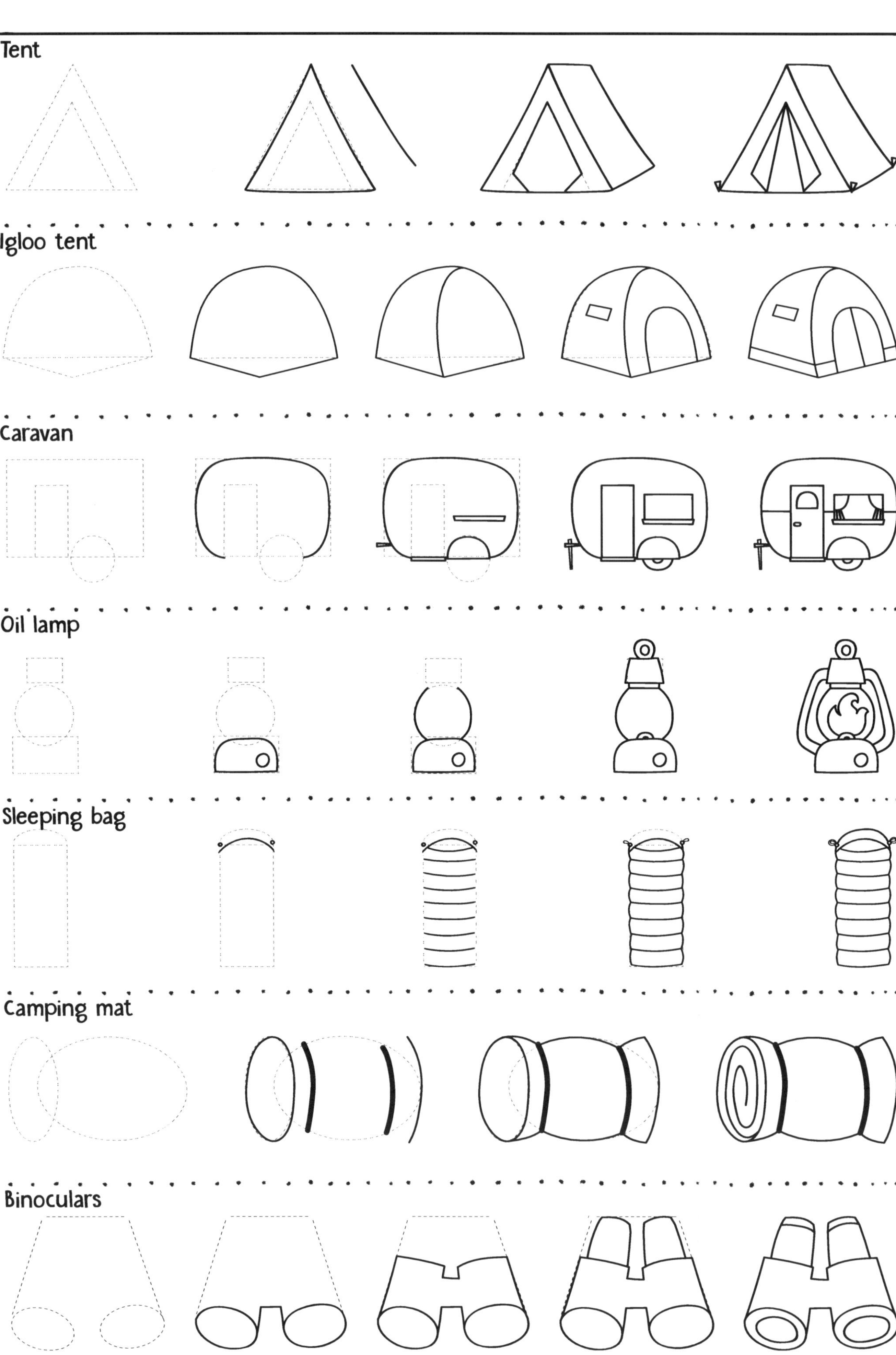
Tent
Igloo tent
Caravan
Oil lamp
Sleeping bag
Camping mat
Binoculars

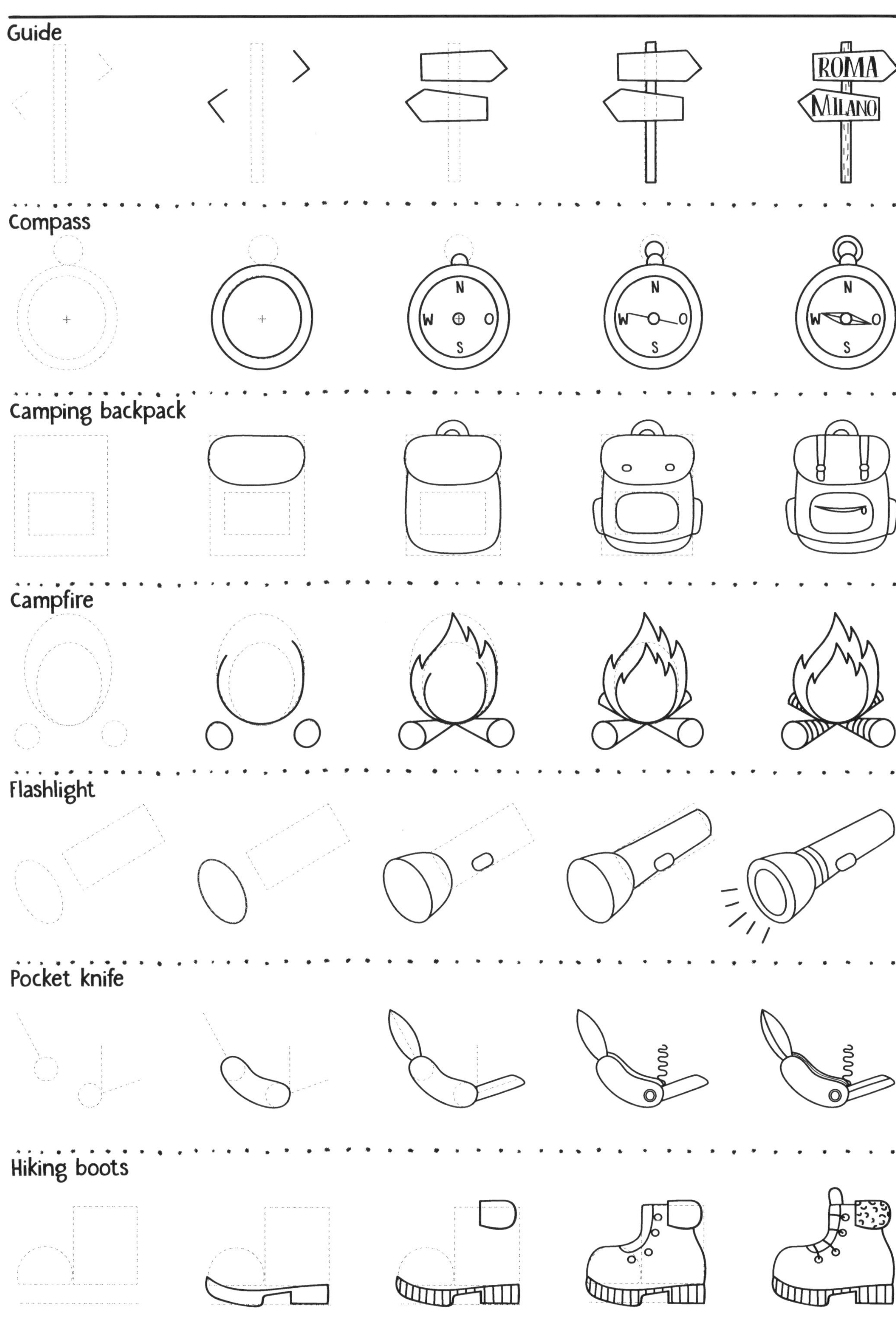
Guide
ROMA
MILANO
Compass
N
W
O
S
Camping backpack
Campfire
Flashlight
Pocket knife
Hiking boots

Farm

Haystack

Bales of straw

Pasture fence

Scarecrow

Well

Milk can

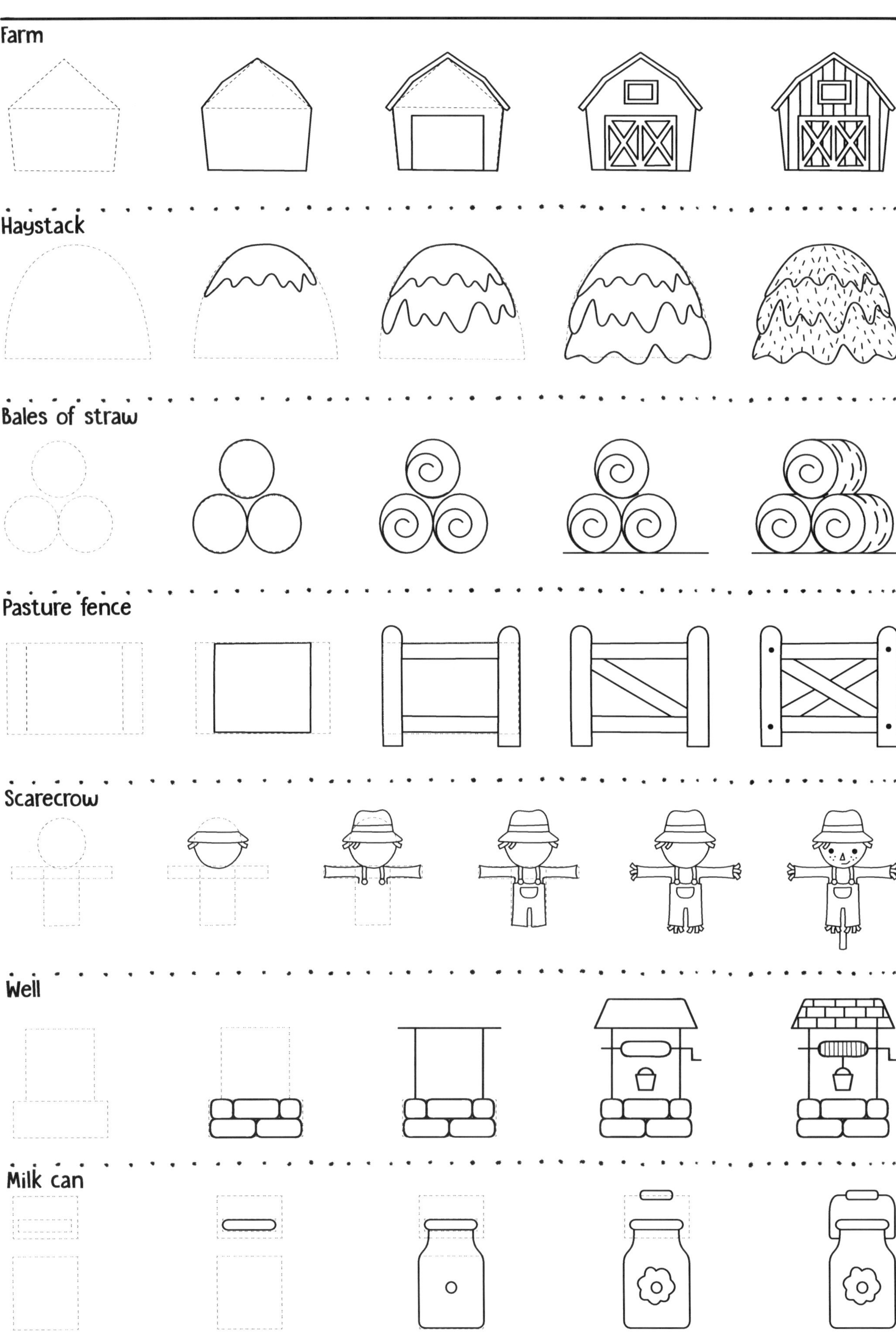

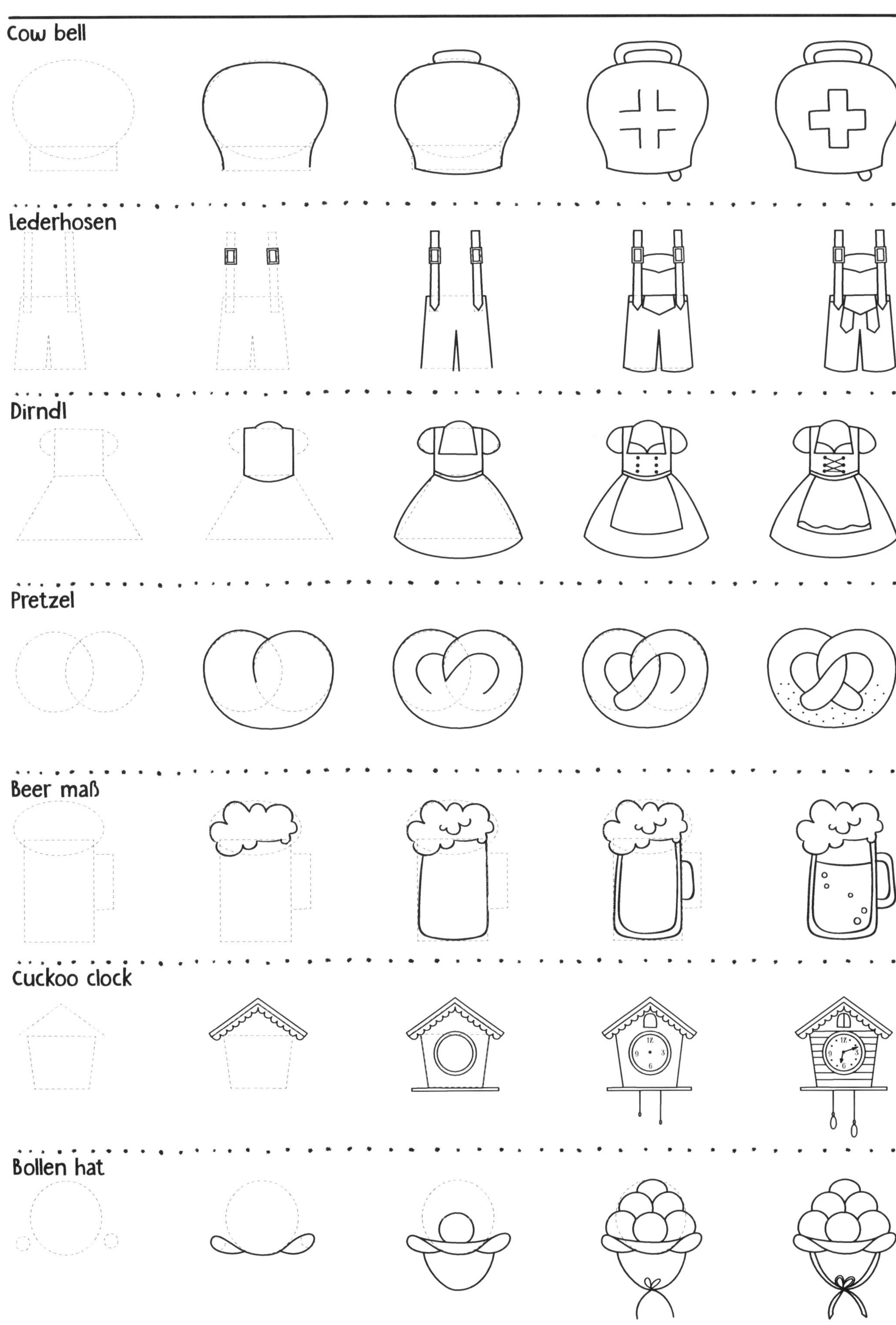
Cow bell
Lederhosen
Dirndl
Pretzel
Beer maß
Cuckoo clock
Bollen hat

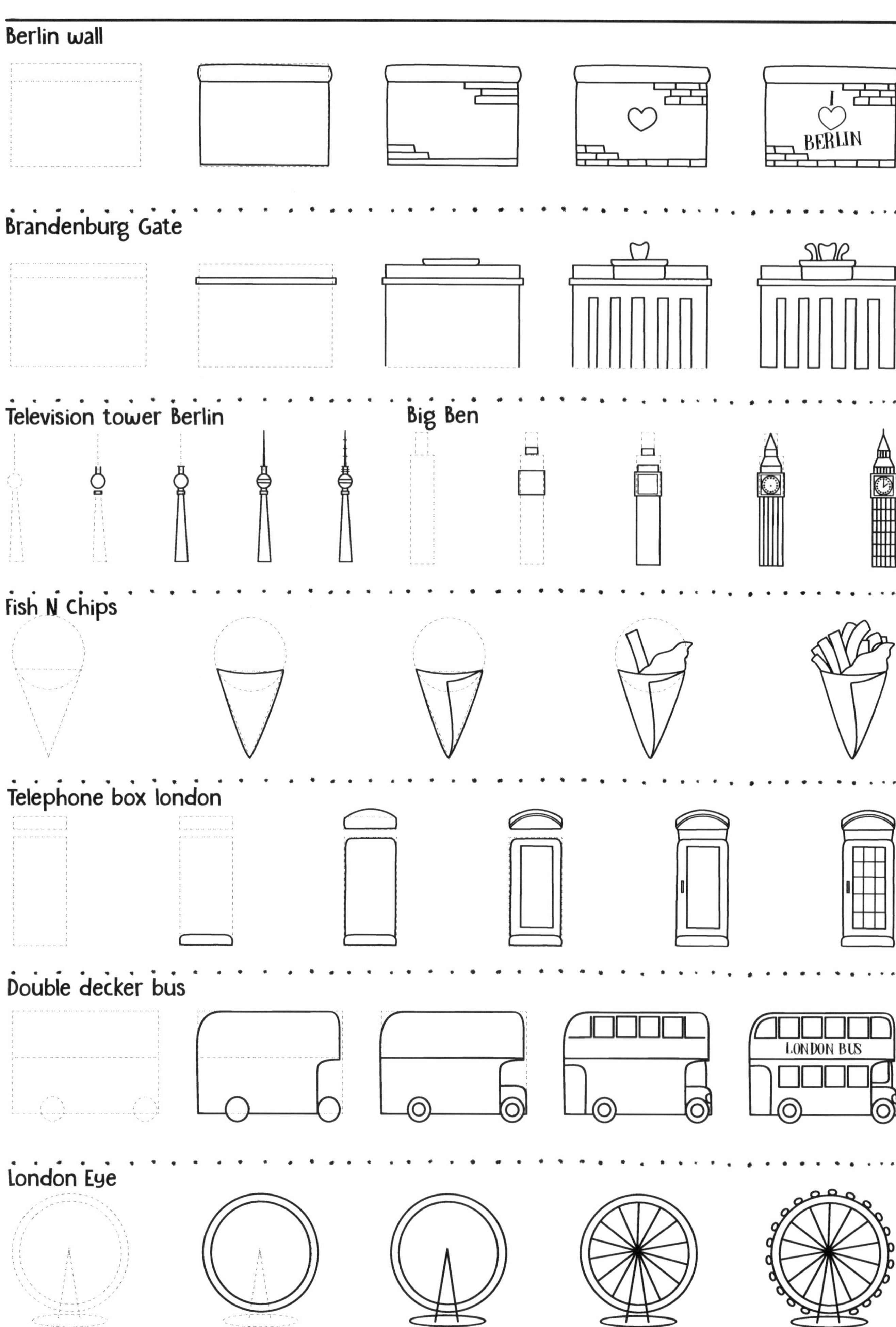
Berlin wall
I
BERLIN
Brandenburg Gate
Television tower Berlin
Big Ben
Fish N Chips
Telephone box london
Double decker bus
LONDON BUS
London Eye

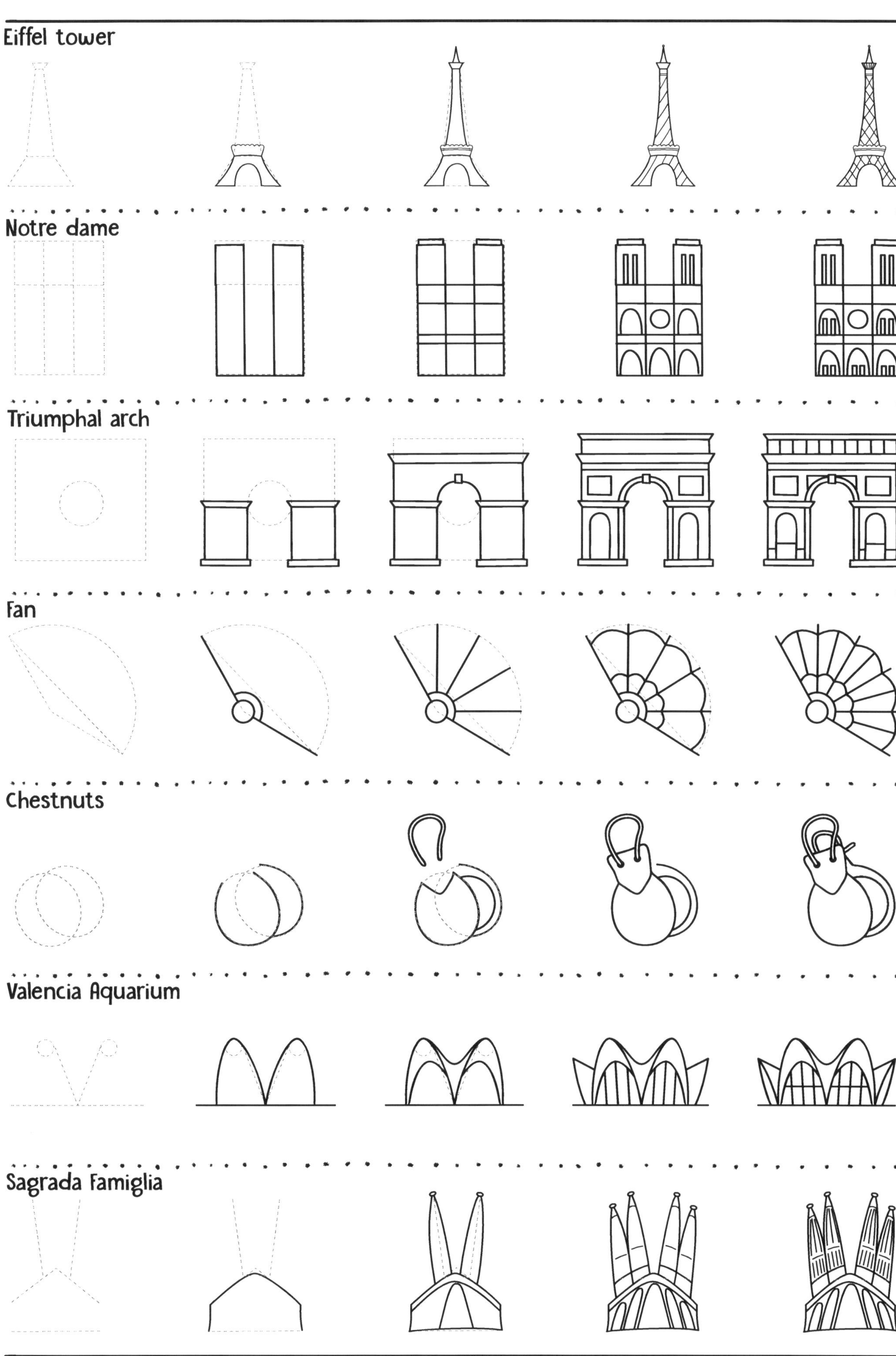
Eiffel tower
Notre dame
Triumphal arch
Fan
Chestnuts
Valencia Aquarium
Sagrada Famiglia

Gondola

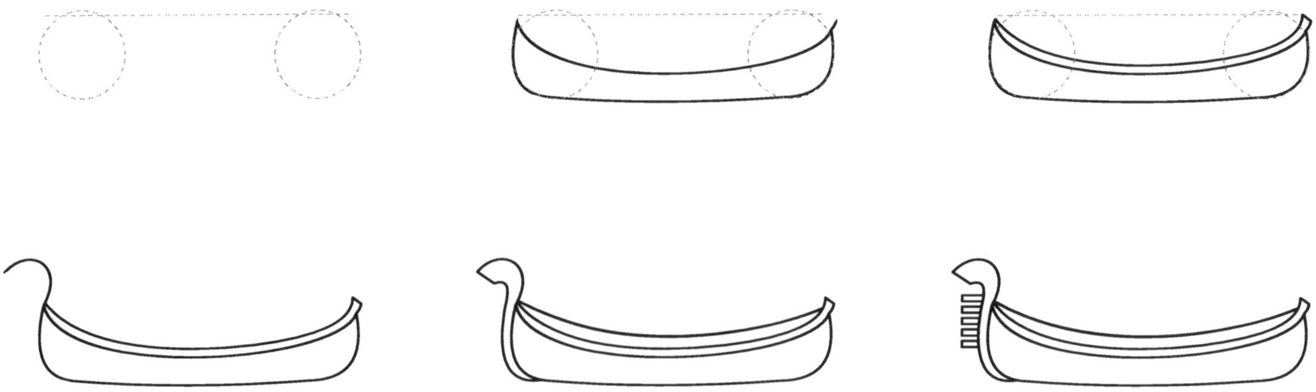

Colosseum

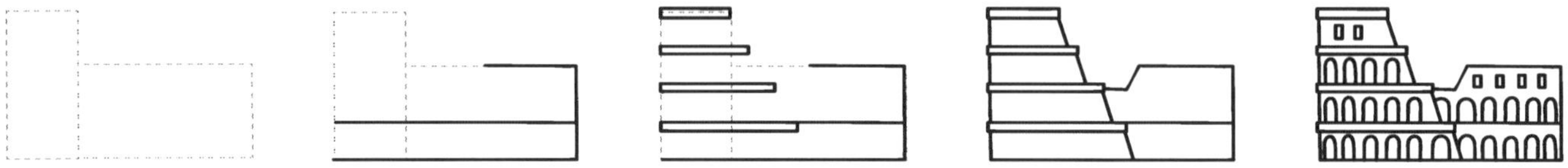

Pisa tower

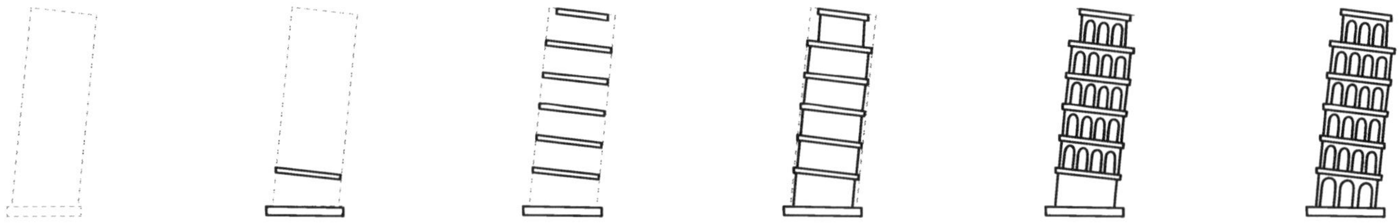

Pizza

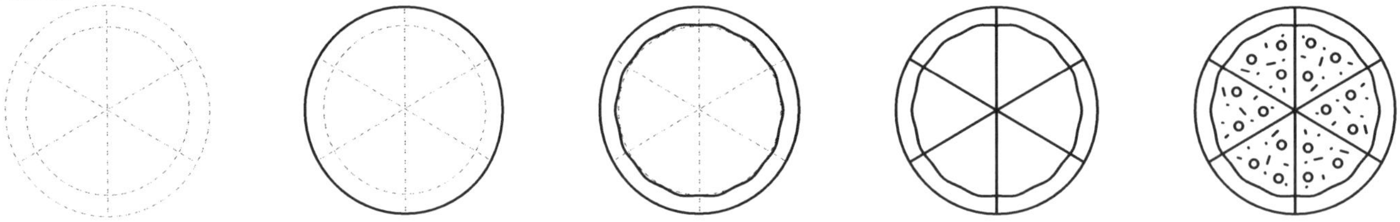

Wine glass

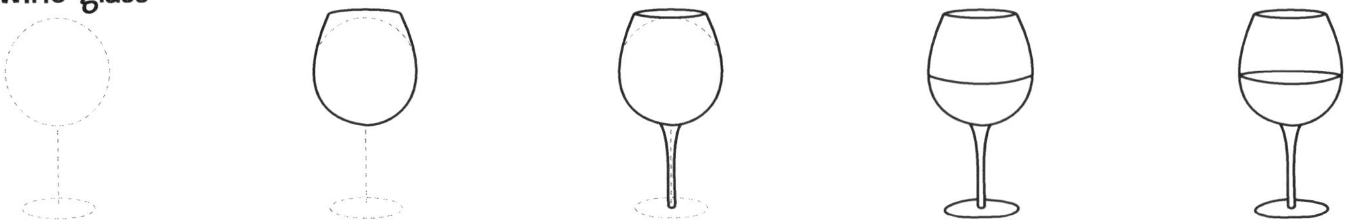

Flag

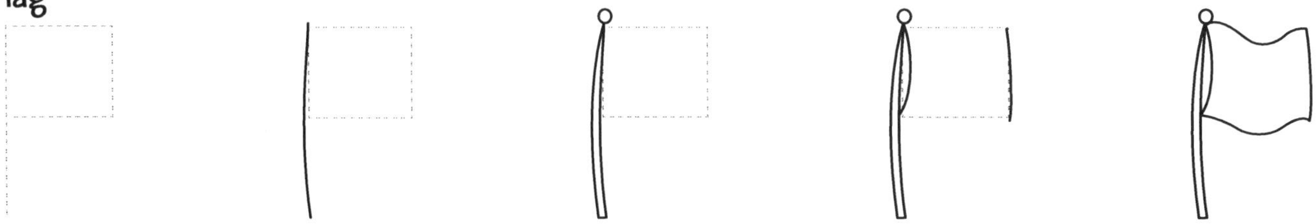

Pyramid

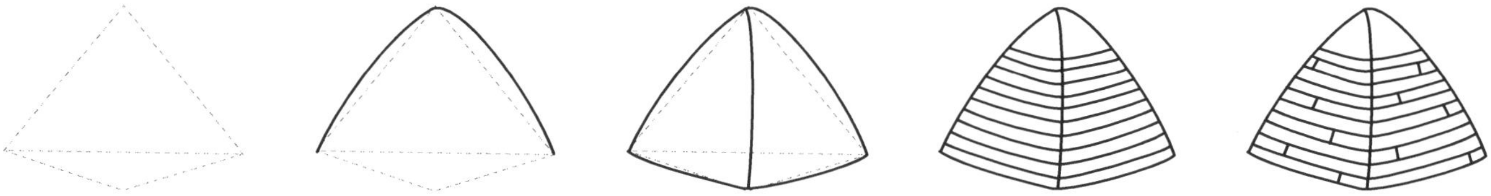

Sphinx

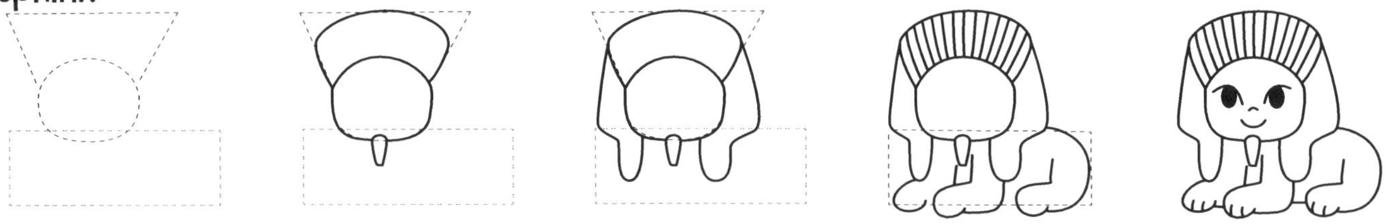

Amphora

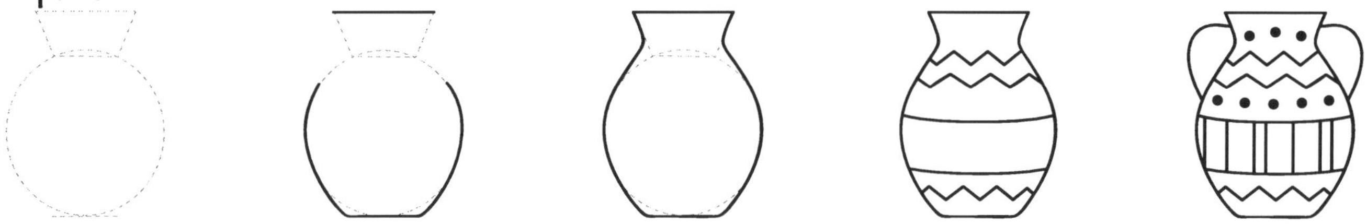

Burj al Arab

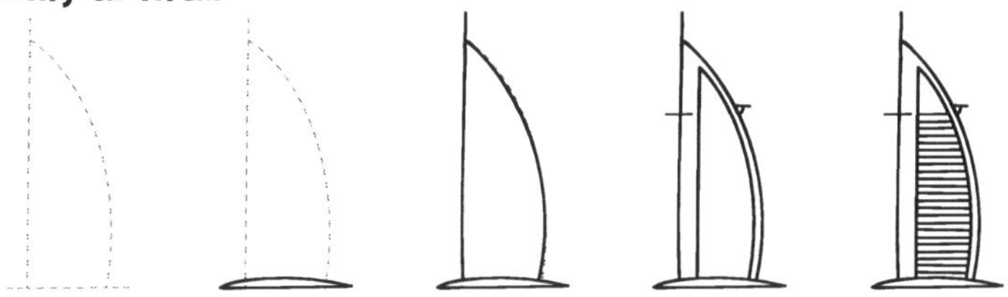

Fortune cookie

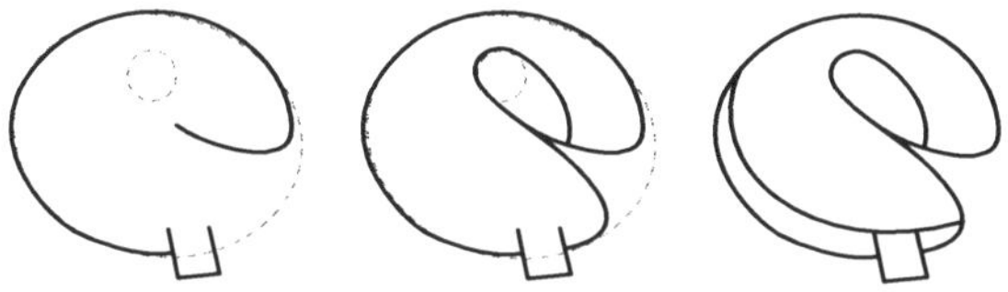

Sumo wrestler

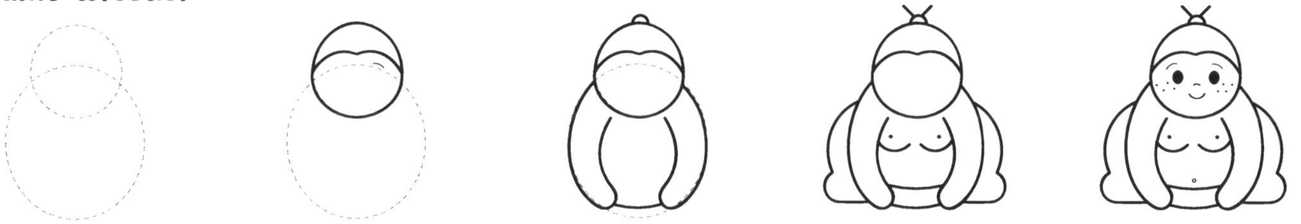

Pagoda

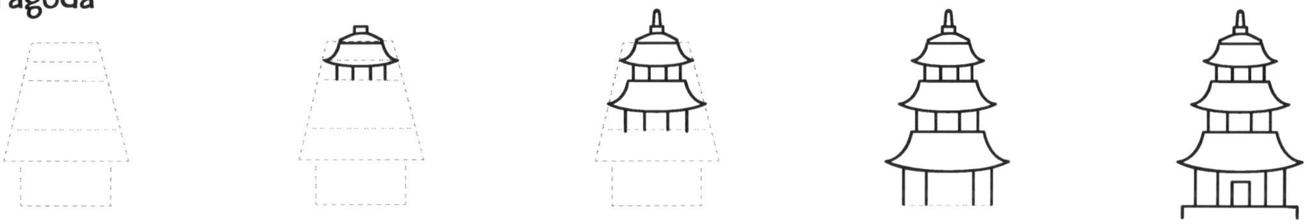

Statue of Jesus

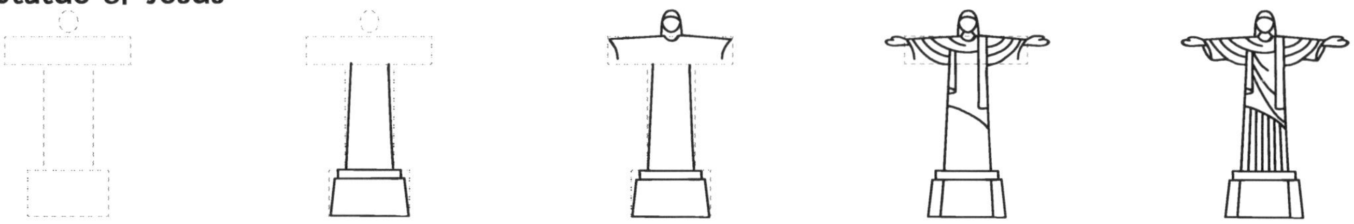

Statue of liberty

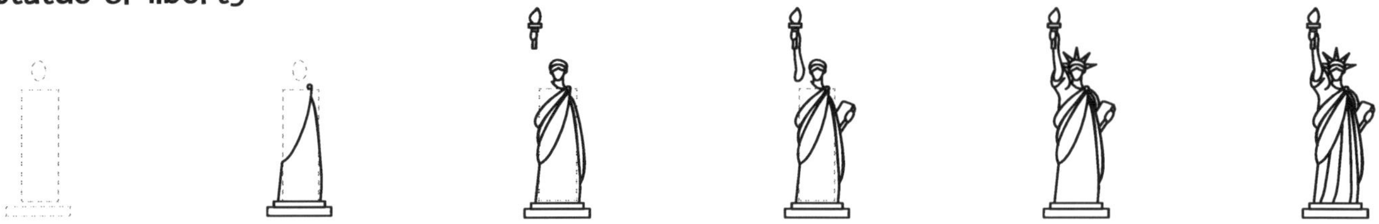

Empire state building

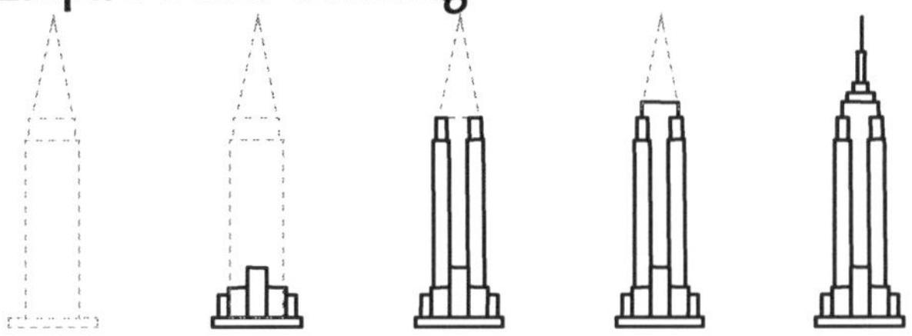

Chrysler building

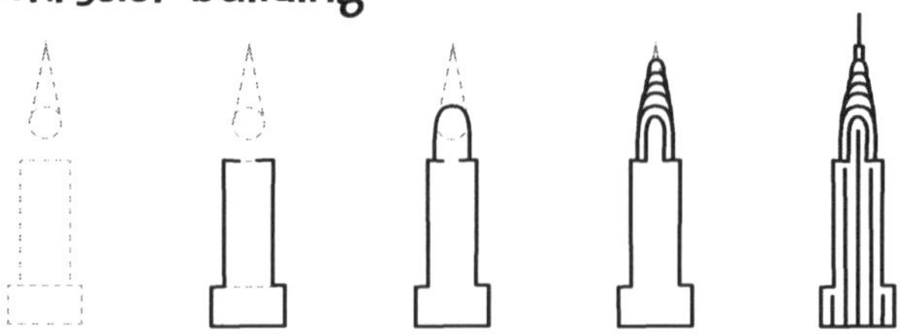

Capitol building

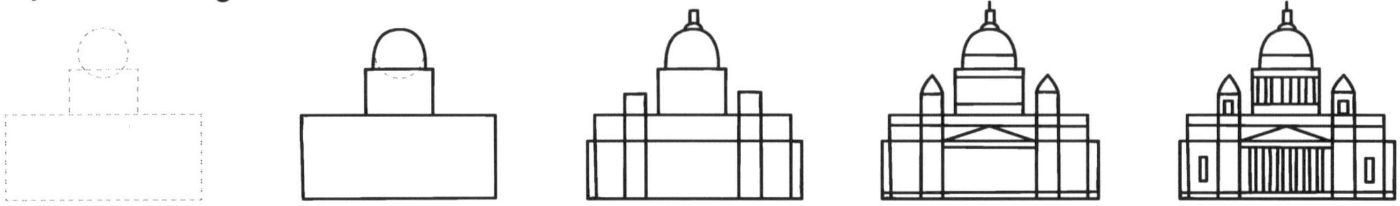

Sombrero

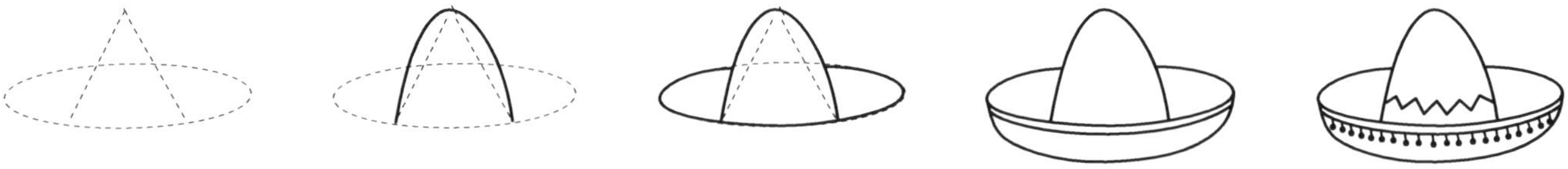

Maya pyramid

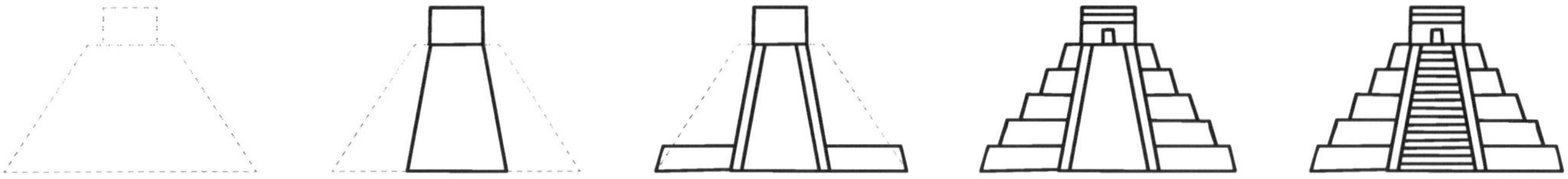

Matryoshka

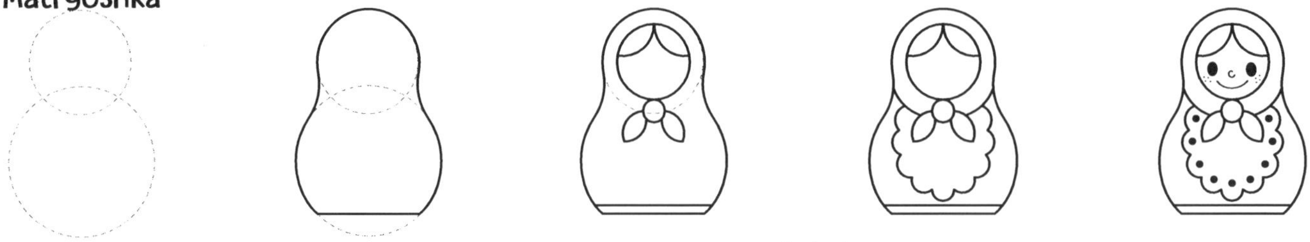

Kremlin

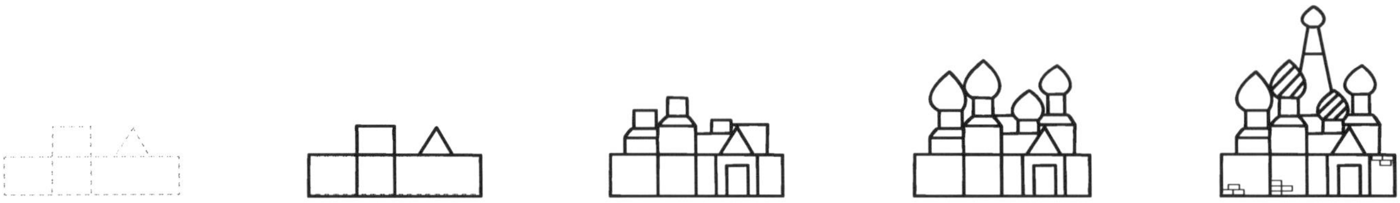

House

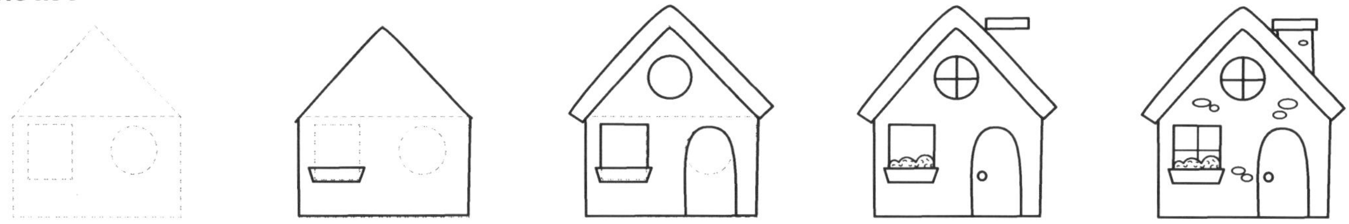

School

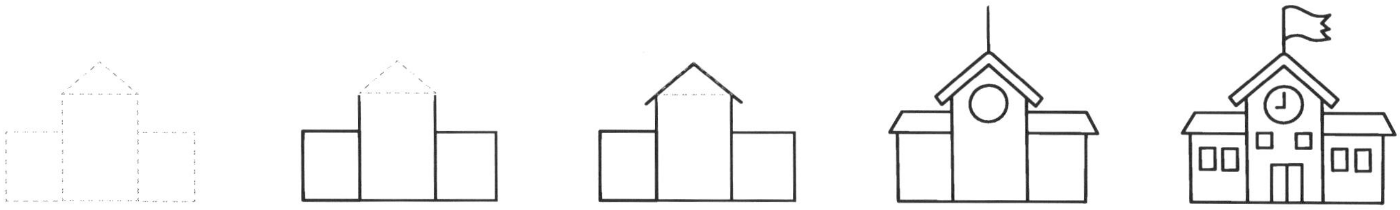

Half-timbered house

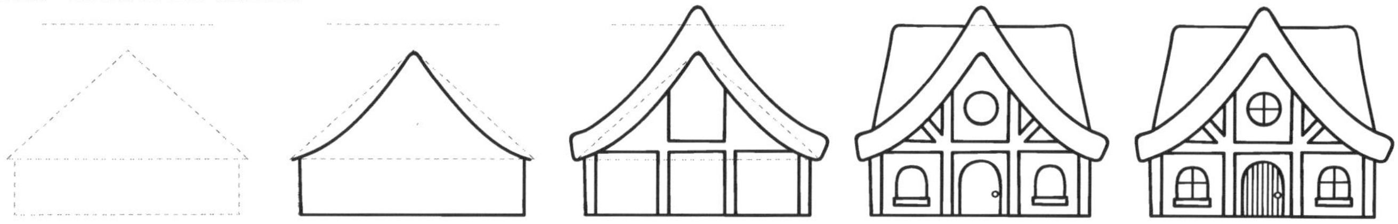

Log cabin

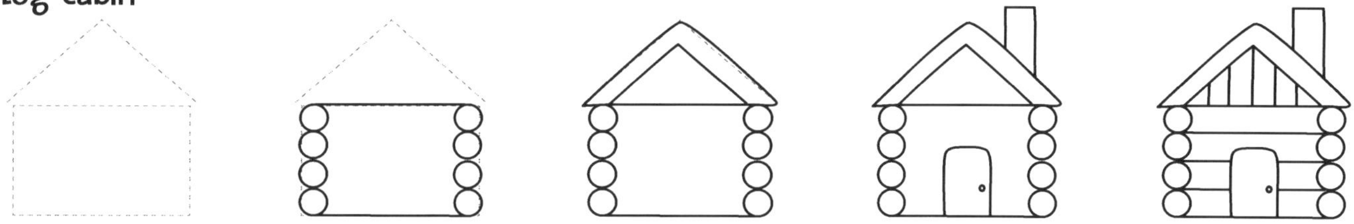

Igloo

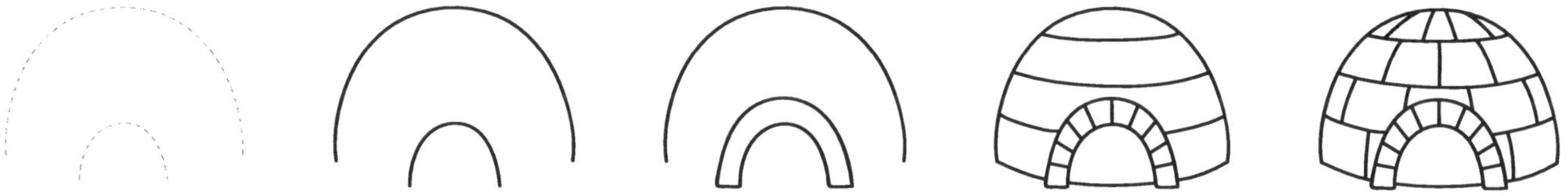

Church

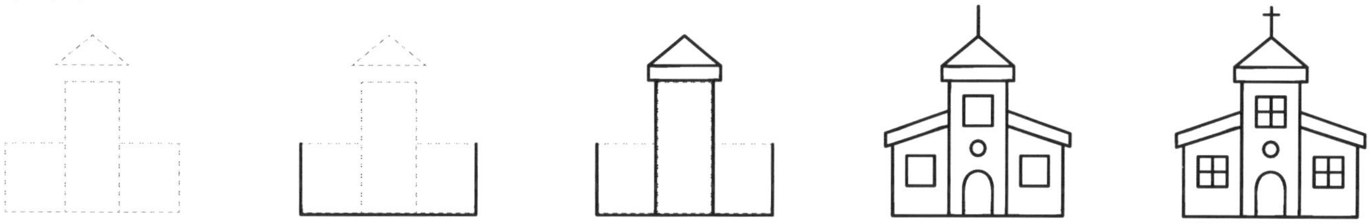

Mosque

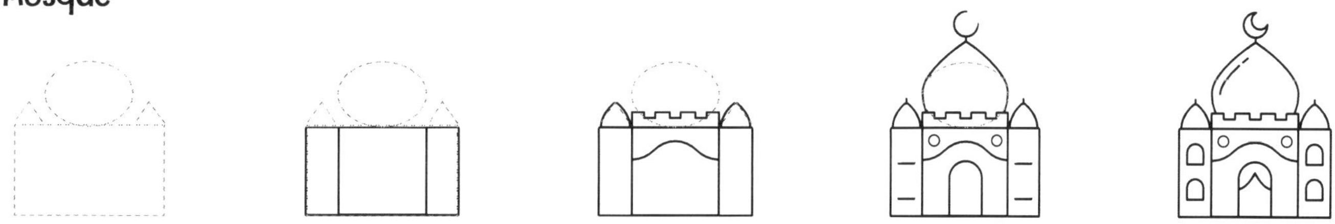

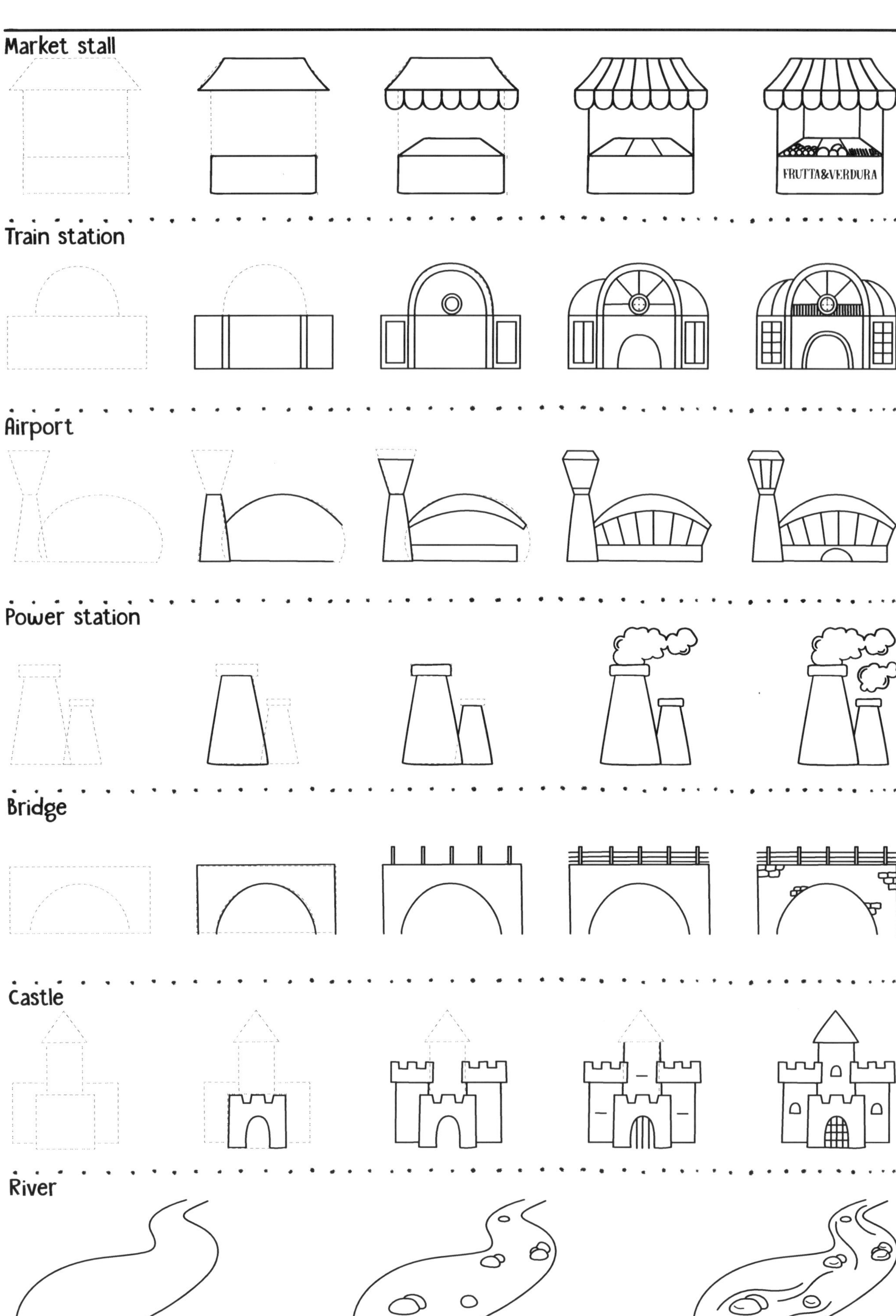
Market stall
FRUTTA&VERDURA
Train station
Airport
Power station
Bridge
Castle
River

Lake

Waterfall

Pebbles

Rocks

Mountains

Puddle

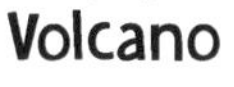

Volcano

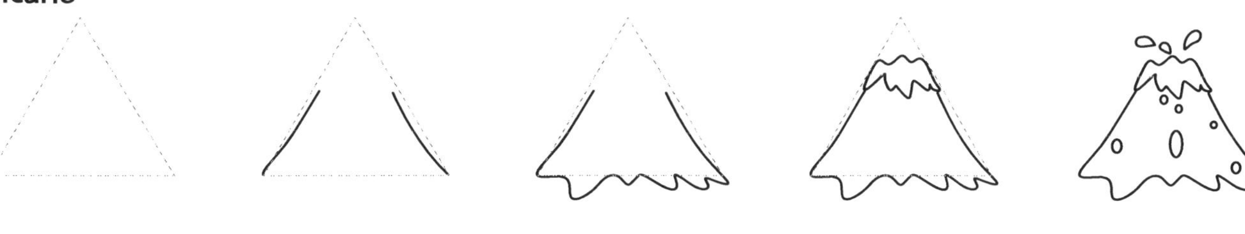

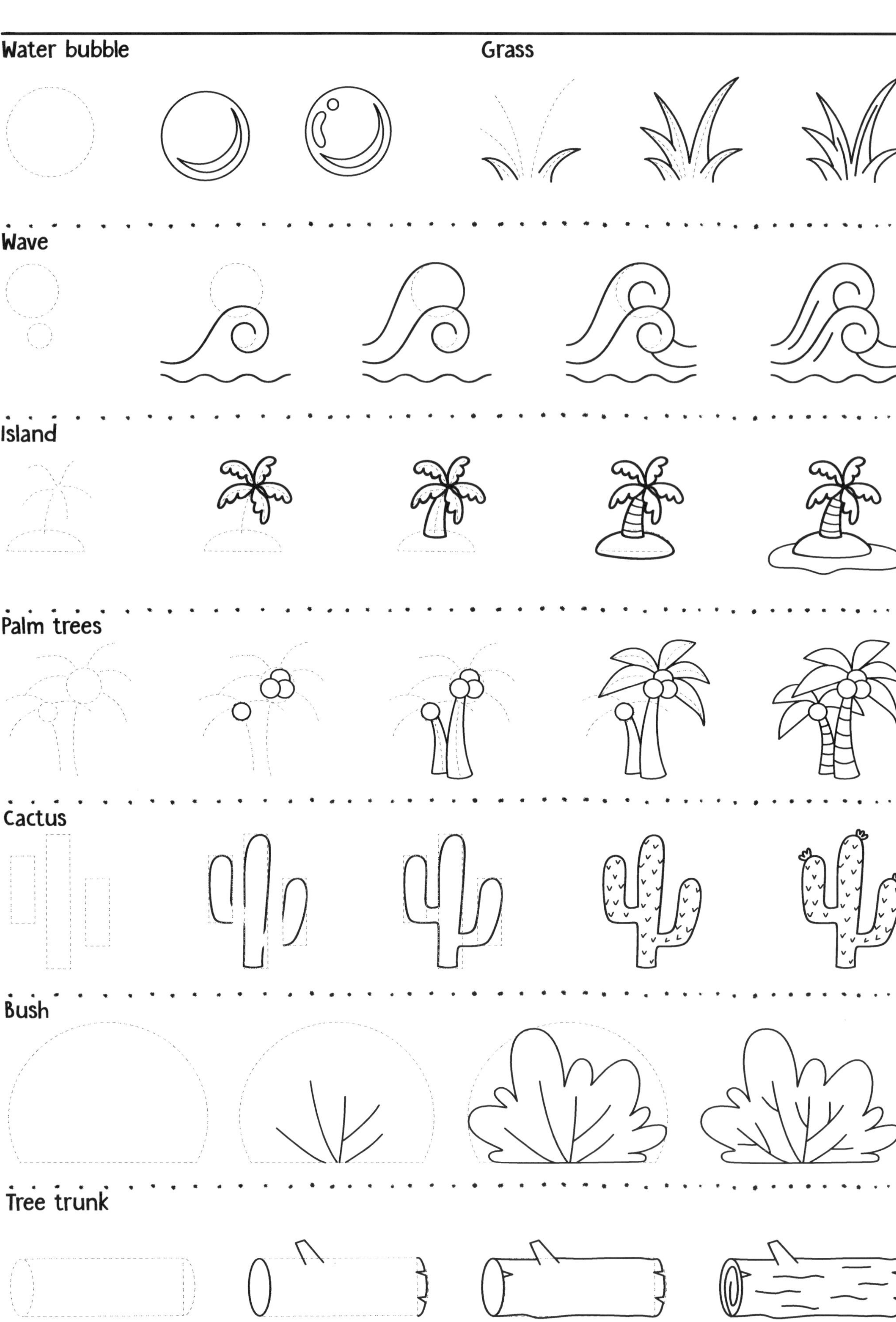
Water bubble
Grass
Wave
Island
Palm trees
Cactus
Bush
Tree trunk

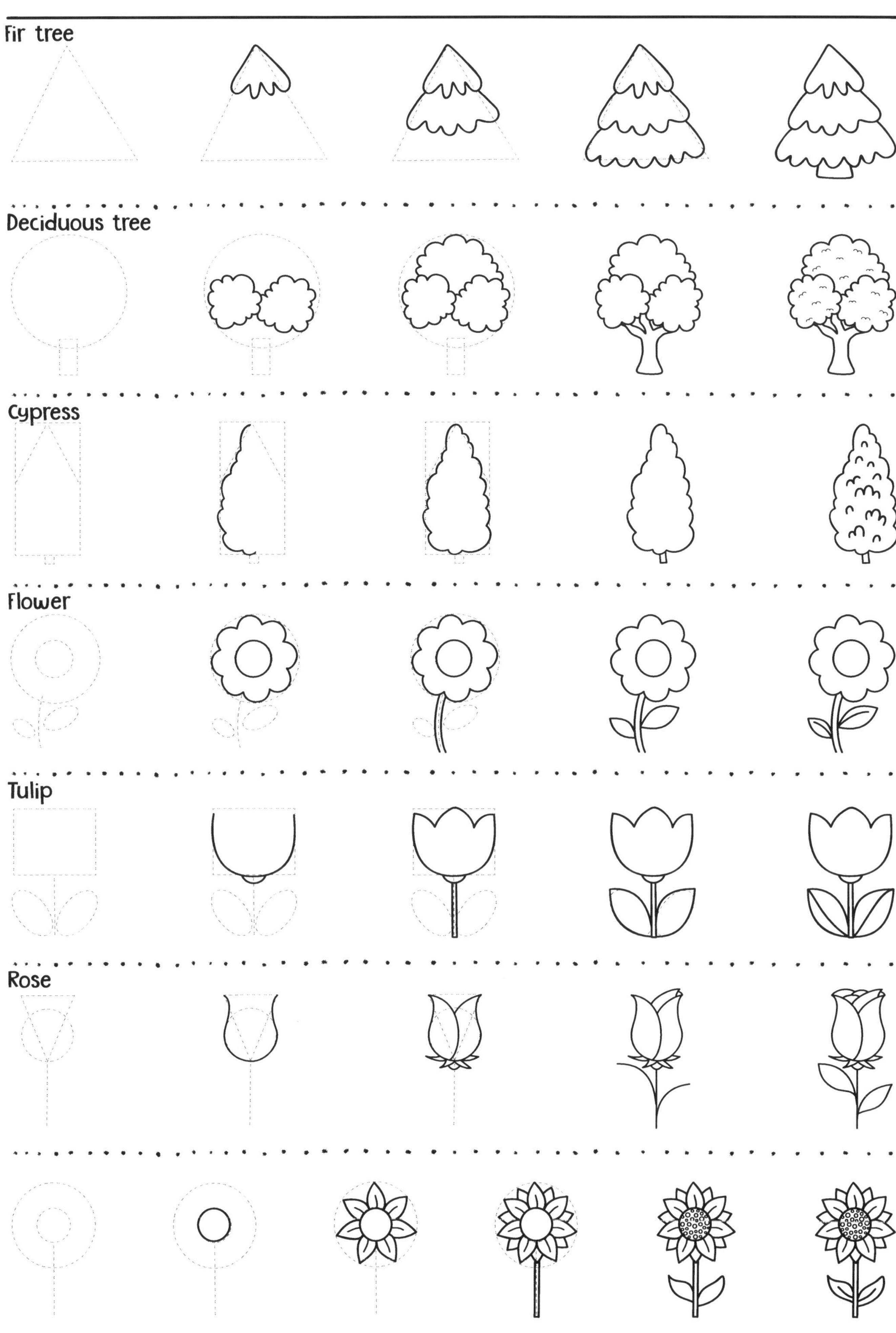
Fir tree
Deciduous tree
Cypress
Flower
Tulip
Rose

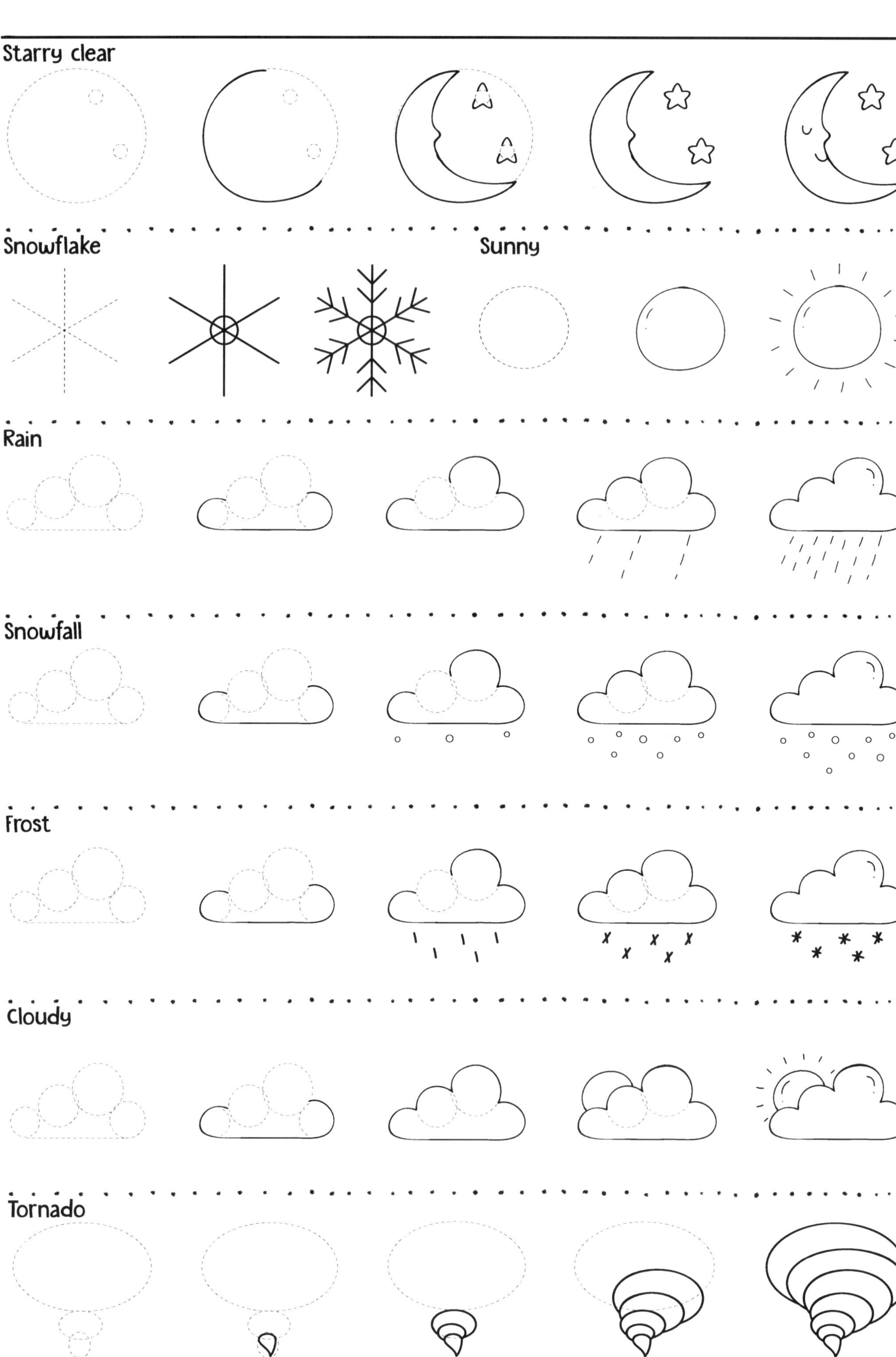

Starry clear
Snowflake
Sunny
Rain
Snowfall
Frost
Cloudy
Tornado

Cloud

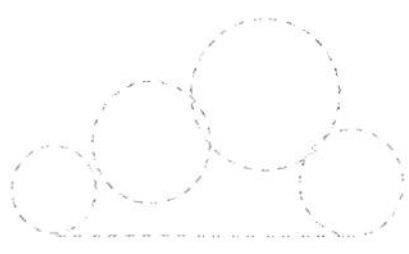
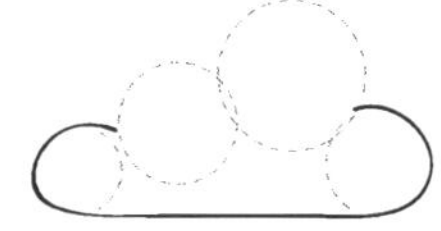
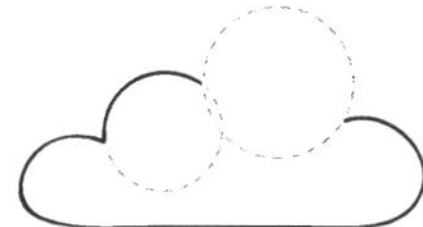
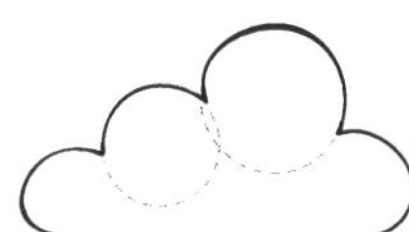
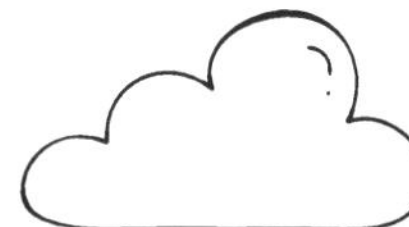

Rainbow

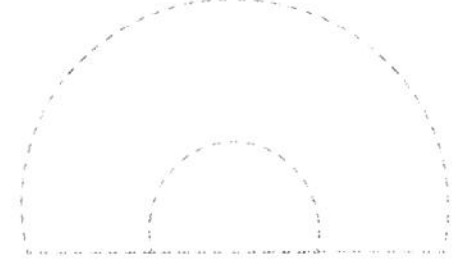
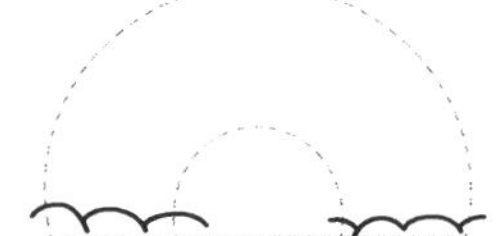
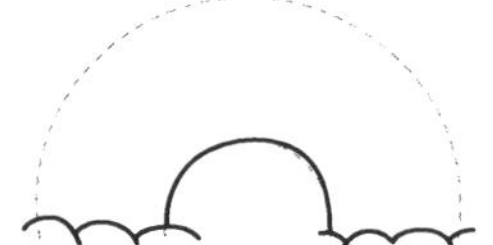
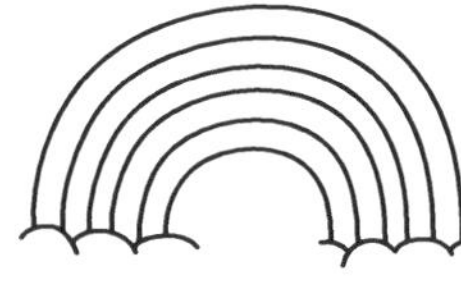

Star

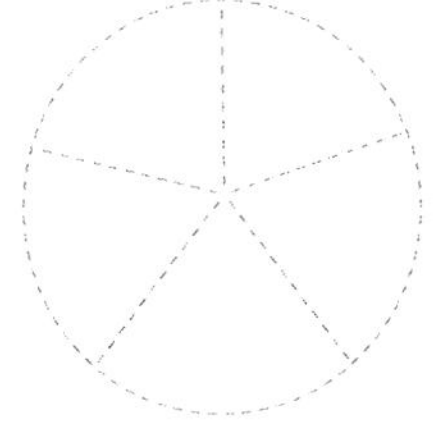
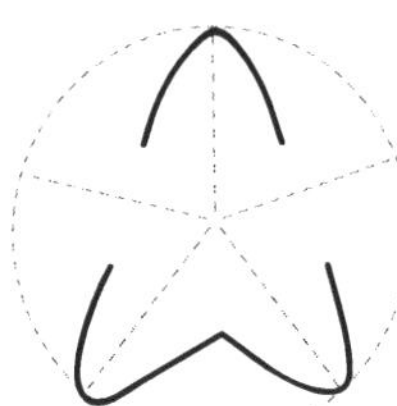
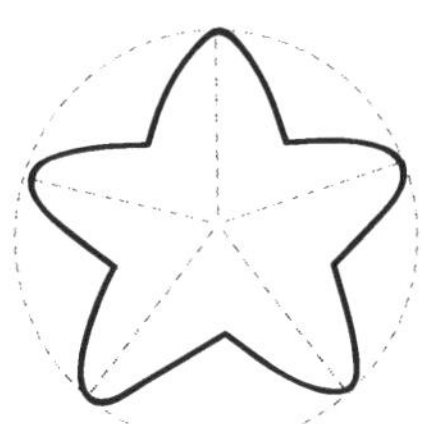

Shooting star

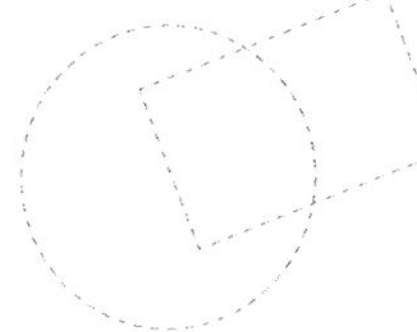
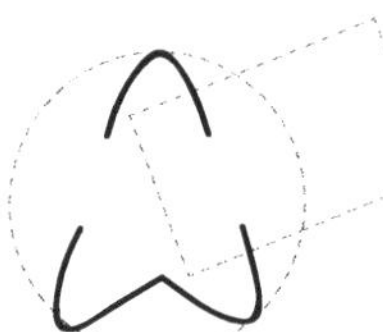
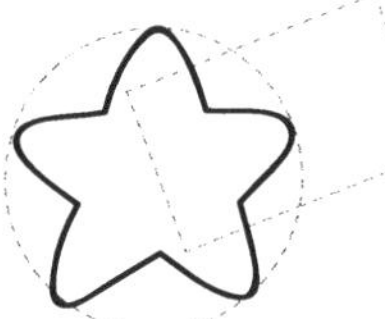
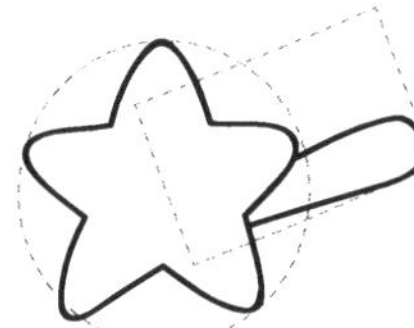

Comet

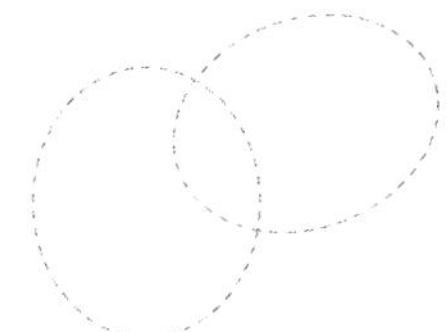
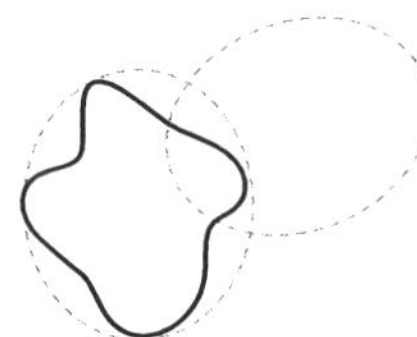
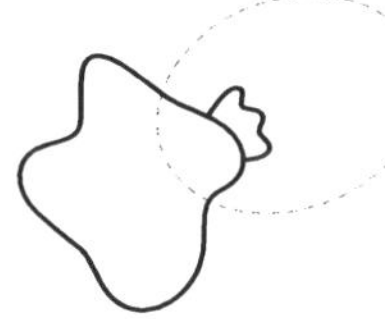
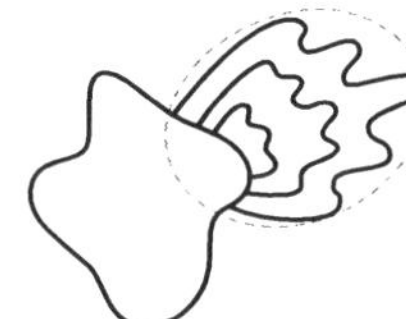
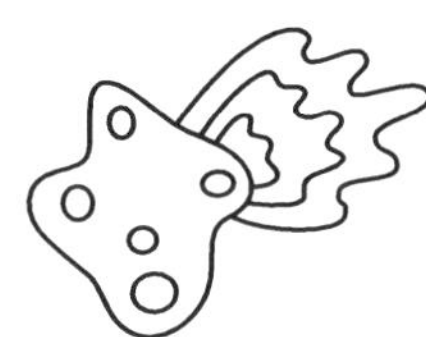

Constellation

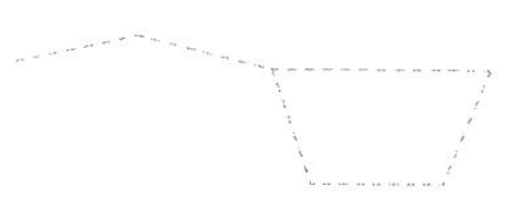
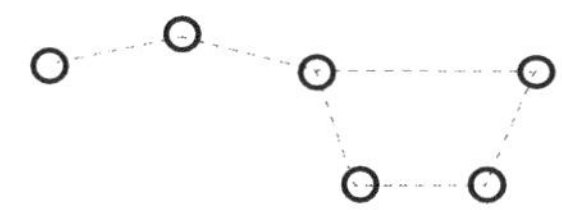
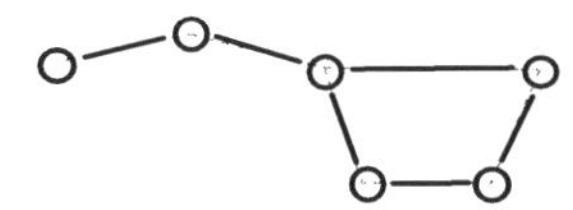
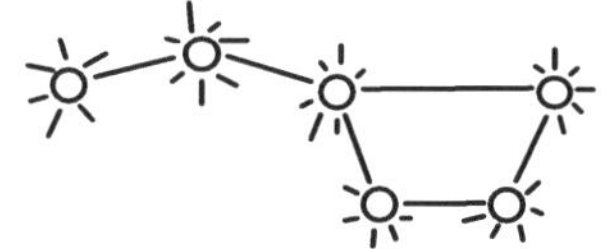

Galaxy

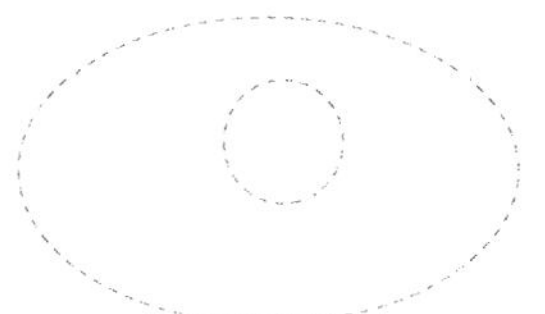
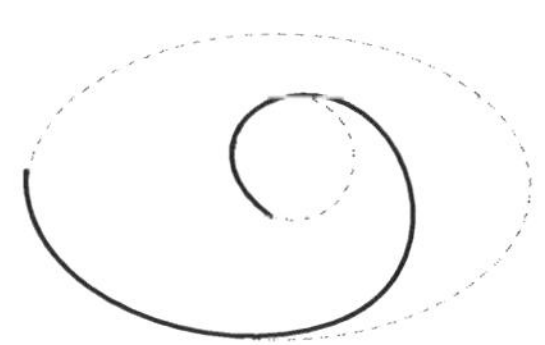
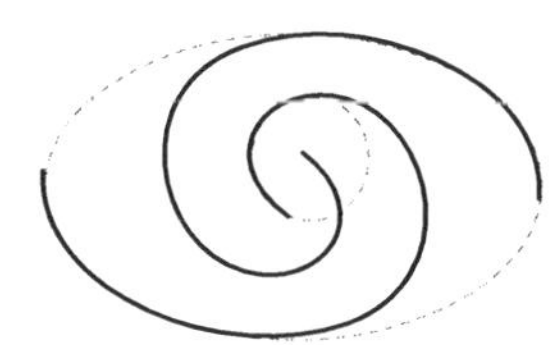
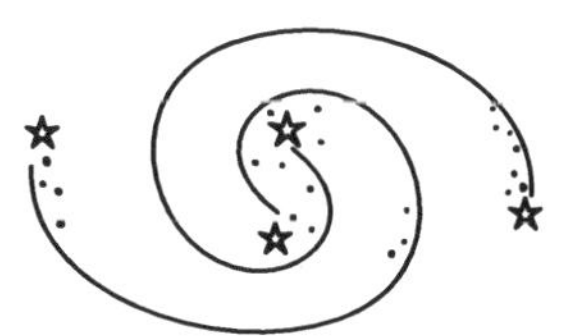

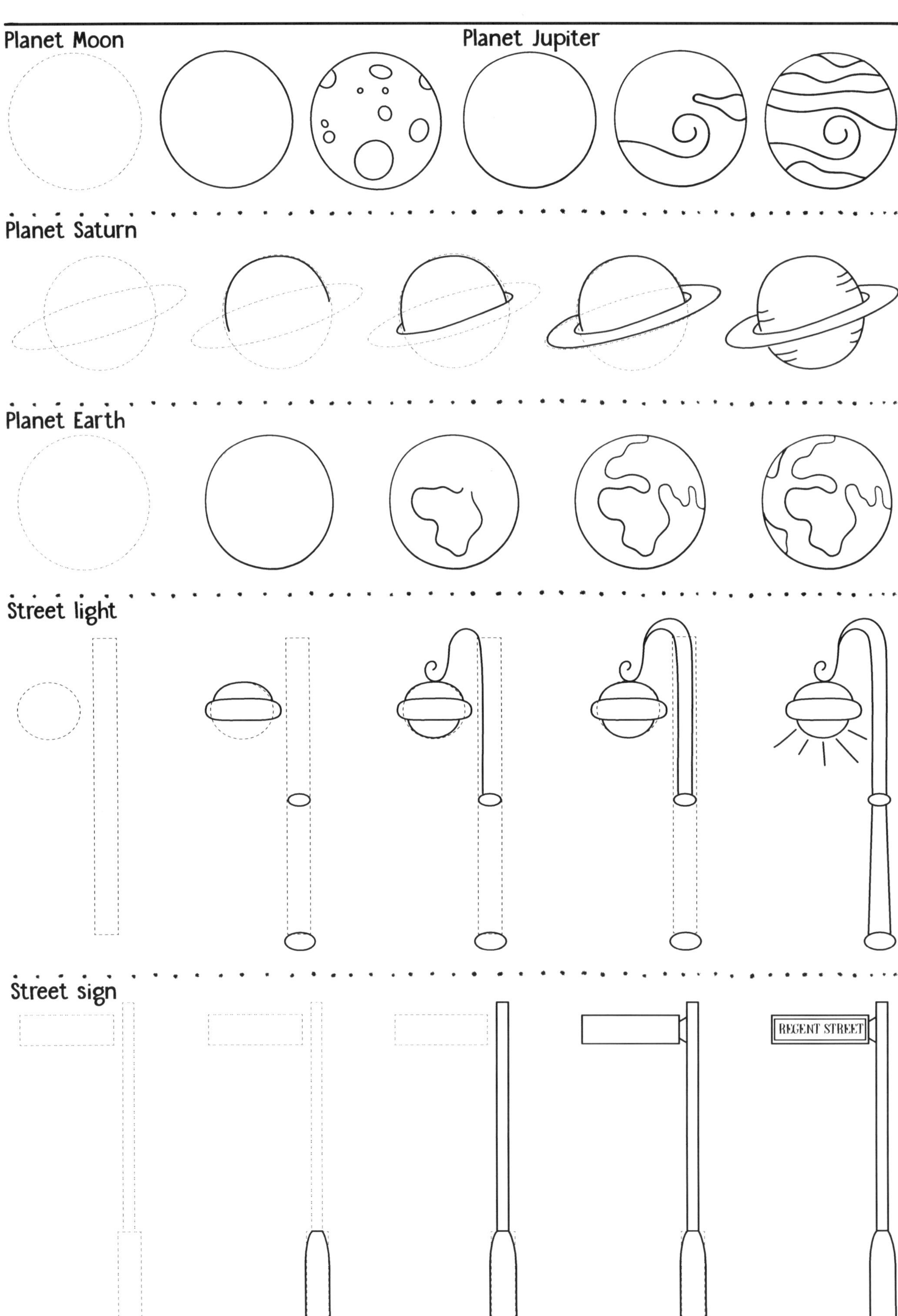
Planet Moon
Planet Jupiter
Planet Saturn
Planet Earth
Street light
Street sign
REGENT STREET

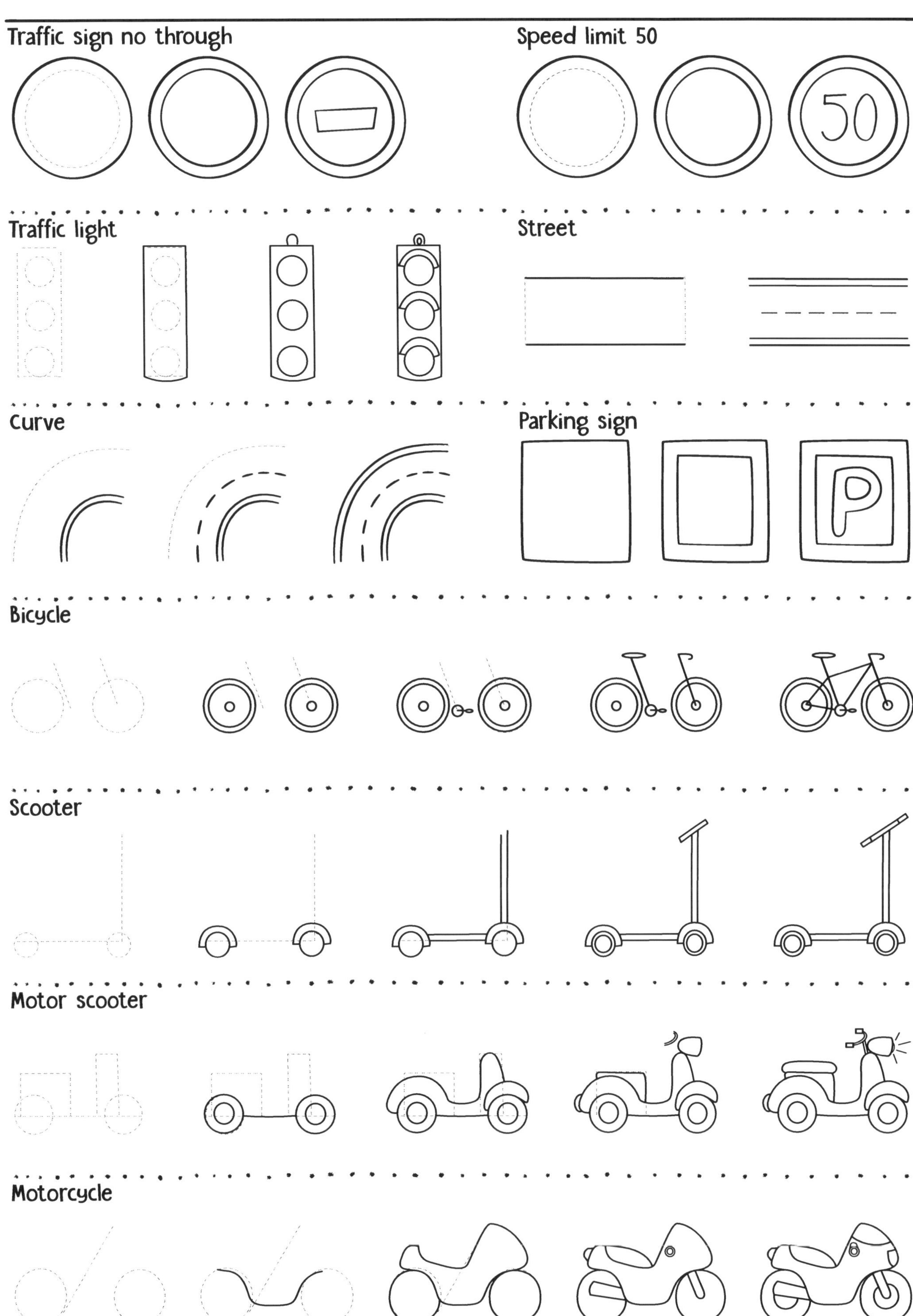
Traffic sign no through
Speed limit 50
50
Traffic light
Street
Curve
Parking sign
P
Bicycle
Scooter
Motor scooter
Motorcycle

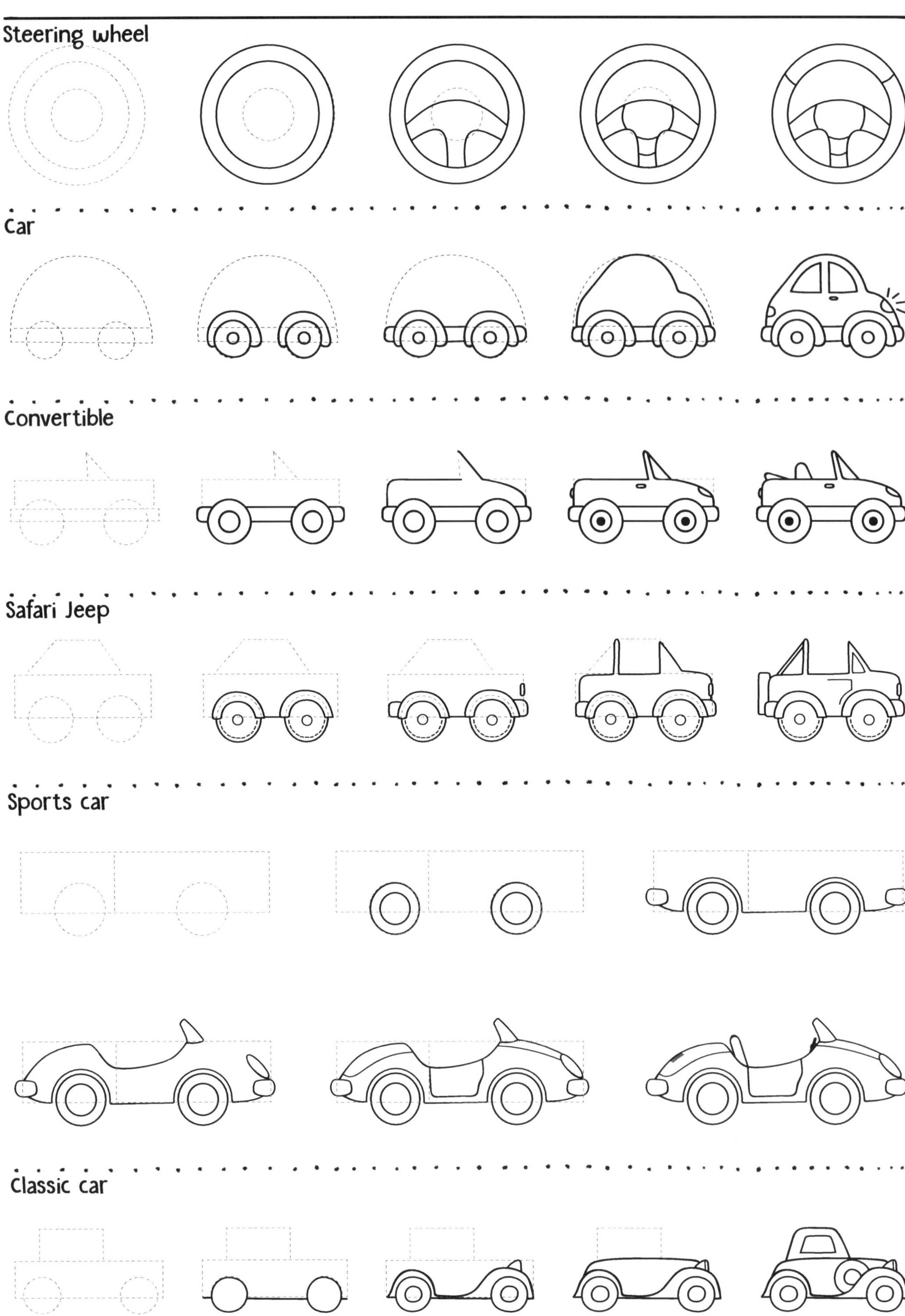
Steering wheel
Car
Convertible
Safari Jeep
Sports car
Classic car

Lamborghini

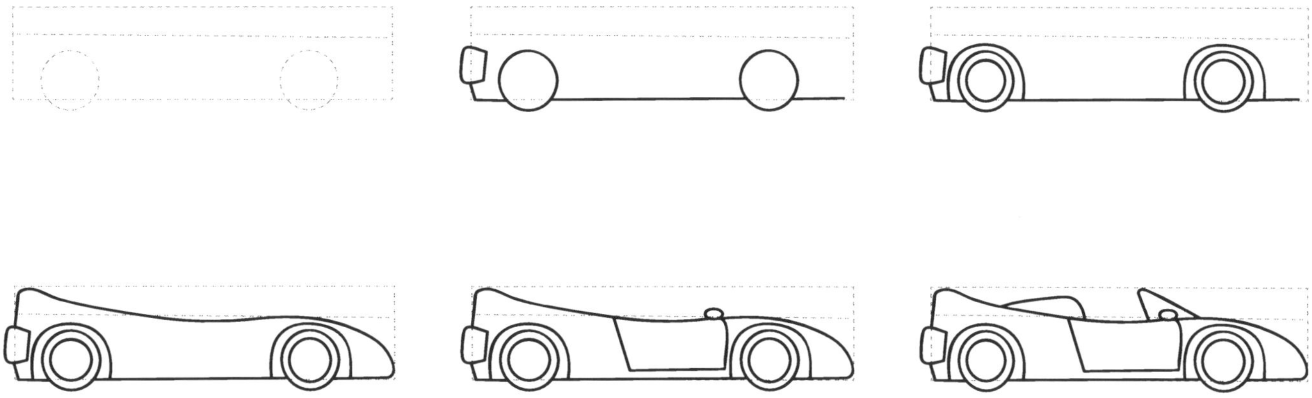

Formula 1 racing car

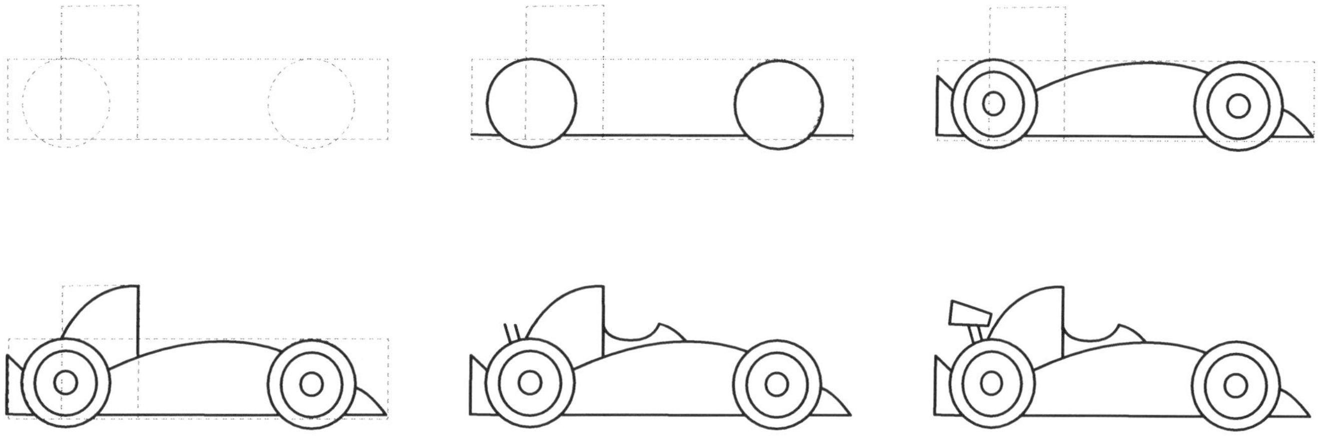

Bus

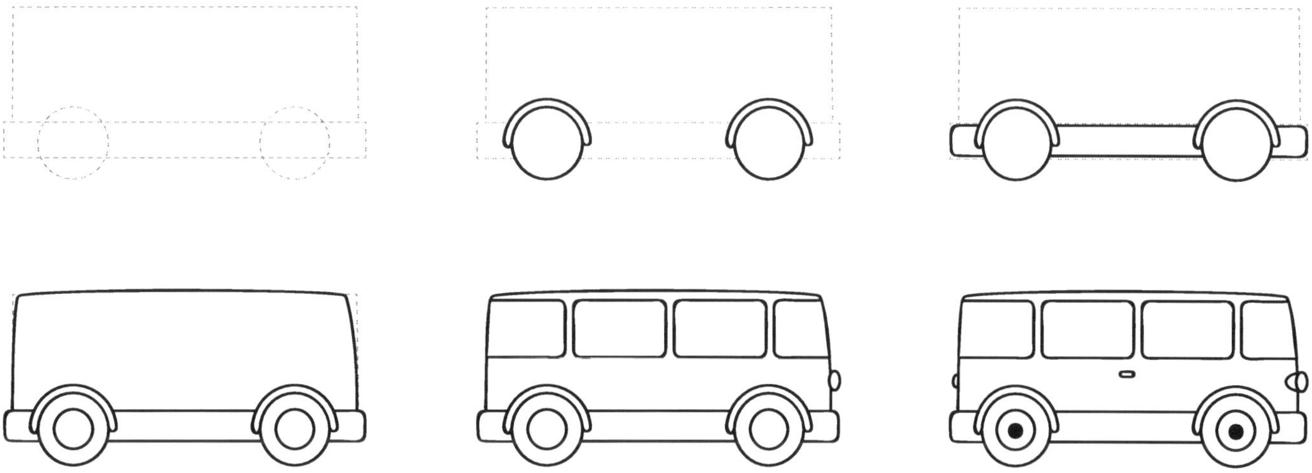

Camping bus

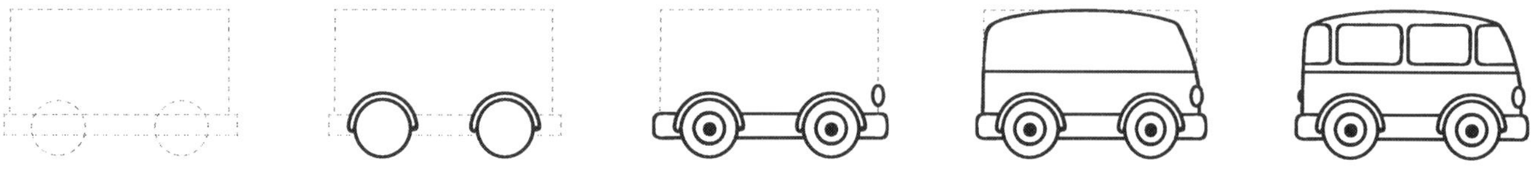

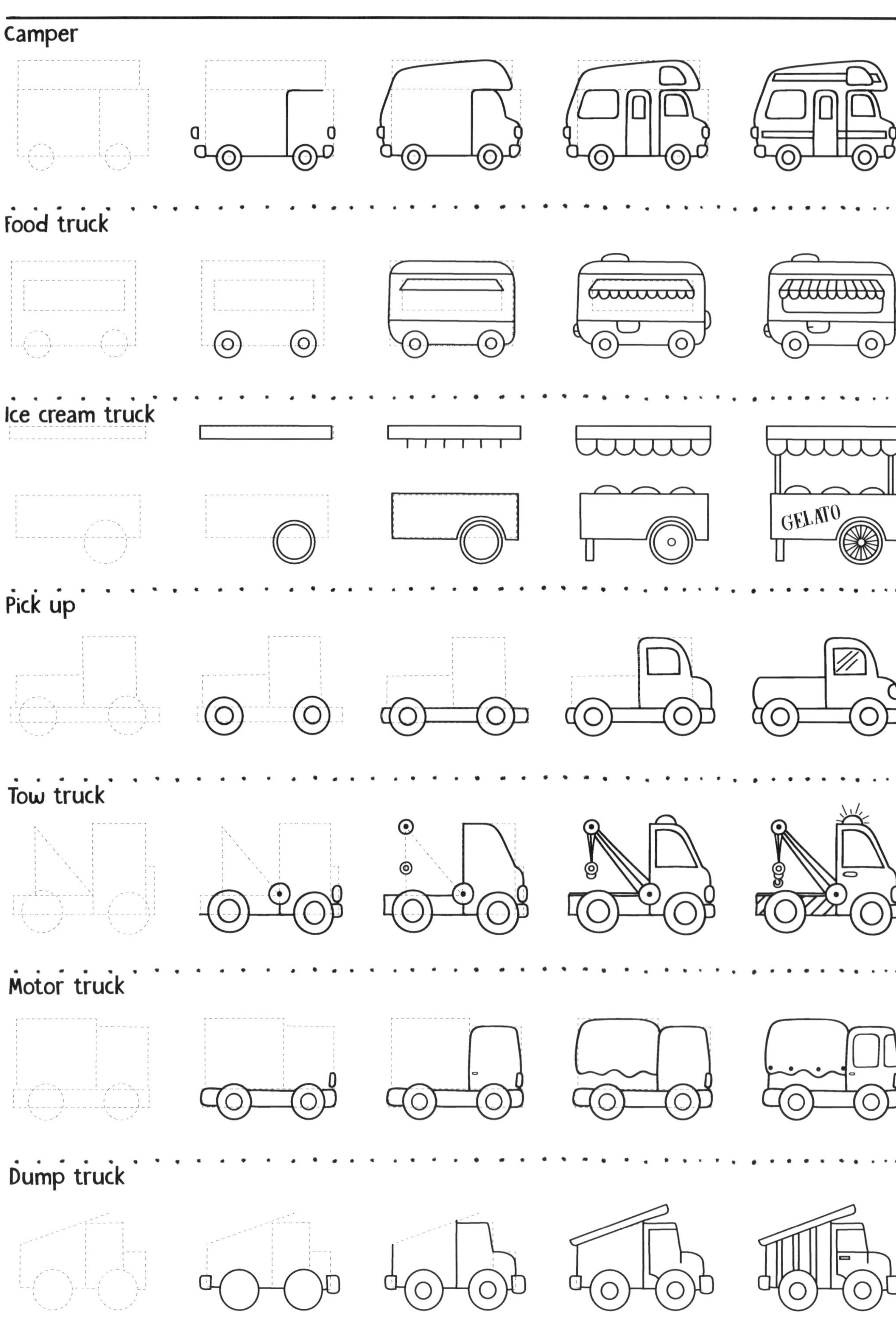
Camper
Food truck
Ice cream truck
GELATO
Pick up
Tow truck
Motor truck
Dump truck

Concrete mixer

Mini excavator

Snow removal vehicle

Forklift truck

Tractor

Combine harvester

Steam train

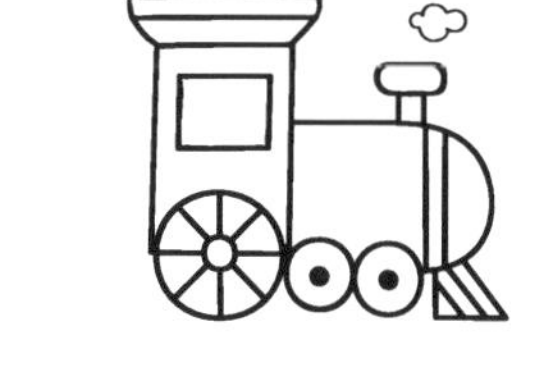

Train wagon

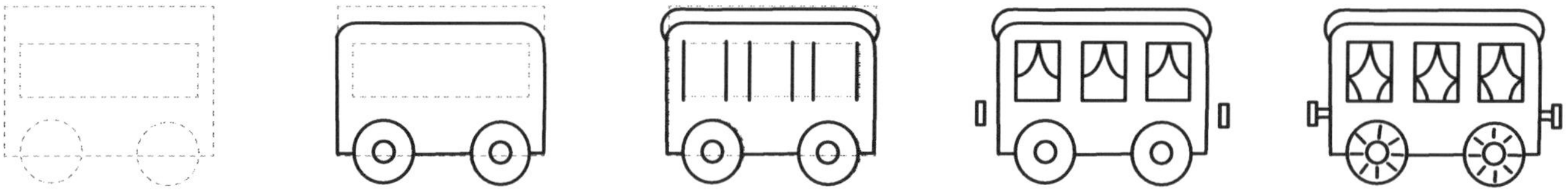

Speed train

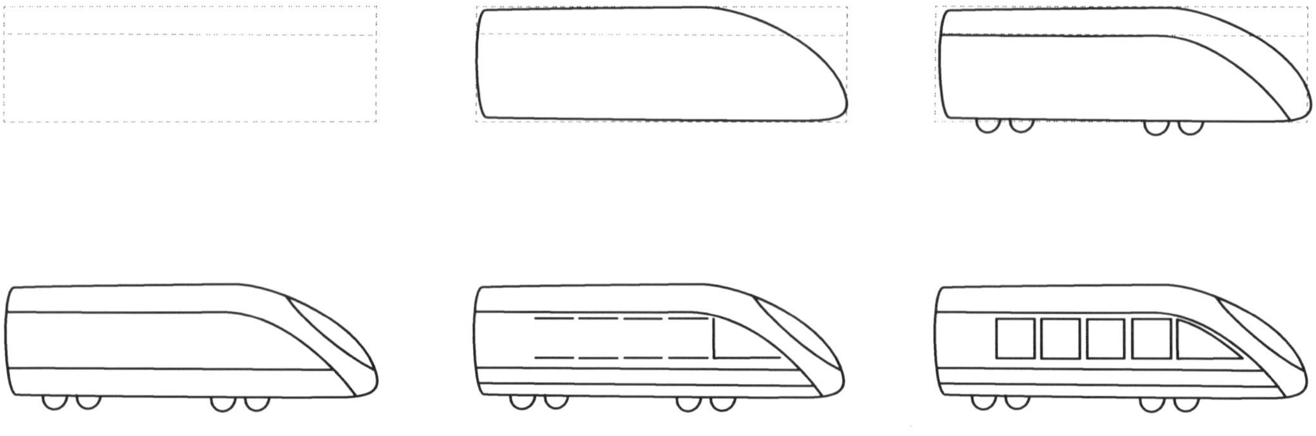

Speed train wagon

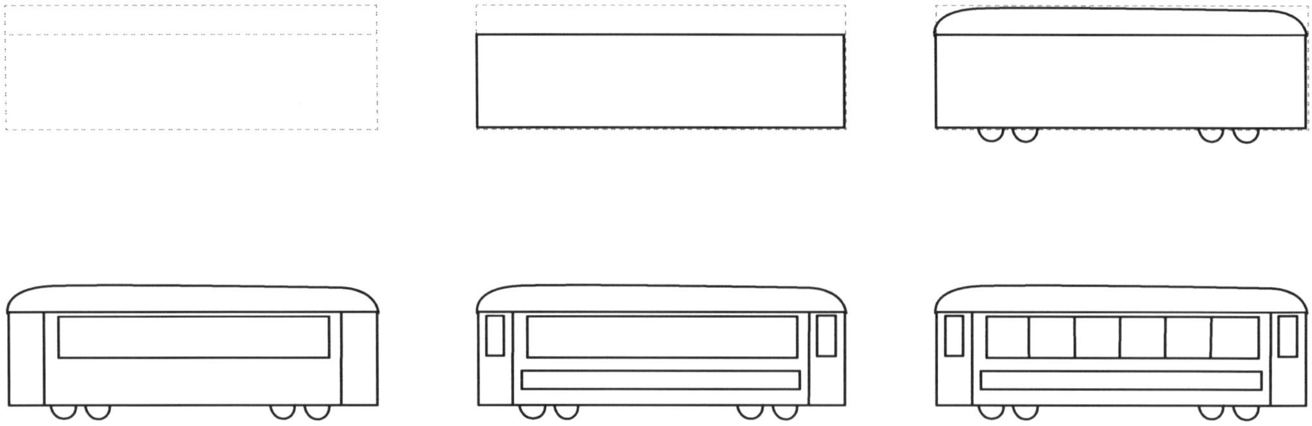

Tank

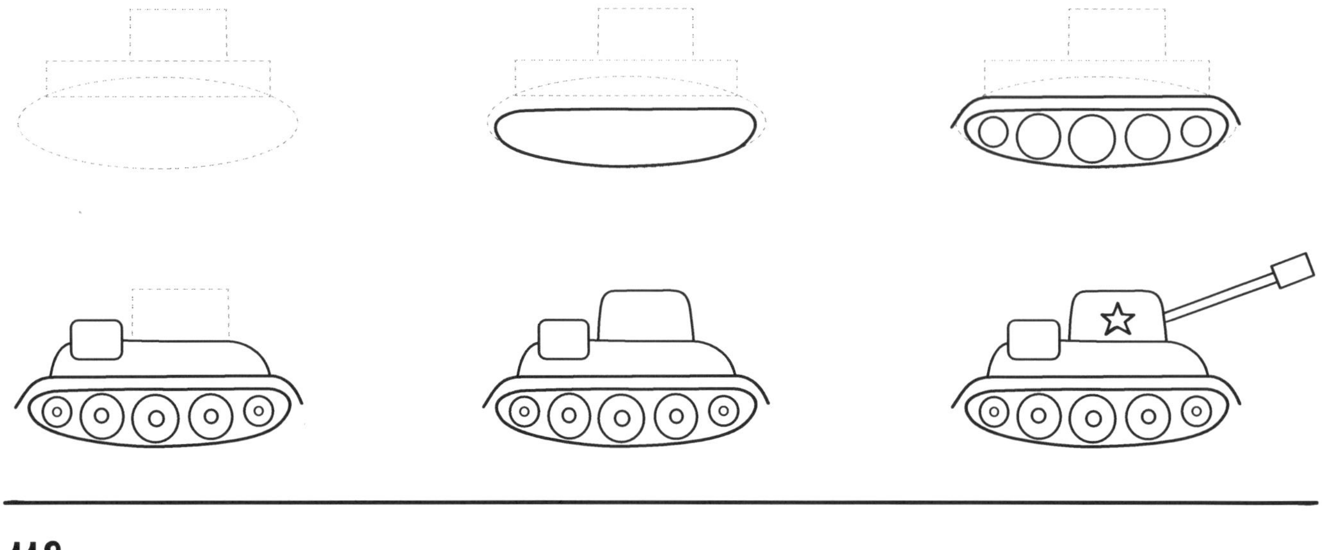

Radar

Airplane

Biplane airplane

Propeller plane

Hot air balloon

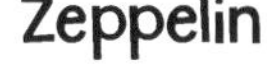

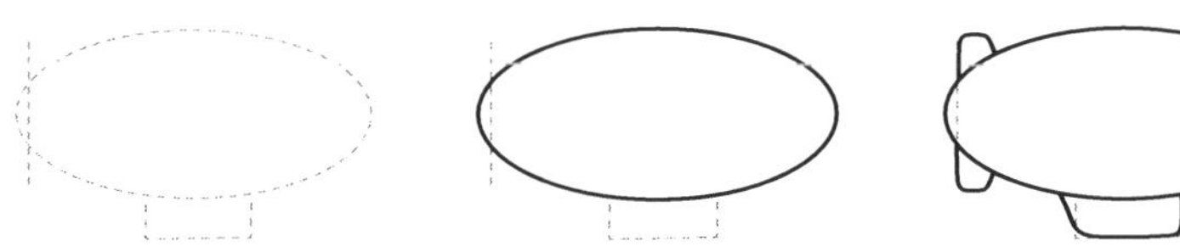

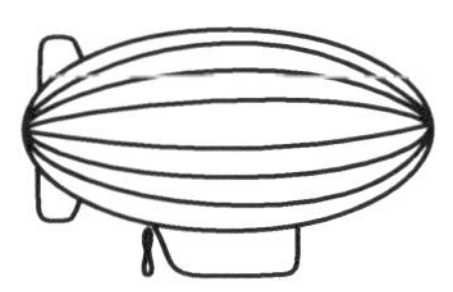

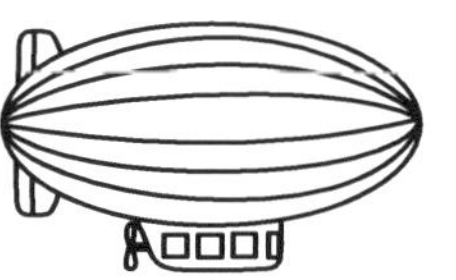

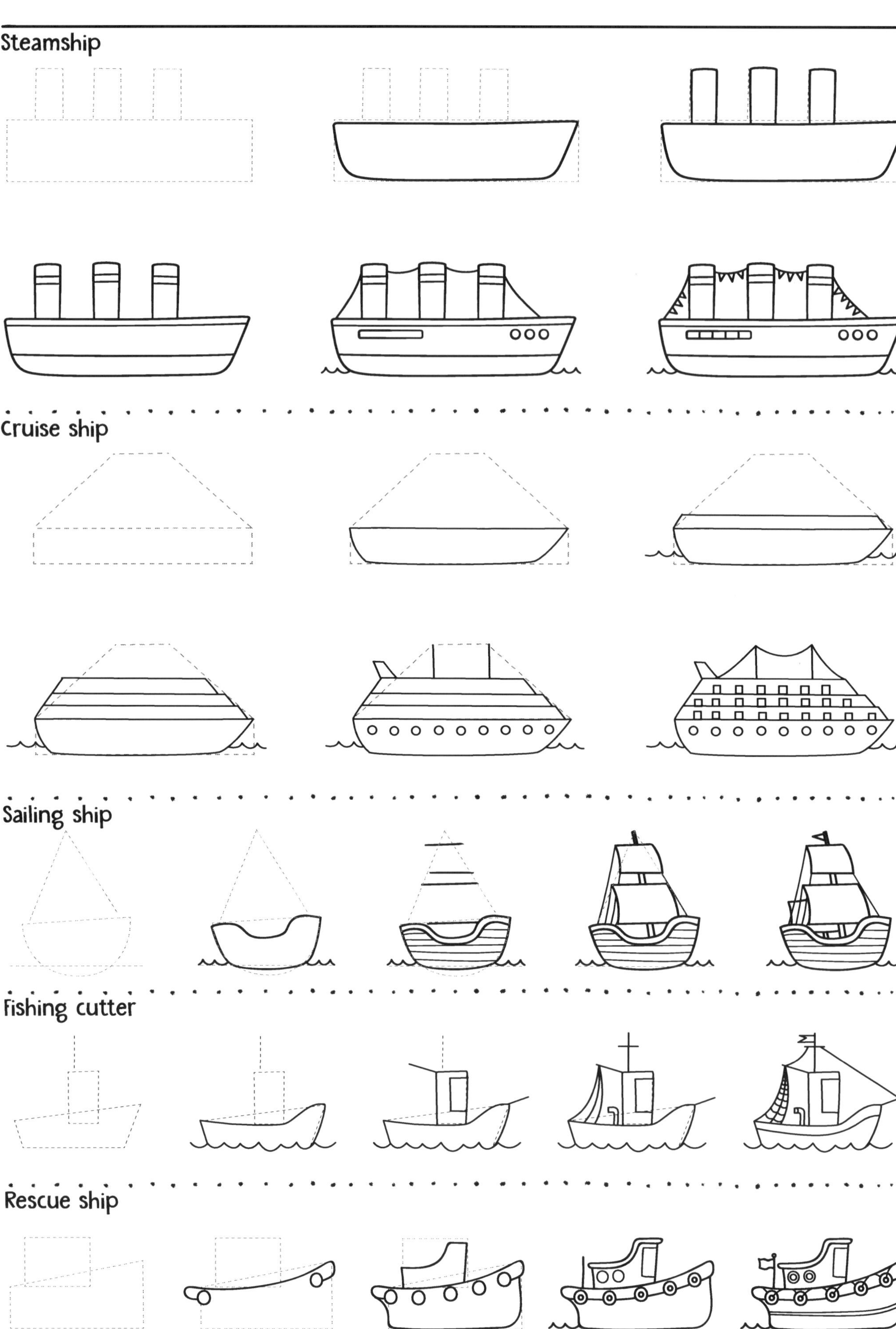
Steamship
Cruise ship
Sailing ship
Fishing cutter
Rescue ship

Ark

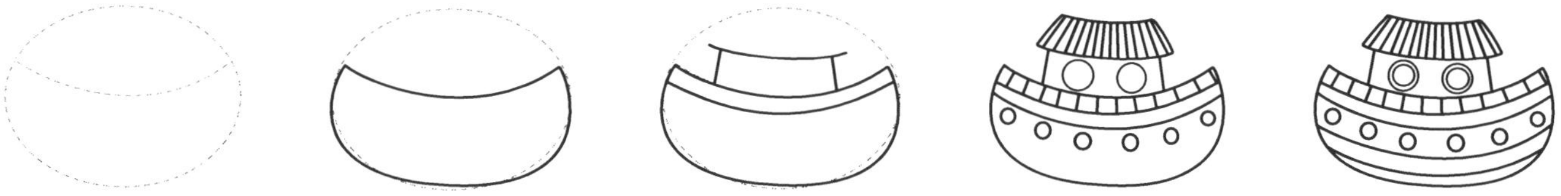

Canoe

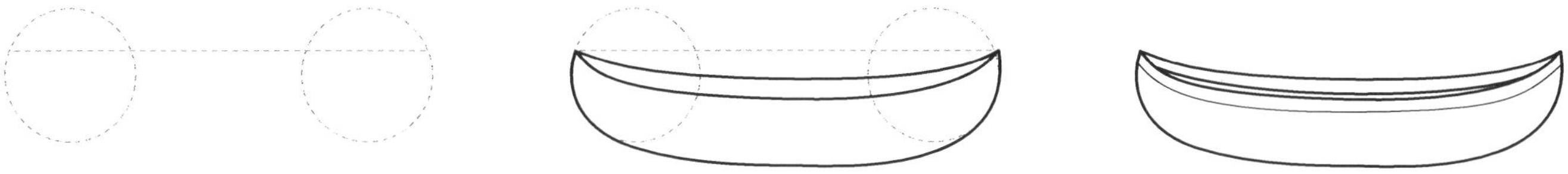

Inflatable boat

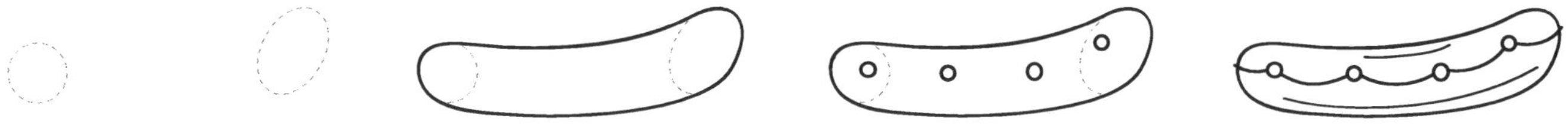

Oar

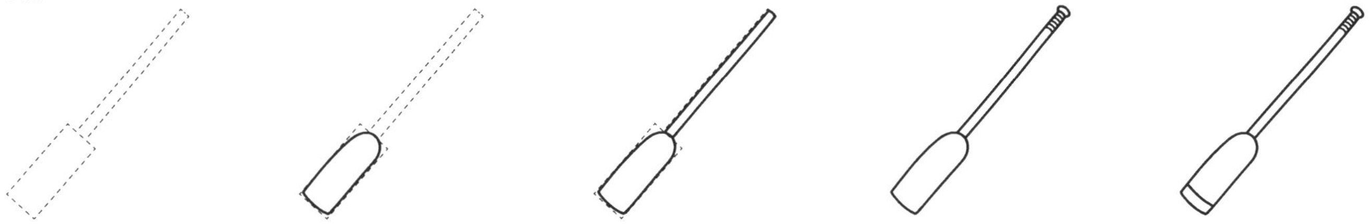

Submarine

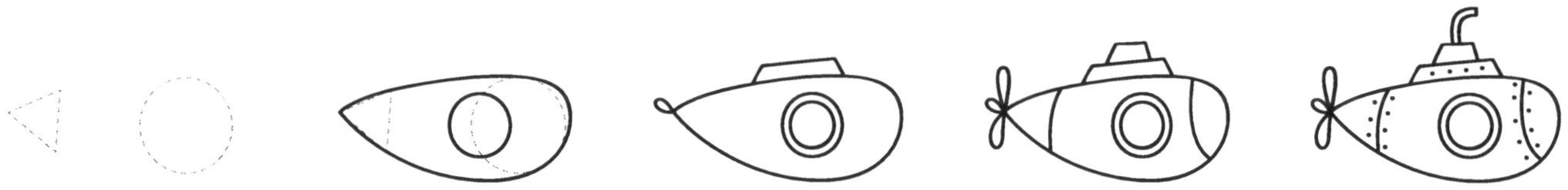

Steering wheel

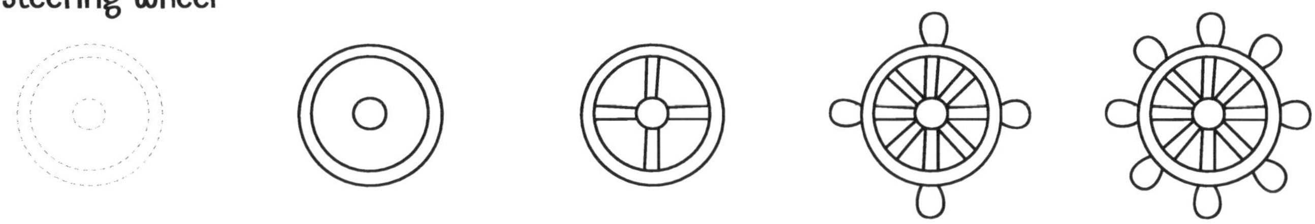

Cockle

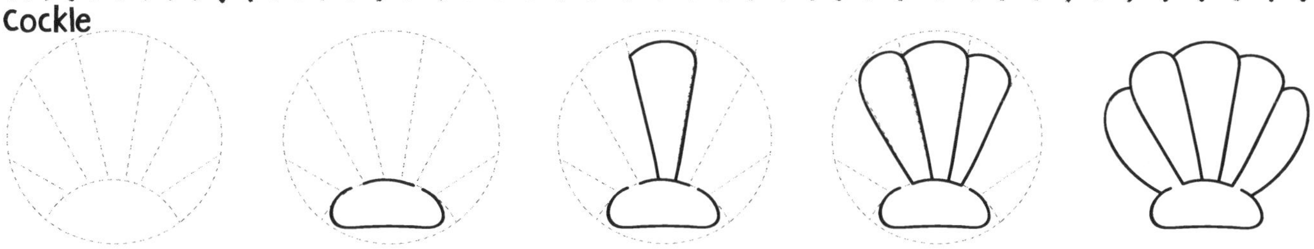

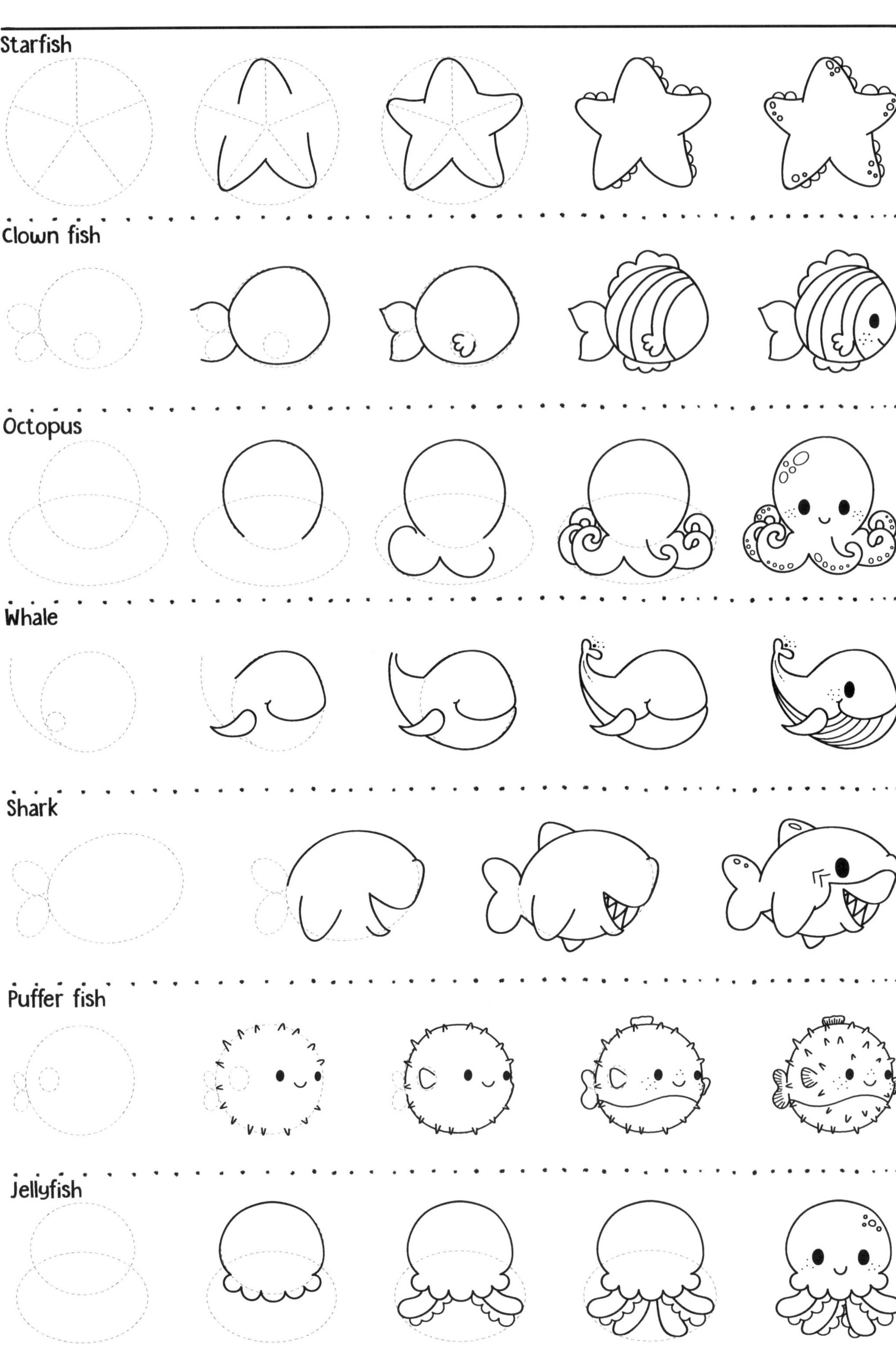
Starfish
Clown fish
Octopus
Whale
Shark
Puffer fish
Jellyfish

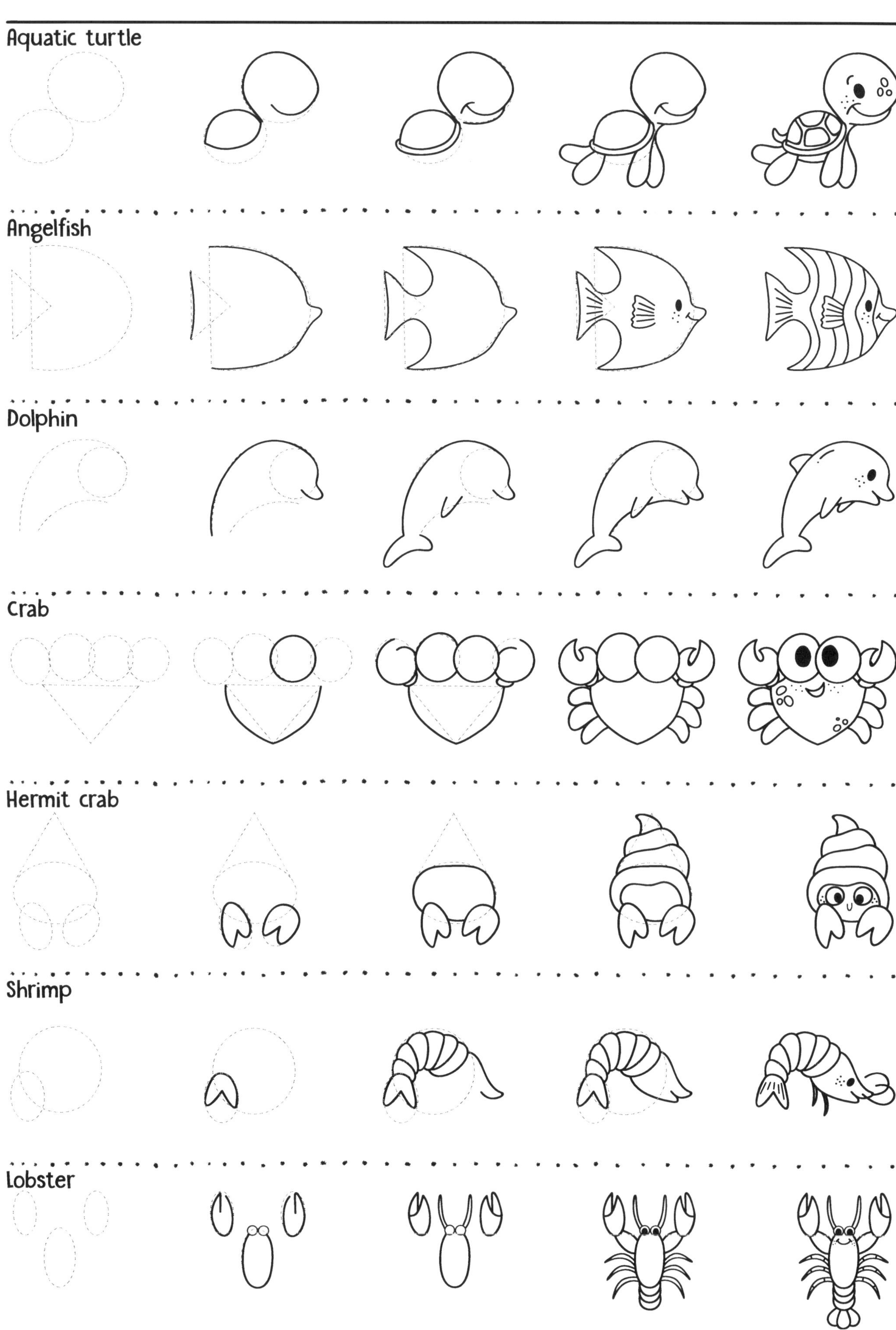
Aquatic turtle
Angelfish
Dolphin
Crab
Hermit crab
Shrimp
Lobster

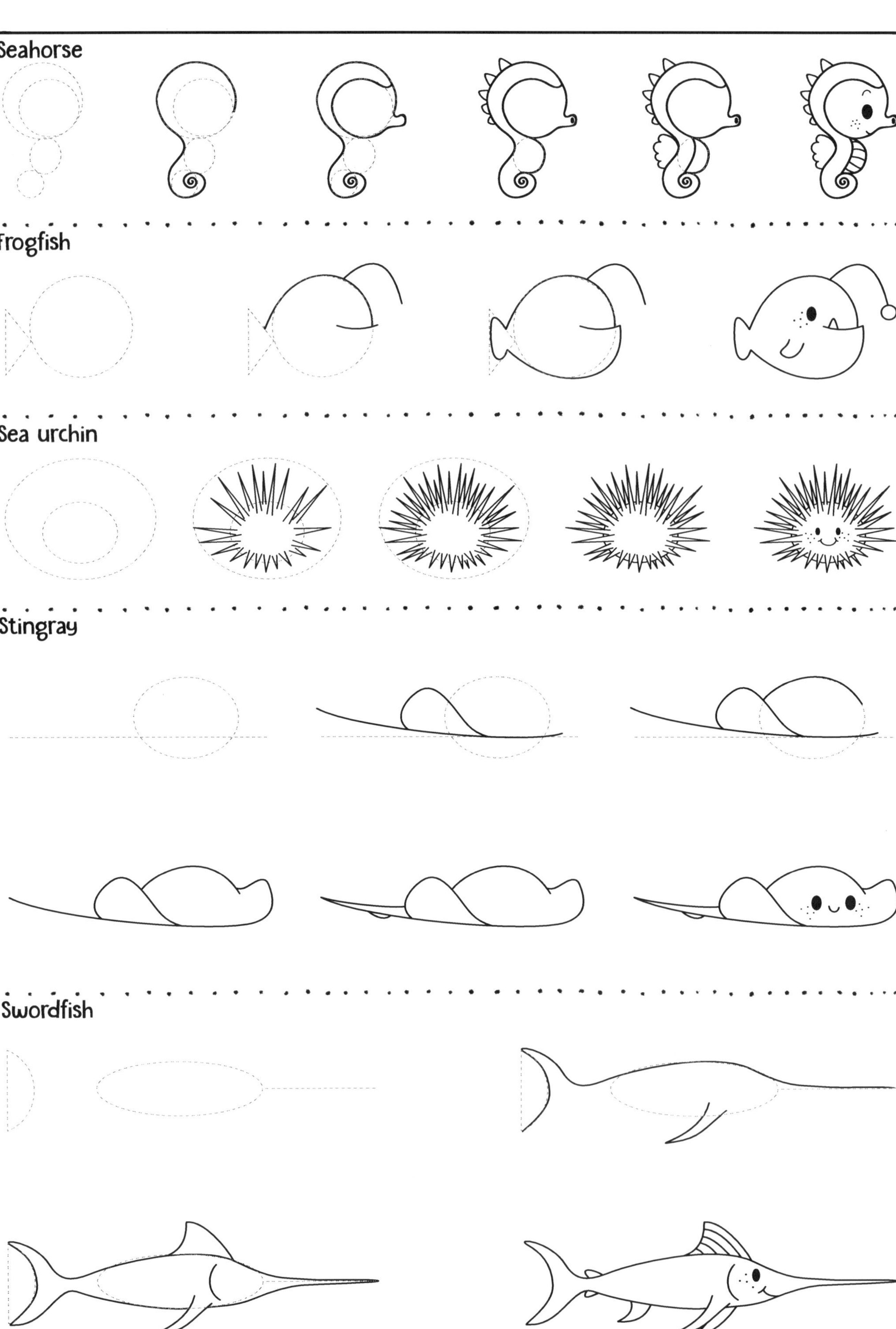
Seahorse
Frogfish
Sea urchin
Stingray
Swordfish

Walrus

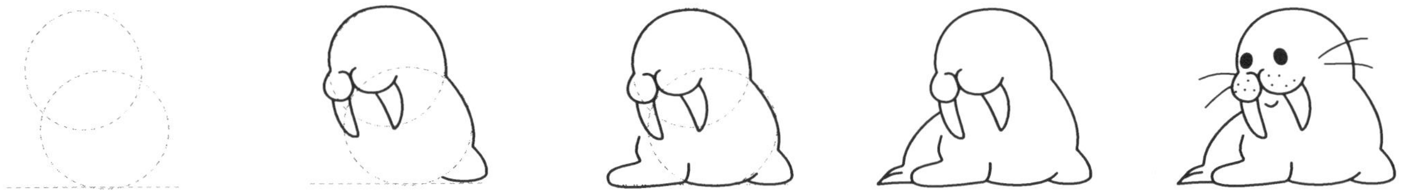

Pinniped

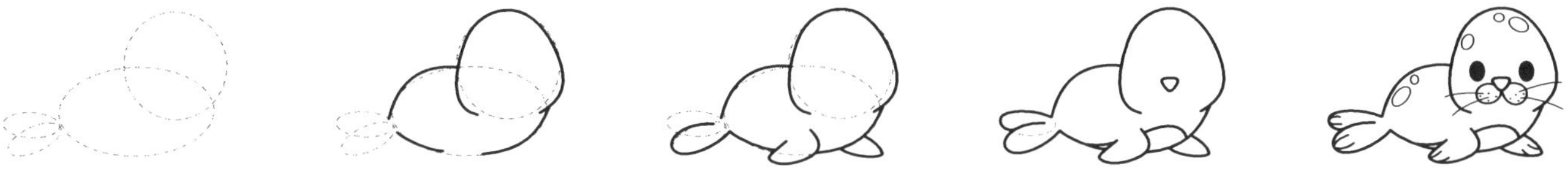

Penguin

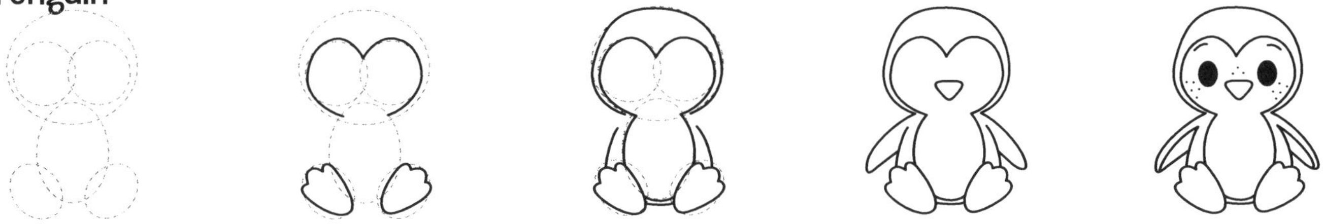

Pelican

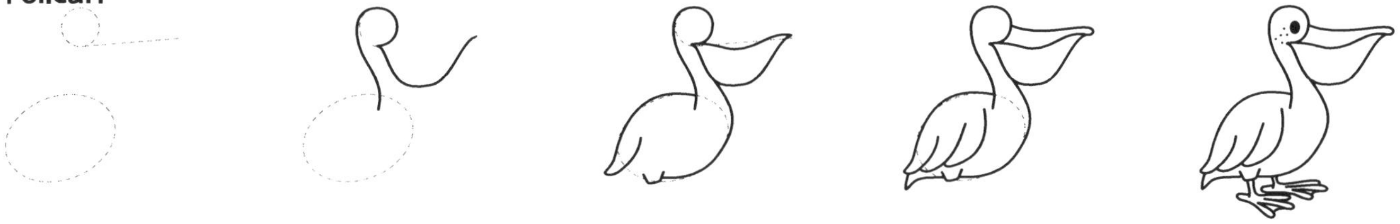

Stork

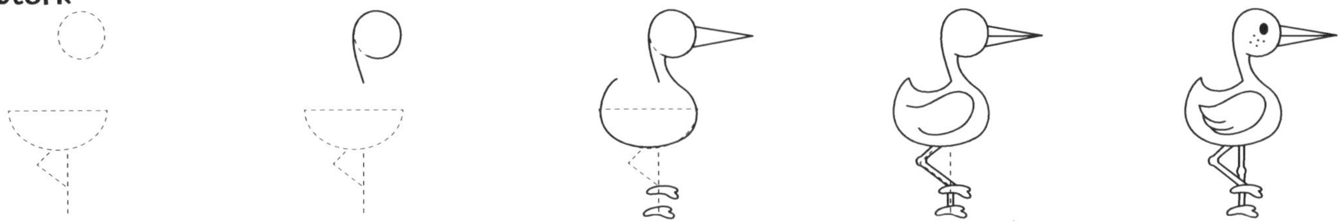

Swan

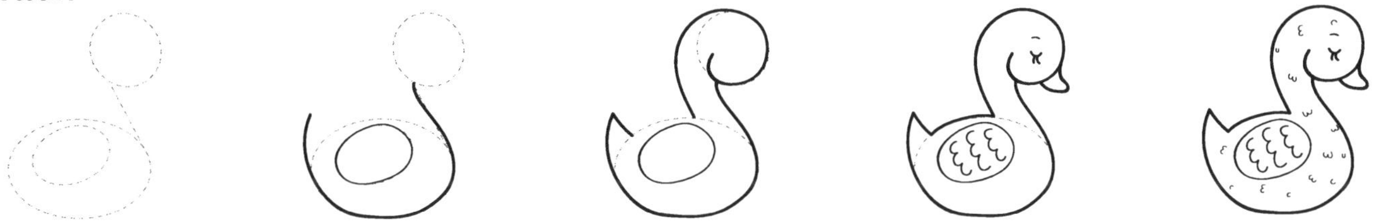

Horse

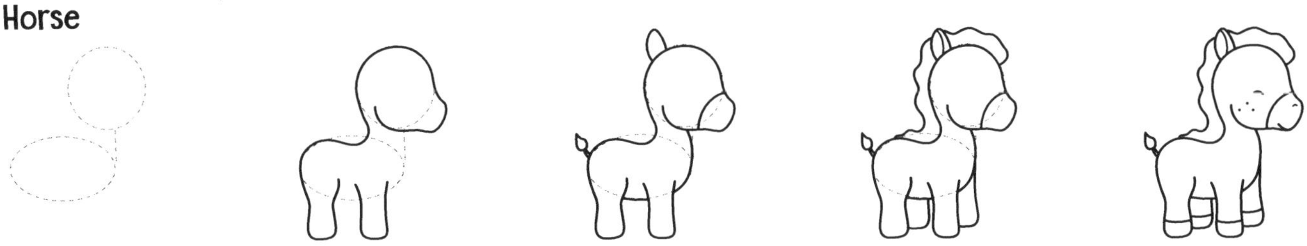

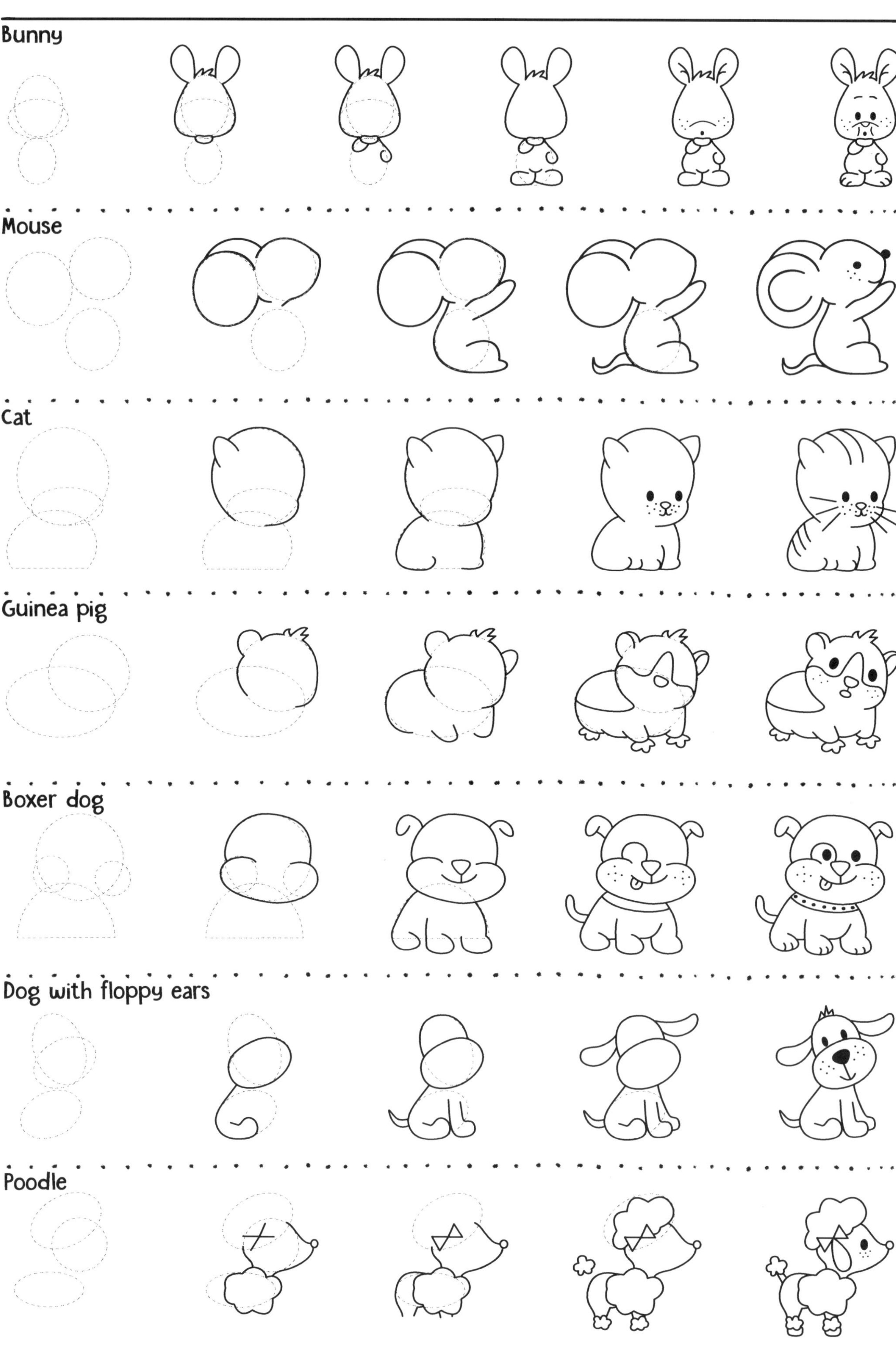
Bunny
Mouse
Cat
Guinea pig
Boxer dog
Dog with floppy ears
Poodle

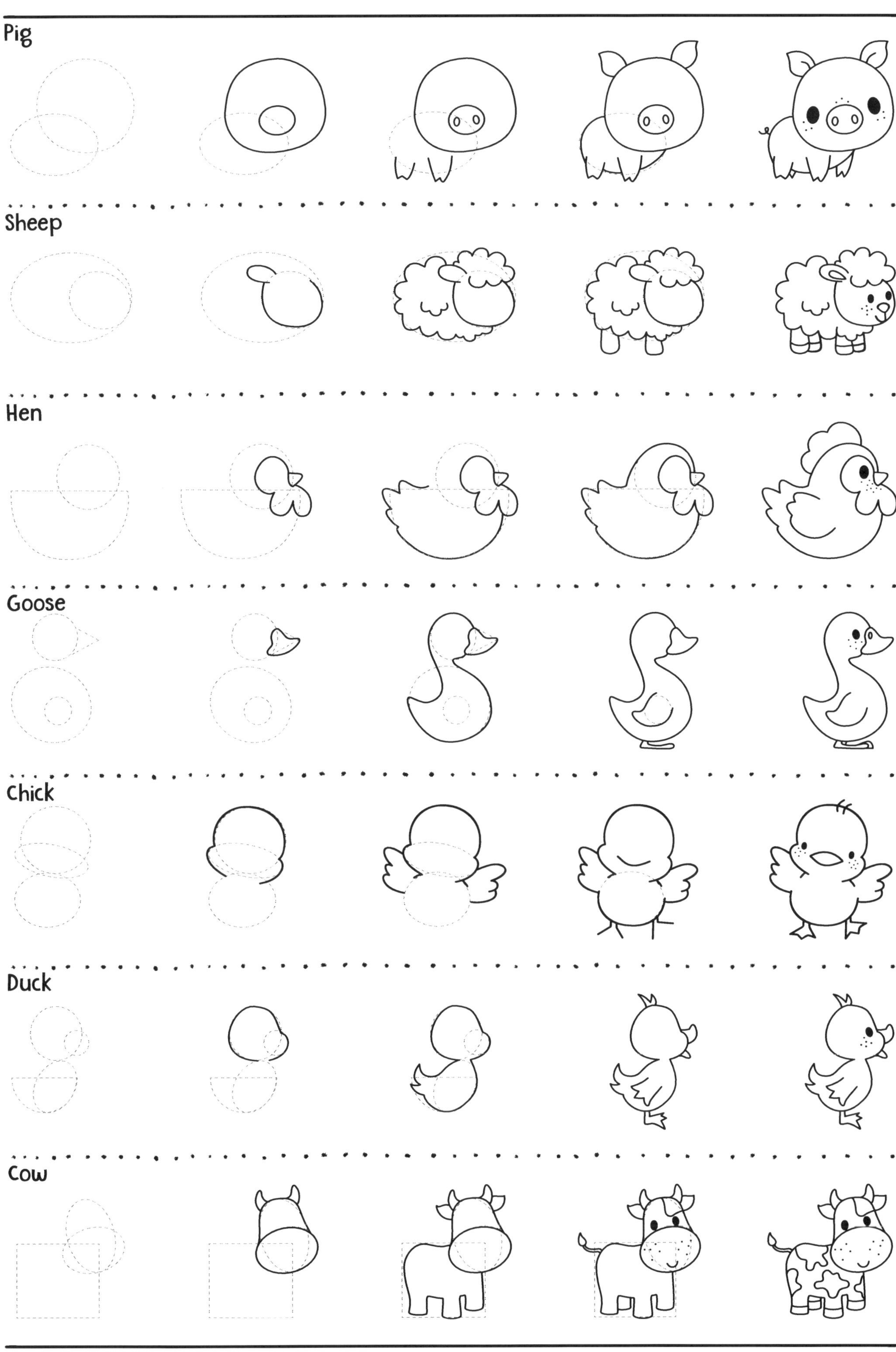
Pig
Sheep
Hen
Goose
Chick
Duck
Cow

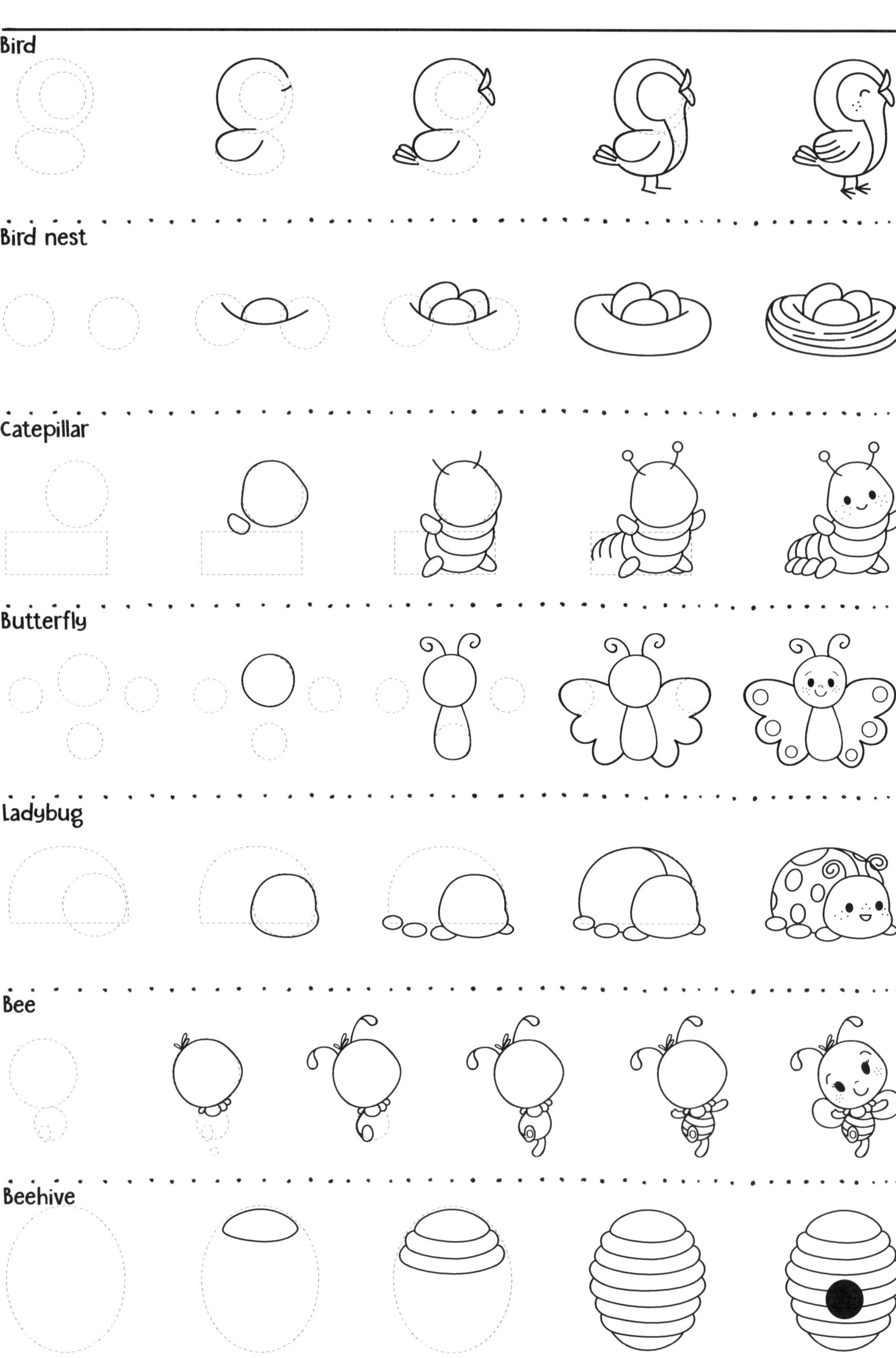
Bird
Bird nest
Catepillar
Butterfly
Ladybug
Bee
Beehive

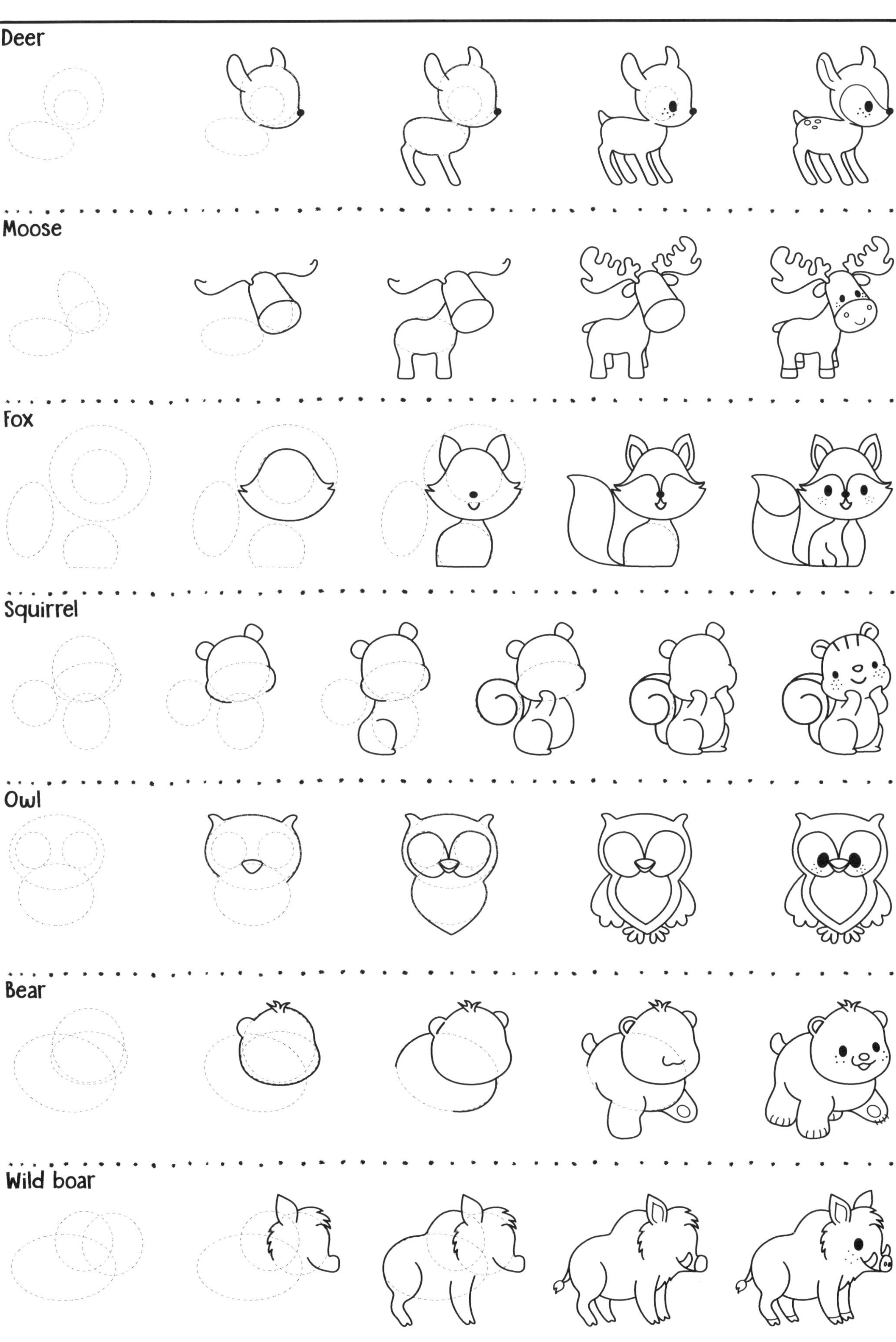
Deer
Moose
Fox
Squirrel
Owl
Bear
Wild boar

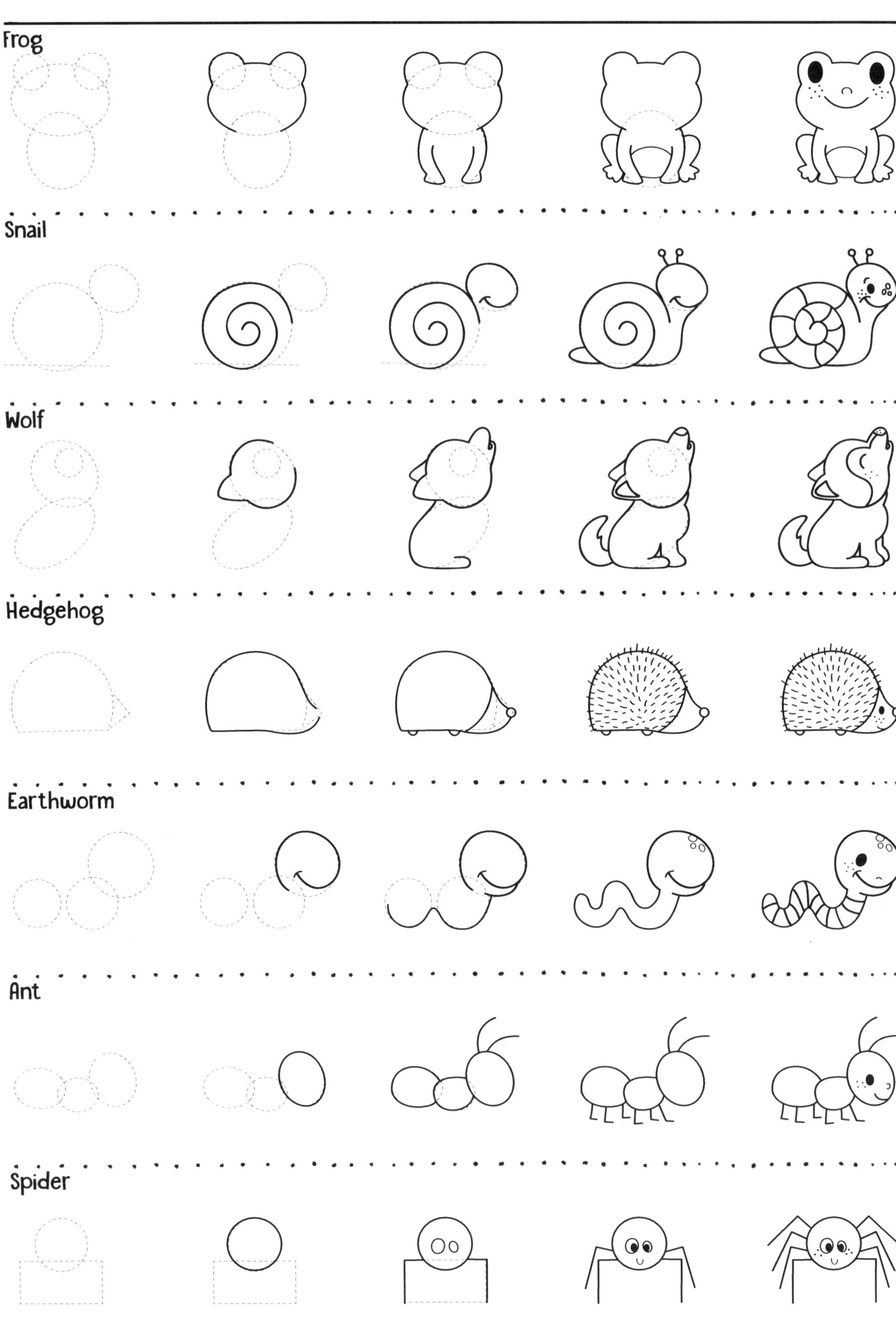
Frog
Snail
Wolf
Hedgehog
Earthworm
Ant
Spider

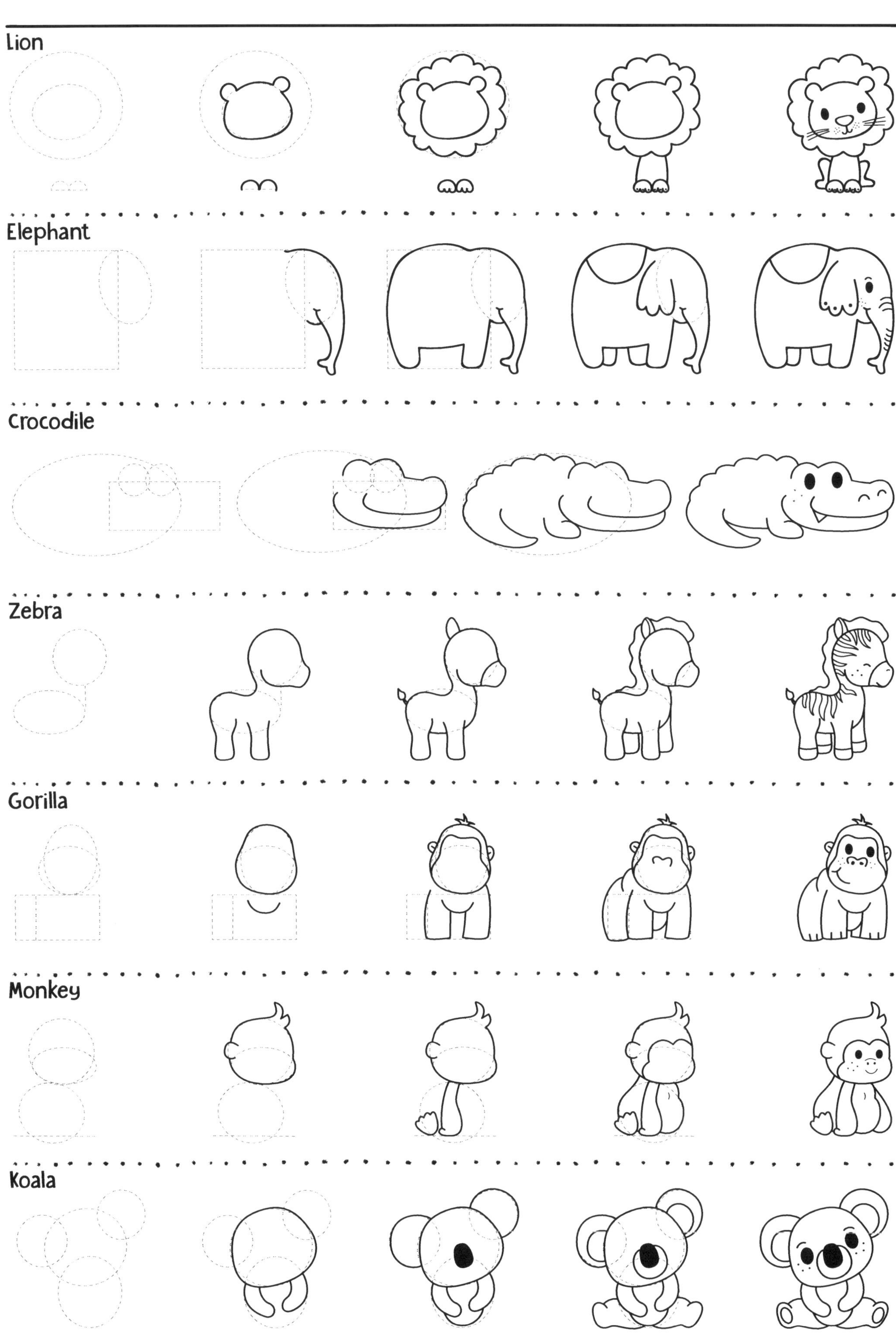
Lion
Elephant
Crocodile
Zebra
Gorilla
Monkey
Koala

Turtle

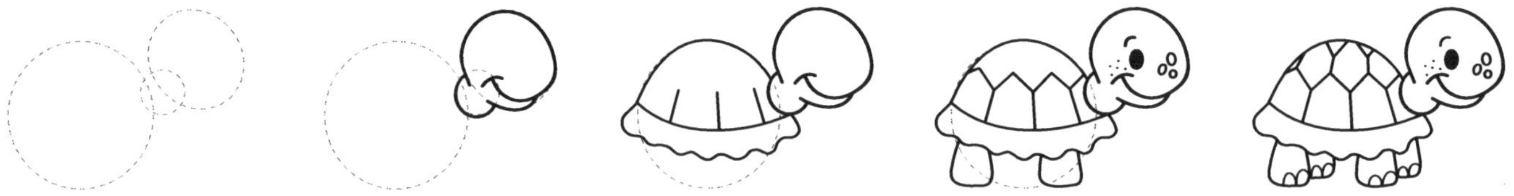

Flamingo

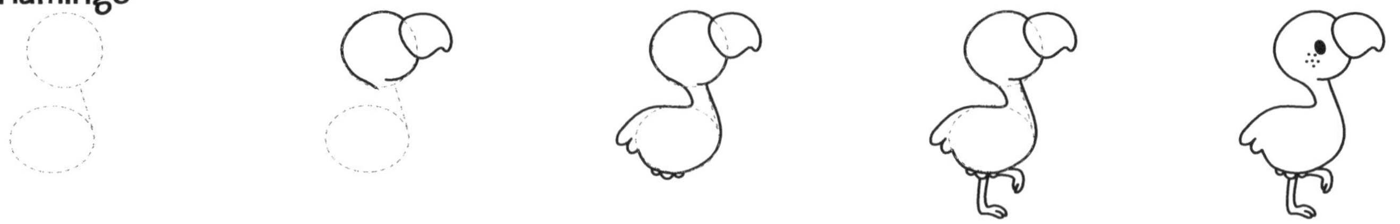

Peacock

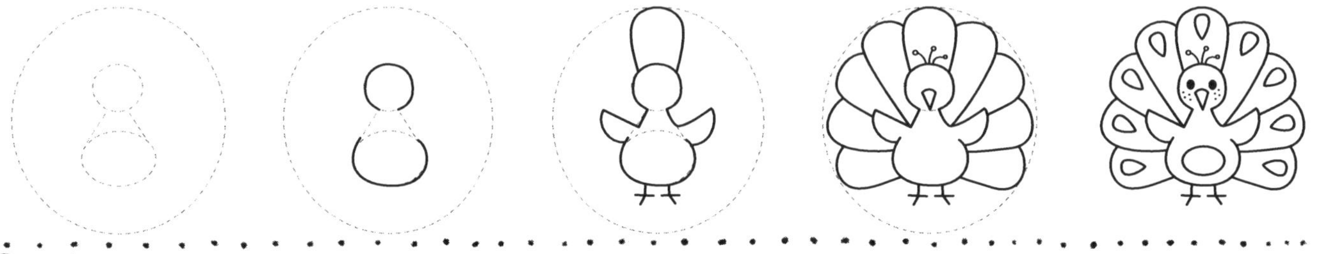

Parrot

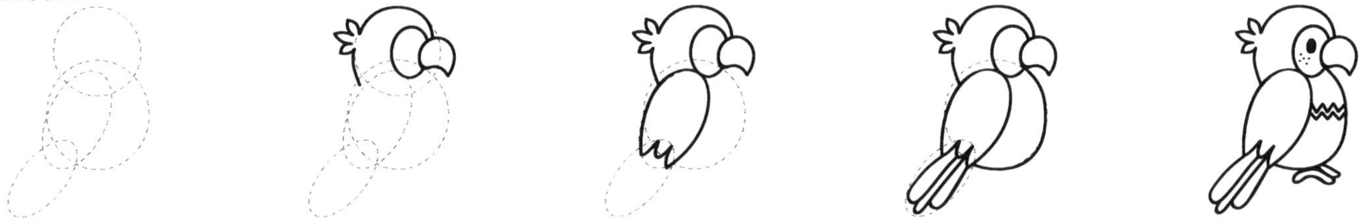

Camel

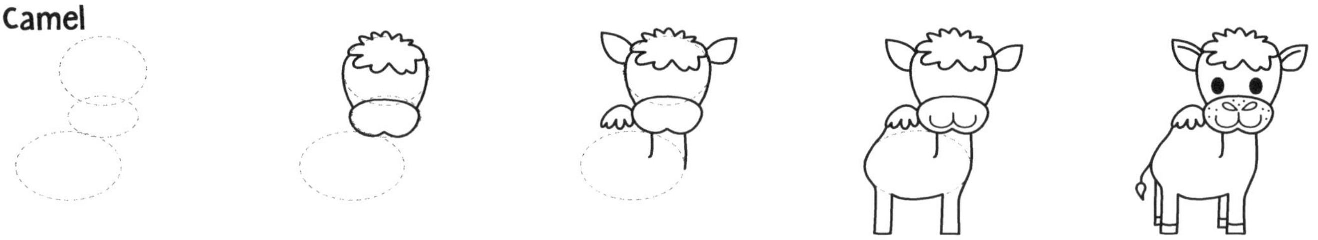

Giraffe

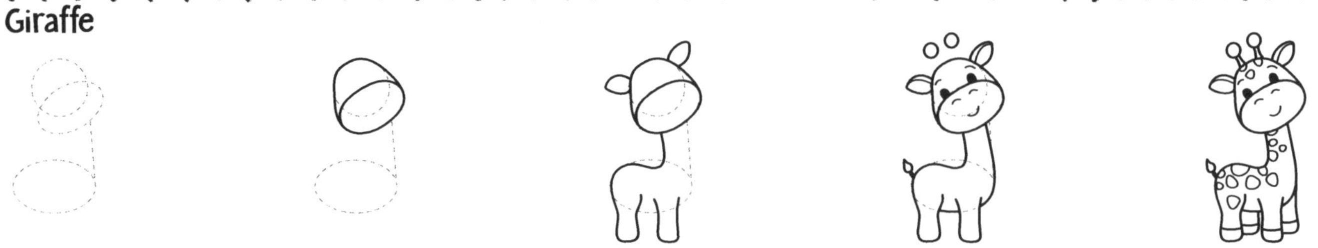

Sloth

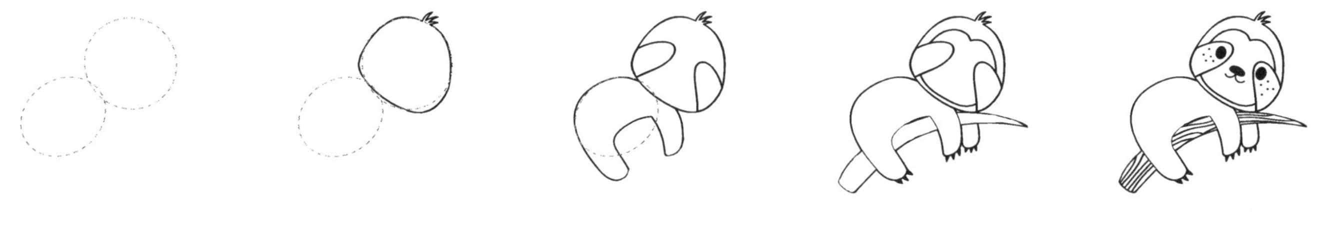

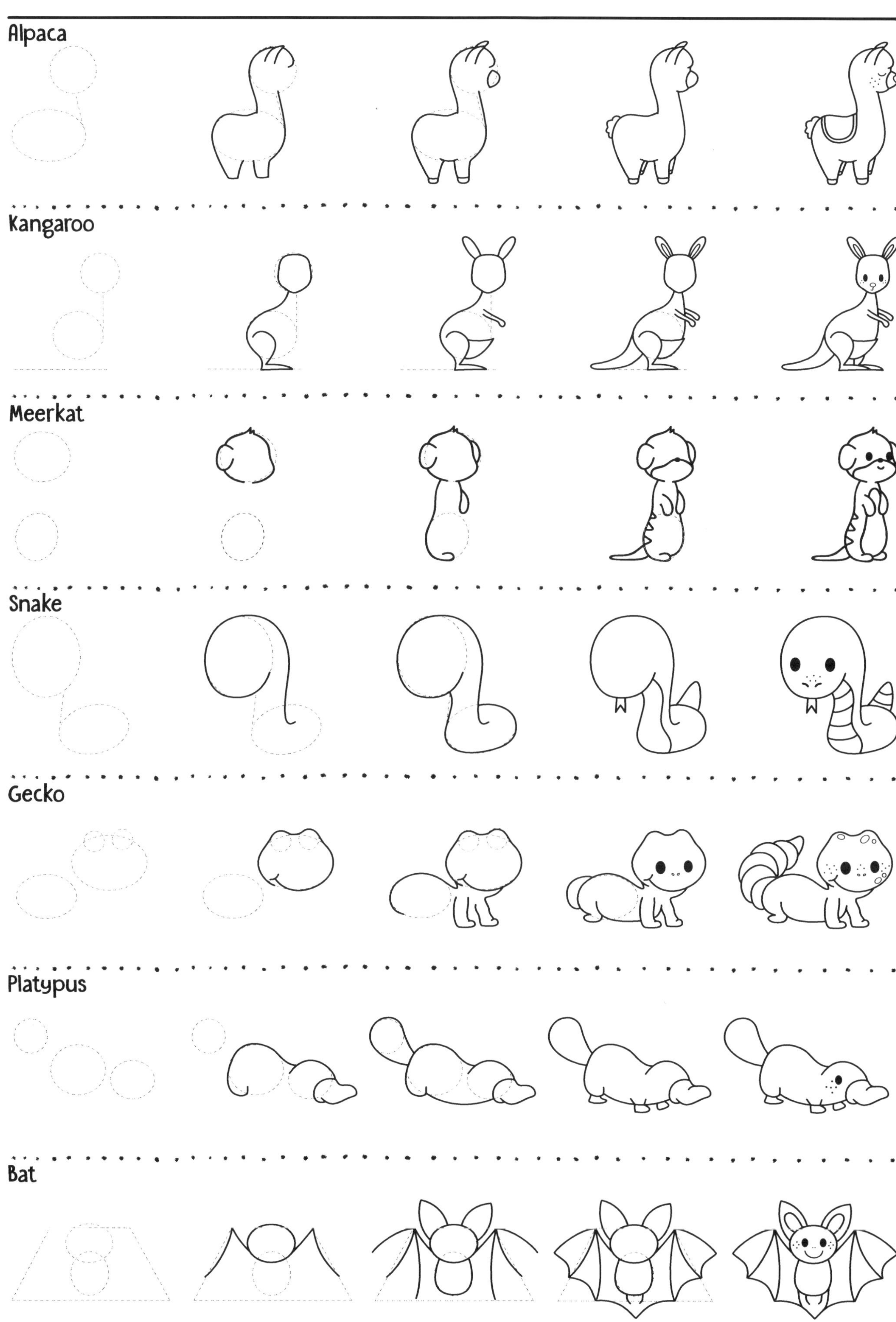
Alpaca
Kangaroo
Meerkat
Snake
Gecko
Platypus
Bat

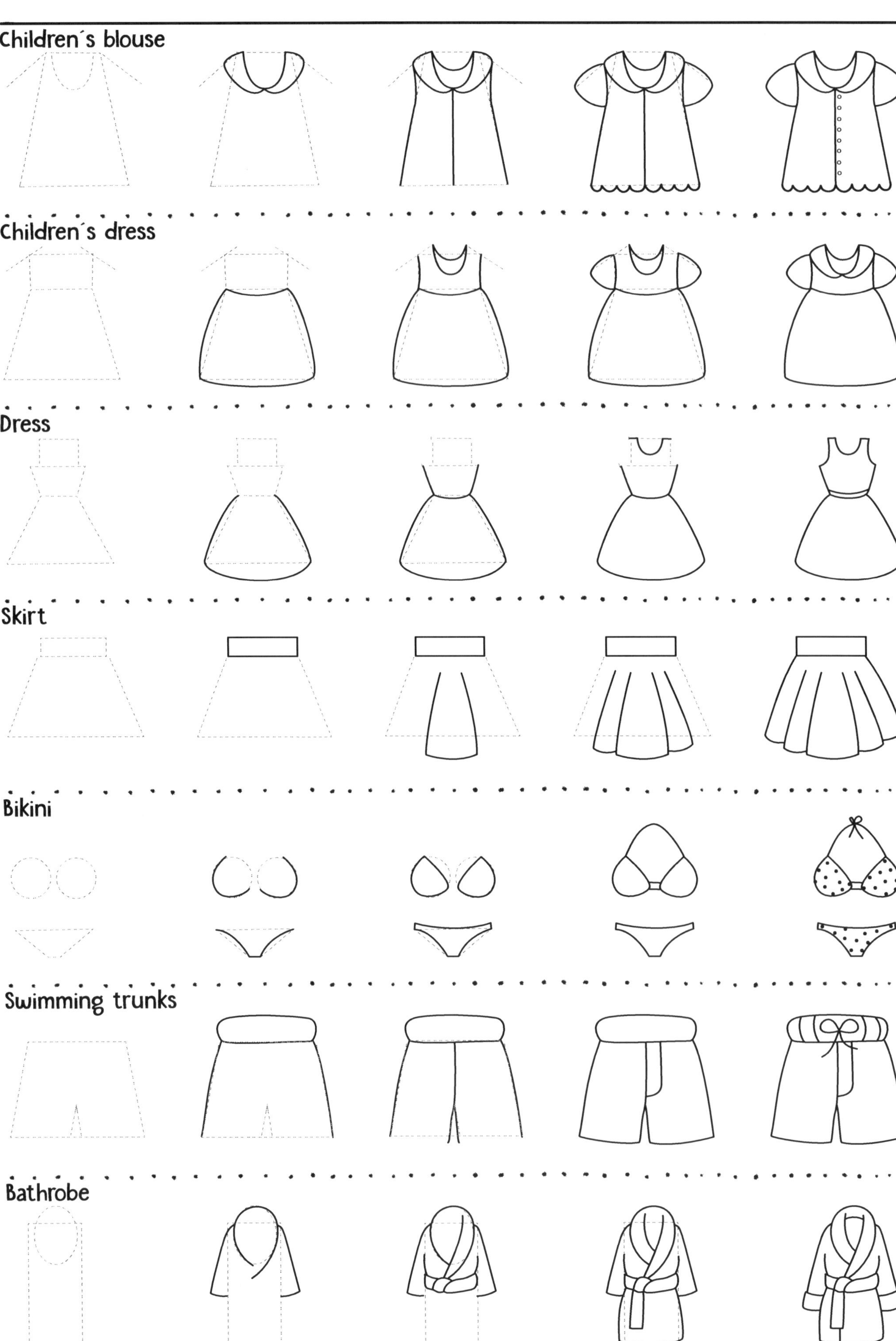
Children´s blouse
Children´s dress
Dress
Skirt
Bikini
Swimming trunks
Bathrobe

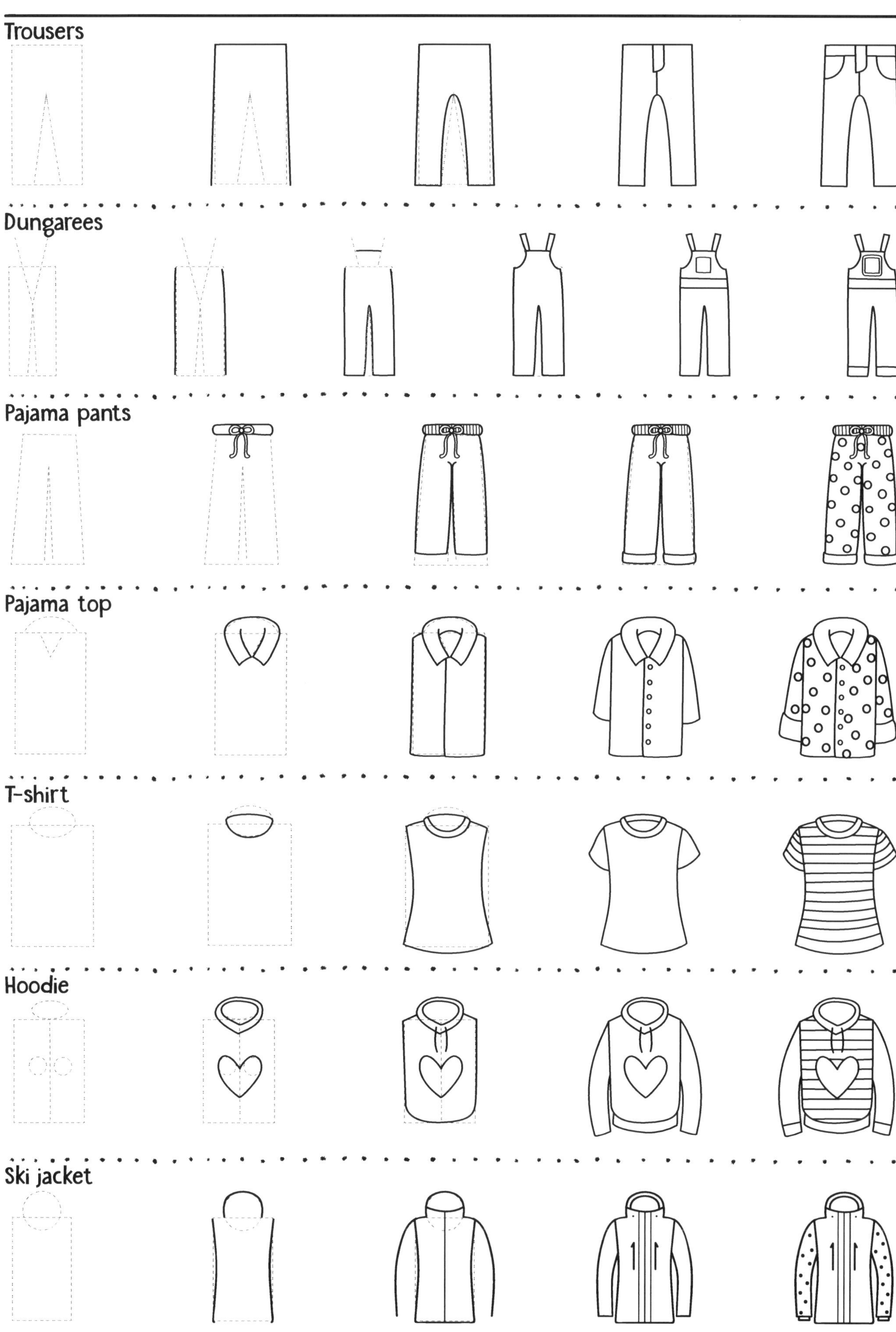
Trousers
Dungarees
Pajama pants
Pajama top
T-shirt
Hoodie
Ski jacket

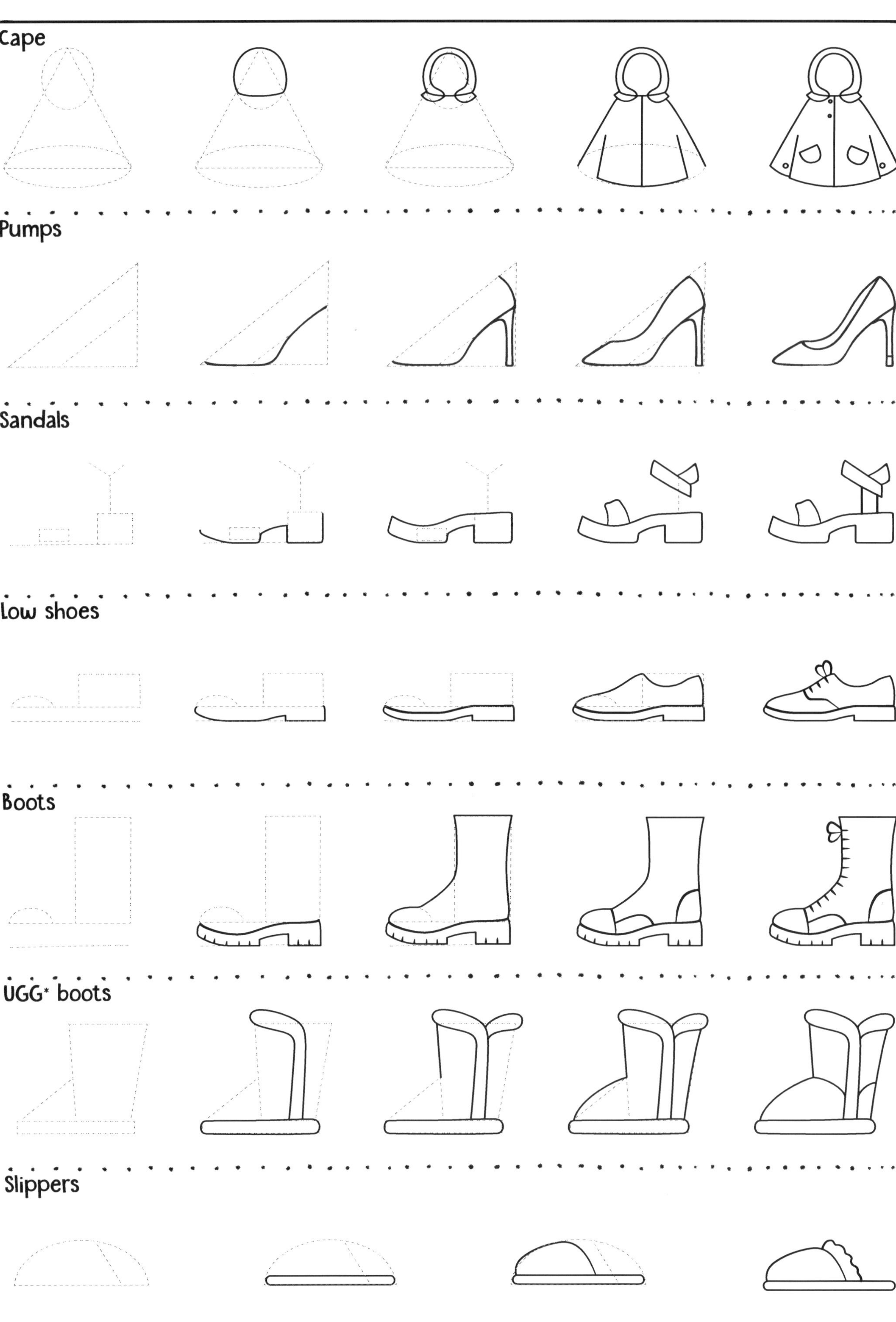
Cape
Pumps
Sandals
Low shoes
Boots
UGG* boots
Slippers

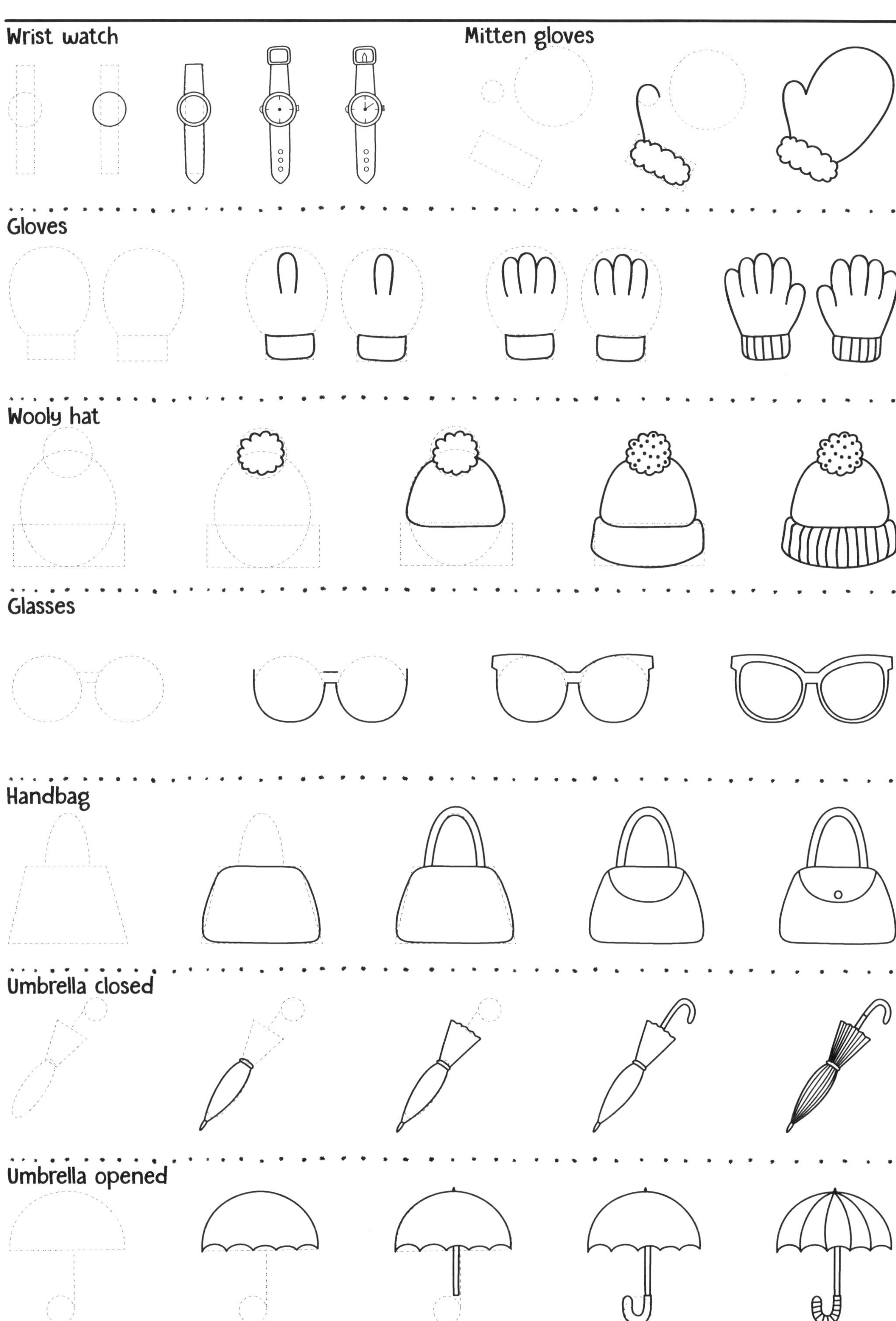
Wrist watch
Mitten gloves
Gloves
Wooly hat
Glasses
Handbag
Umbrella closed
Umbrella opened

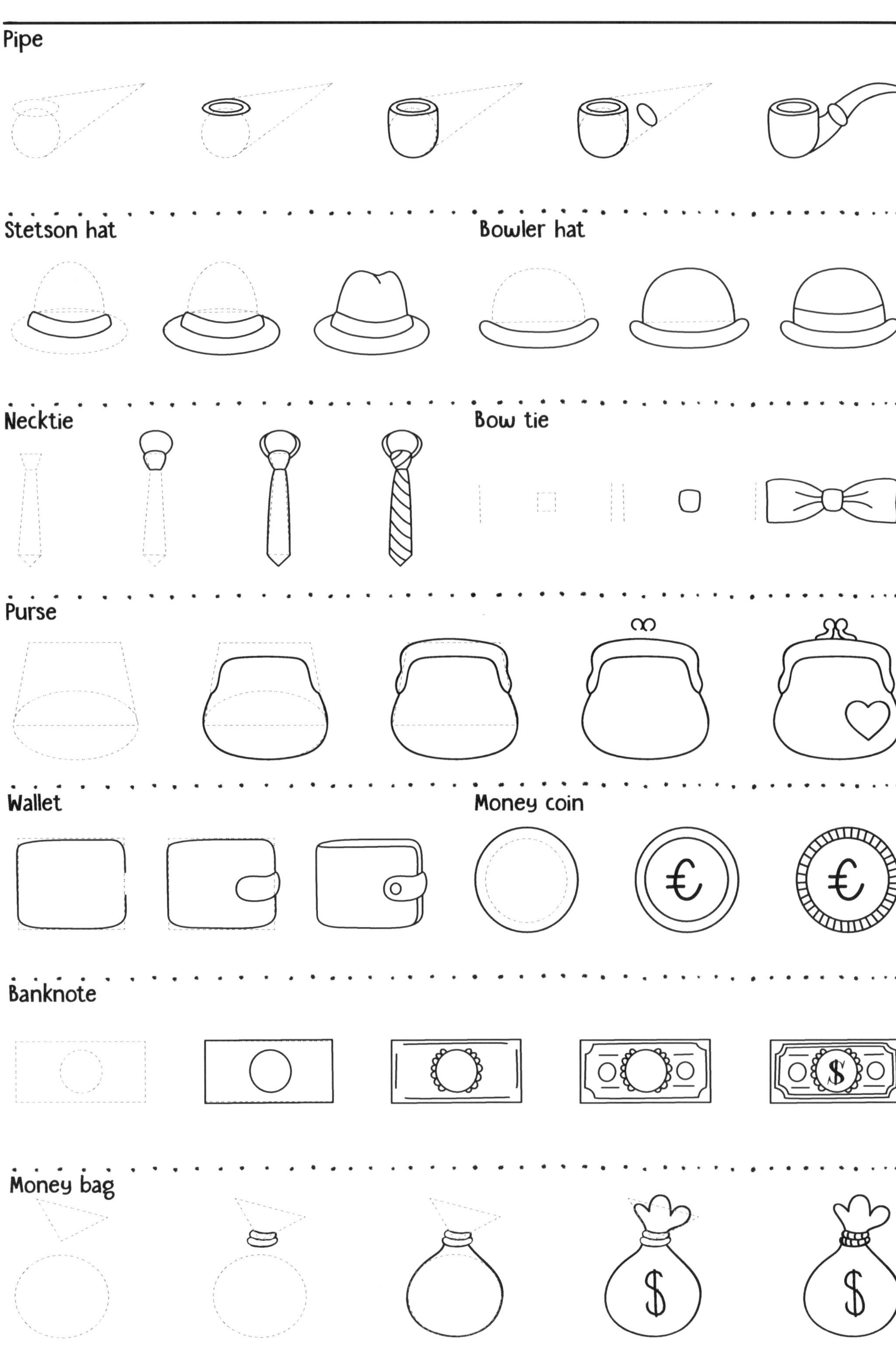
Pipe
Stetson hat
Bowler hat
Necktie
Bow tie
Purse
Wallet
Money coin
Banknote
Money bag

Index

A

Accordion 44
Afraid 7
Aggressive 7
Airplane 119
Airport 106
Alarm clock 53
Albus* 25
Alien 16
Alpaca 133
Ambulance 18
Amphora 103
Anchor 95
Angel 45
Angelfish 123
Angler 85
Angry 7
Anna 34
Ant 130
Anxious 7
Apple 70
Apron 15
Aquarium 73
Aquatic turtle 123
Ark 121
Armchair 72
Artichoke 69
Ash* 23
Astronaut 16
Atom 19

B

Baby 50
Baby bodysuit 51
Baby bottle 51
Baby mobile 52
Baby rattle 51
Baby shoes 51
Baby socks 51
Baby stroller 52
Baguette 63
Bales of straw 98
Ballerina 11
Ballet shoes 37
Ball gown 35
Ballpoint pen 79
Banana 70
Banknote 138
Barrier 13
Baseball 87
Baseball glove 89
Baseball jersey 89
Basketball 87
Basketball hoop 90
Basketball jersey 90
Bat 133
Bathrobe 134
Bathtub 54
Batman* 21
Beach bag 94
Bean 70
Bear 129
Bed 53
Bedside table 54
Bee 128
Beehive 128
Beer maß 99
Beet 68
Berlin wall 100
Bib 52
Bibi Blocksberg 33
Bicycle 113
Big Ben 100
Big top 42
Bike helmet 87
Bikini 134
Binoculars 96
Biplane airplane 119
Bird 128
Bird cage 73
Birdfeeder 74
Bird nest 128
Birthday cake 49
Birthday card 49
Blackboard 80
Bollen hat 99
Bomb 29
Bombette 22
Bombette* 22
Bone 74
Book closed 38
Boots 136
Bouncy castle 40
Bouquet 49
Bow 50
Bow and arrow 31
Bowl 61
Bowler hat 138
Bowling ball 86
Bowling pin 86
Bow tie 138
Boxer dog 126
Boxing gloves 92
Boy 9
Boy with curls 8
Boy with straight hair 8
Braces 19
Brachiosaurus 31
Brandenburg Gate 100
Bridge 106
Broccoli 68
Broom 58
Brush 82
Bucket 58
Bull´s eye 95
Bumper car 41
Bunny 126
Burj al Arab 103
Bus 115
Bush 108
Butter 65
Butter cookie 63
Butterfly 128
Button 83

C

C-3PO 24
C-3PO* 24
Cabbage 69
Cabinet 72
Cabriolet 114
Cactus 108
Cake plate 61
Calculator 78
Calendar 79
Camel 132
Camera 78
Camper 116
Campfire 97
Camping backpack 97
Camping bus 115
Camping mat 96
Candle 75
Candy 63
Candy cane 45
Canned fish 66
Cannon 30
Canoe 121
Cape 136
Cape King 36
Capitol building 104
Captain´s cap 95
Car 114
Caravan 96
Carriage 35
Carrot 68
Castle 35, 106
Cat 126
Catch 85
Catepillar 128
Cauldron 49
Cauliflower 70
Cell phone 76
Chain of lights 46
Chair 72
Chair lift 91
Chairoplane 42
Champagne bottle 47
Champagne flute 47
Chase 21
Chase* 21
Cheeky 7
Cheese 65
Chef hat 15
Cherries 71
Chestnuts 101
Chest protector 89
Chewbacca 24
Chewbacca* 24
Chick 127
Chicken wings 66
Children´s blouse 134
Children´s dress 134
Chinese 6
Chips 67
Chocolate bar 64
Chocolate spread 65
Christ child 46
Christmas baubles 46
Christmas sleigh 45
Christmas stocking 45
Christmas tree 46
Chrysler building 104
Church 105
Cinderella* 34
Cinese 6
Classic car 114
Cleaning brush 58
Clinical thermometer 19
Clone 24
Clone trooper* 24
Cloud 111
Cloudy 110
Clown 6, 42
Clown fish 122
Cockle 121
Coconut 71
Coffee to go 64
Colosseum 102
Comb 55
Combine harvester 117
Comet 111
Compass 97

Computer 77
Computer mouse 77
Concentrated 5
Concrete mixer 117
Constellation 111
Construction helmet 13
Construction trailer 13
Construction worker 13
Controller 39
Convertible 114
Cook 15
Cookie 63
Cooking pot 15
Cooking spoon 15
Cordless screwdriver 84
Cordless telephone 76
Corn 69
Corona 35
Couch 72
Covid-19 Virus 18
Covid Virus 18
Cow 127
Cow bell 99
Cowboy 32
Cowboy hat 32
Crab 123
Craft scissors 81
Crane 13
Cream puff 62
Crib 52
Crocodile 131
Croissant 62
Crown 35
Cruise ship 120
Crying 7
Crystal 36
Cuckoo clock 99
Cucumber 69
Cup 59, 88
Cupcake 62
Curtains 53
Curve 113
Cutlery 60
Cutter knife 81
Cypress 109

D

Daily newspaper 53
Dancing ballet 10
Darth Vader 24
Darth Vader* 24
Deceitful 7
Deciduous tree 109
Deck chair 74
Deer 129
Denture 19
Designer stubble 6
Desk 72
Desk lamp 76
Detergent 56
Devil 6
Diamond 36
Diamond ring 36
Diaper 50
Diary 36
Dinamite 30
Dinosaur Egg 30
Dirndl 99
Dish liquid 58
Diver 93
Diving goggles 93
Dobby 25
Dobby* 25
Doctor 18
Dog basket 73
Doghouse 74
Dog with floppy ears 126
Doll 38
Dolphin 123
Domino 38
Donut 62
Double decker bus 100
Doubting 5
Dough scraper 61
Draco 26
Draco* 26
Dragon 27
Dream 5
Dress 134
Drill 85
Drinking glass 61
Duck 127
Dumbbell 92
Dump truck 116
Dungarees 135
Dustpan 57

E

Earthworm 130
Easel 82
Easter bunny 47
Easter egg 46
Easter nest 47
Eating 5
Eclair 63
Egg cup 59
Eggplant 69
Eggs 65
Eiffel tower 101
Electric guitar 43
Electric toothbrush 56
Elephant 131
Elsa 34
Embarrassed 5
Empire state 104
Envelope back 14
Envelope front 14
Eraser 80
Evil 7

F

Fairy 35
Fairy wand 35
Fan 77, 101
Farfalle 66
Farm 98
Farmhouse bread 63
Feather duster 58
Fence 74
Ferris wheel 41
Figure skating skate 90
Finish line 93
Firebolt 27
Firebolt* 27
Fire extinguisher 20
Firefighter 20
Firefighter boots 20
Fire hose 20
Fire truck 20
Firework 47
Firework rocket 47
Fir tree 109
Fishing cutter 120
Fishing rod 85
Fishing suitcase 85
Fish N Chips 100
Fitness Tracker 92
Flag 102
Flames 20
Flamingo 132
Flash 21
Flash* 21
Flashlight 97
Flip Flops 94
Flippers 93
Floor lamp 76
Flour bag 61
Flower 109
Flower box 12
Flower pot 12
Flute 44
Foam hand 90
Food bowl 73
Food truck 116
Football 87, 89
Football goal 89
Football helmet 89
Football jersey 89
Football pants 89
Forklift truck 117
Formula 1 racing car 115
Fortune cookie 103
Fountain pen 81
Fox 129
French 6
French fries 67
Fried egg 65
Frog 130
Frogfish 124
Front door 52
Frost 110
Frozen 34
Full beard 6
Furious 7

G

Galaxy 111
Gangster 6
Gardener 12
Garden Gnome 12
Garden hose 12
Garden parasol 75
Garland 49
Gecko 133
Genie 32
Ghost 48
Giant 27
Giant swingboat 41
Gift 49
Giggle 5
Gingerbread man 45
Giraffe 132
Girl 9
Girl with chignons 8
Girl with curls 8
Girl with glasses 8
Girl with headscarf 8
Girl with straight hair 8
Glasses 137
Globe 81
Gloves 137
Glue stick 80
Goldfish bowl 73
Golf ball 86
Golf caddy 86
Golf club 86
Golf hole 86
Gondola 91, 102
Goomba 23
Goomba* 23
Goose 127
Gorilla 131
Grandma 9
Grandpa 9
Grapes 71
Grass 108
Grater 60
Guide 97
Guinea pig 126
Guitar 43

H

Hagrid 25
Hagrid* 25
Hairbrush 55
Hair dryer 55
Half-timbered house 105
Halloween pumpkin 48
Hamburger 67

Hammer 84
Hammock 95
Handbag 137
Hand blender 59
Hand broom 57
Handcart 41
Handcuffs 17
Handheld microphone 43
Hand mirror 36
Hand truck 14
Hanger 57
Hanging lamp 76
Harry 25
Harry* 25
Harry Potter 25
Hatchet 85
Haystack 98
Hazelnut 71
Headphones 78
Hedgehog 130
Hello Kitty 37
Hello Kitty* 37
Hen 127
Hermione 25
Hermione* 25
Hermit crab 123
High-visibility vest 13
Hiker 11
Hiking boots 97
Hobby 82
Hockey goal 90
Hockey skate 90
Hockey stick 90
Hoodie 135
Hook 30
Horse 125
Hot air balloon 119
Hot Dog 67
Hot glue gun 82
Hot-water bag 56
House 105
Hungry 5
Hydrant 20

I

Ice cream cone 64
Ice cream sundae 64
Ice cream truck 116
Igloo 105
Igloo tent 96
Inflatable boat 121
Inline skates 86
In love 6
Intelligent 5
Iron 57
Ironing board 57
Island 108
Italia 102

J

Jedi 24
Jedi* 24
Jelly 65
Jellyfish 122
Jigglypuff 23
Jigglypuff* 23
Jigsaw Puzzle 38
Joshi 22
Joshi* 22
Jumping 10

K

Kangaroo 133
Ketchup 67
Kettle barbecue 74
Key 52
Keyboard 44
Kids cutlery 52
Kissing 5
Kitchen Aid* 15
Kitchen glove 15
Knight 28
Knight castle 27
Knight helmet 28
Knitting needles 82
Koala 131
Kremlin 104

L

Ladder 74
Ladybug 128
Lake 107
Lamborghini 115
Lantern 75
Laptop 77
Laugh 5
Laundry basket 57
Lederhosen 99
Lego 38
LEGO* brick 38
Leia 24
Leia* 24
Lemon 71
Letterbox 14
Lettuce 70
Life ring 95
Light bulb 75
Lighthouse 95
Lion 131
Lipstick 56
Little Red Riding Hood 33
Lobster 123
Locker 81
Log cabin 105
Lollipop 63
London Eye 100
Low shoes 136
Luigi 22
Luigi* 22

M

Macaroni 66
Macho 6
Magic lamp 32
Magic potion 26
Magnifying glass 79
Make up brush 56
Mammoth 27
Mammut 27
Man 9
Mario 22
Mario* 22
Market stall 106
Marshall 21
Marshall* 21
Martins lantern 41
Mask 18
Matryoshka 104
Maya pyramid 104
McGonagall* 25
McGranitt 25
Medal 93
Meerkat 133
Mermaid 37
Message in a bottle 29
Microphone 78
Milk 64
Milk can 98
Milkshake 64
Mini excavator 117
Minion 33
Miraculous 21
Miraculous* 21
Mitten gloves 137
Money bag 138
Money coin 138
Monkey 131
Monster 33
Moose 129
Mosque 105
Motorcycle 113
Motor scooter 113
Motor truck 116
Mountains 107
Mouse 33, 126
Moustache 6
Movie ticket 42
Mummy 48
Mushroom 68
Musical notes 43

N

Nagini 26
Nagini* 26
Nail 84
Native American 31
Necklace 36
Neck pillow 53
Necktie 138
Nintendo Switch 39
Nintendo Switch* 39
Notebook 80
Notre dame 101
Nurse 19

O

Oar 121
Octopus 122
Offended 7
Oil lamp 96
Olaf 34
Old telephone 76
Orange slice 70
Owl 129

P

Pacifier 51
Pacifier clip 51
Package closed 14
Package open 14
Paddle 87
Paddling pool 40
Pagoda 103
Pain 7
Paint brush 83
Paint bucket 83
Painting 73
Paint palette 82
Pajama pants 135
Pajama top 135
Palace 32
Palm trees 108
Paper airplane 39
Paper boat 39
Paper clip 79
Paper kite 39
Paprika 69
Parasol 94
Parchment 26
Parking sign 113
Parrot 132
Party blowout 47
Party hat 49
Pasta strainer 60
Pastry bag 61
Pasture fence 98
Pause 78
Pavone 132
Paw Patrol 21
PC 77
Peach 71
Peacock 132
Peanut 71
Pear 70
Pearl shell 37

Peas 69
Pebbles 107
Pelican 125
Pencil 79
Pencil case 81
Penguin 125
Pepper 69
Perplexed 5
Peter Pan 32
Photo 78
Pick up 116
Pick-up 116
Picnic basket 75
Pie 62
Piece of cake 61
Piece of Pizza 66
Pie slice 61
Pig 127
Pikatchu 23
Pikatchu* 23
Pile of dirt 13
Pillow 53
Pincushion 83
Pineapple 70
Pinniped 125
Pipe 138
Pippi Longstocking 33
Piranha Plant* 23
Pirate 28
Pirate hat 30
Pirate ship 29
Pisa tower 102
Pistol 17
Pizza 66, 102
Pizza delivery service 66
Pizza wheel 60
Planet Earth 112
Planet Jupiter 112
Planet Moon 112
Planet Saturn 112
Plaster 19
Plaster leg 18
Plate 60
Platypus 133
Play 78
Playing card 39
Playing soccer 10
Pocket knife 97
Pointe shoes 37
Pokeball 23
Pokeball* 23
Pokemon 23
Police badge 17
Police cap 17
Police car 17
Policeman 17
Poodle 126
Popcorn 42
Popsicle 64
Postman 14
Potato 68
Power saw 84
Power station 106
Pretzel 99
Prince 34
Princess 34
Princess Peach* 22
Printer 77
Professor 6
Propeller plane 119
Puck 90
Puddle 107
Puffer fish 122
Pumpkin 68
Pumps 136
Punk 6
Purse 138
Puzzle 38
Pylon 13
Pyramid 103

R

Radar 119
Radio 17, 76
Rafting 42
Rain 110
Rainbow 111
Rattles 43
Ravioli 66
Record 43
Refrigerator 59
Rescue ship 120
Revolver 30
Risante 5
River 106
River ride 42
Rocker 6, 11
Rocket 16
Rocking 10
Rocks 107
Roll 63
Roller skates 86
Rolling pin 60
Ron 25
Ron* 25
Rose 109
Rubber duck 55
Rubik´s cube 39
Rye bread 63

S

Saber 30
Sad 7
Saddle 86
Safari Jeep 114
Safety needle 83
Sagrada Famiglia 101
Sailing ship 120
Sandals 136
Sandbox 40
Sand bucket 94
Sand castle 94
Sandglass 39
Santa Claus 45
Satellite 16
Satellite dish 16
Sausage 66
Saw 84
Scarecrow 98
School 105
School backpack 80
Schoolbag 80
School cone 80
Scooter 113
Scotch tape 79
Screw 84
Screwdriver 85
SD Card 77
Seahorse 124
Sea urchin 124
Seedling 12
Shampoo 55
Shark 122
Sharpener 80
Sheep 127
Shooting star 111
Shovel 85
Shower pouf 55
Shrimp 123
Shuttlecock 87
Single Dice 38
Sink 54
Sitting 10
Skeptical 7
Ski 92
Ski boot 91
Skier 11
Ski goggles 91
Ski helmet 91
Ski jacket 135
Ski pass 91
Ski-pass 91
Ski poles 92
Skirt 134
Skull 29
Sled 91
Sleeping bag 96
Sleep mask 53
Slide 40
Slippers 136
Sloth 132
Smile 5
Smoker 6
Snack bag 60
Snail 130
Snake 133
Snape* 26
Snitch* 27
Snorkel 93
Snowboard 92
Snowfall 110
Snowflake 110
Snow globe 46
Snowman 46
Snow removal vehicle 117
Snow White* 34
Soap 55
Soap dispenser 55
Soccer ball 88
Soccer field 88
Soccer goal 88
Soccer player 11
Soccer shoes 88
Soccer stadium 88
Socket 76
Soda pop 67
Sombrero 104
Space shuttle 16
Speed limit 50 113
Speed train 118
Speed train wagon 118
Sphinx 103
Spider 130
Spider-Man 21
Spider-Man* 21
Spider web 48
Spinning top 38
Spirit level 83
Spiteful 7
Sponge 58
Spoon 60
Sport 85
Sports car 114
Spray bottle 58
Spray can 82
Squirrel 129
Squirt gun 41
Stachi 23
Stachi* 23
Stage 42
Stamp 14
Standing 10
Stapler 79
Star 111
Starfish 122
Starry clear 110
Star Wars 24
Statue of Jesus 103
Statue of liberty 104
Steak 66
Steamship 120
Steam train 117
Steering wheel 114, 121
Stegosaurus 31
Stethoscope 18
Stetoscopio 18
Stetson hat 138
Stingray 124
Stone age man 30
Stop 78
Stopplay 78
Stopwatch 92

Stork 125
Stove 59
Strawberry 71
Street 113
Street light 112
Street sign 112
String lights 75
Submarine 121
Suitcase 94
Sultan 32
Sumo wrestler 103
Sunflower 109
Sunny 110
Sunscreen 56
Supereroe 21
Superfungo 23
Superman 21
Superman* 21
Super Mario 22
Super mushroom* 23
Super Star 22
Superstella 22
Surfboard 93
Surprised 5
Sushi 68
Swan 125
Sweet pastries 62
Swimming ring 95
Swimming trunks 134
Swing 40
Sword 28
Swordfish 124
Syringe 19

T

Table 72
Table lamp 75
Tablet 76
Tablets 18
Tacco 67
Taco 67
Talking hat* 26
Tank 118
Tape dispenser 79
Tape measure 84
Target 41
Tartaruga 132
Tea bag 65
Teapot 59
Teddy bear 38
Teether 51
Telephone box 100
Telescope 29
Television tower 100
Tenda 96
Tennis ball 87
Tennis racket 87
Tent 96
Tepee 31
Tetra Pak 65
Thread spool 83
Tiara 35
Tipi 31
Toad 22
Toad* 22
Toast 63
Toaster 59
Toddler 9
Toilet 54
Toilet paper 54
Toilette 54
Tomato 69
Tool box 84
Tooth 19
Toothbrush 56
Toothpaste 56
Tornado 110
Tournament loop 36
Towel rack 54
Tow truck 116
Tractor 117
Traffic light 113
Train station 106
Train wagon 118
Trampoline 40
Trampolinist 11
Transverse Flute 44
Trash can 54
Treasure chest 29
Treasure map 29
Tree trunk 108
Triangle 44
Trick or treat bucket 48
Triumphal arch 101
Troll 33
Trolley 94
Trousers 135
Trumpet 43
T-shirt 135
Tulip 109
Tulipano 109
Turkey 66
Turtle 132
Tutu 37
TV 77
Tyrannosaurus 31

U

Ufo 16
UGG* boots 136
Umbrella closed 137
Umbrella opened 137
Unicorn 37

V

Vacuum cleaner 58
Valencia Aquarium 101
Vampire 48
Vanity mirror 55
Viking 28
Viking helmet 28
Viking ship 28
Violin 44
Volcano 107
Voldemort 26
Voldemort* 26
Volleyball 87
Vulcano 107

W

Walking 10
Wallet 138
Wallpaper 83
Wall shelf 73
Walnut 71
Walrus 125
Washing machine 57
Waste container 59
Water bottle 68
Water bubble 108
Watercolors 81
Waterfall 107
Watering can 12
Wave 108
Wax crayon 82
Wedding cake 50
Wedding car 50
Wedding dress 50
Wedding rings 50
Well 98
Whale 122
Wheelbarrow 12
Wheelchair user 11
Whisk 15
Whistle 88
Wild boar 129
Window 52
Wine glass 102
Wink 5
Winner podium 93
Witch 48
Witch hat 49
Wolf 130
Woman 9
Wool 82
Wool wound up 82
Wooly hat 137
Wrap 67
Wrench 85
Wrist watch 137

X

Xylophone 44

Y

Yeast plait 62
Yeti 27
Yoda 24
Yoda* 24

Z

Zebra 131
Zeppelin 119

1. Edition 2022
ISBN: 978-3962232306

Author: LILLYLOO
Publisher: PALEROMA

PALEROMA
Kapellenweg. 15
72401 Haigerloch
kontakt(at)Paleroma.de
Germany

Made in the USA
Las Vegas, NV
07 June 2023

73111679R00083